LIZZIE

ALSO BY FRANK SPIERING

Berserker

Prince Jack:
The True Story of Jack the Ripper

The Man Who Got Capone

LIZZIE

FRANK SPIERING

RANDOM HOUSE NEW YORK

Published in the United States by Random House, Inc., New York, and
simultaneously in Canada by Random House of Canada Limited, Toronto.

Library of Congress Cataloging in Publication Data

Spiering, Frank.
Lizzie.

1. Borden, Lizzie, 1860–1927. 2. Crime and criminals—
Massachusetts—Fall River—Biography. 3. Murder—Massa-
chusetts—Fall River—Case studies. 4. Sisters—Massa-
chusetts—Fall River—Case studies. I. Title.
HV6248.B66S64 1984 364.1'523'0924 [B] 83-43199
ISBN 0-394-51477-7

Manufactured in the United States of America
24689753
First Edition

For Davis Grubb,
a wonderful author and friend,
who was the first to encourage me to write about Lizzie
and tell what really happened

And for my son, John, with all my love

All of the quoted conversations in the pages that follow are from transcripts of trial testimony, newspaper accounts, contemporary interviews and statements of living witnesses.

I wish to acknowledge and thank the people of Fall River, Massachusetts, and Newmarket, New Hampshire, who shared with me their time and their memories. *Lizzie* was fortunate in having the finest editor possible, Robert Loomis of Random House, as well as an exceptional supporter, my agent, Freya Manston, whose words of encouragement were always there.

CONTENTS

I

92 SECOND STREET

1

THE POISON

ON A WARM WHITE-HONEYSUCKLE-SCENTED AUGUST morning in 1892, Lizzie Borden sat in her room on the top floor of the narrow wooden frame house at 92 Second Street planning how to murder her father and stepmother.

She and her sister, Emma, had been overwhelmed by their father's sudden betrayal. Behind their backs he had given his interest in a house he owned on Fourth Street to his wife's sister Sarah Whitehead. They had learned about it only through the chance comment of a friend. It was their father's secrecy which had enraged them. Their stepmother's family had wormed their way in, and he had calmly gone along with it.

And then they discovered that he was planning to place his farm in Swansea in his wife's name.

The farm had been theirs. They had gone there each summer. When Lizzie was a child her father had taught her to fish on the bank of the stream which ran through it.

She was close to her father. She felt that she meant much more to him than her stepmother did. But her father's response to her fury had been indignant and cold. There was no explanation. He offered Emma and her twenty-five hundred dollars each for a house he had given them years before. Lizzie put two thousand dollars in her checking account and five hundred in savings. But this did not pacify her. The incident had erupted into a bitter family argument. It was clear to Lizzie and Emma what their father intended to do. Under the influence of their uncle, John Vinnicum Morse, Andrew Borden was planning a will depriving them of the bulk of his fortune.

As his wife, Abby, retreated to her room, Andrew Borden heatedly refused to speak anymore about it. He attempted to soothe Lizzie by reassuring her that he had not made a will favoring her stepmother.

It had all happened less than a week ago.

On the day following the argument with their father, the two sisters left the house on Second Street. Lizzie had planned to visit acquaintances in Marion and Emma was to stay with her friends the Brownells in Fairhaven. They had journeyed as far as New Bedford when Lizzie decided to turn back. The endless crisis pitting them against their stepmother was intolerable. Something had to be done swiftly as Morse would be arriving from South Dartmouth in another week.

Emma continued on to the Brownells in Fairhaven.

Lizzie returned to Fall River, where she took a room in a small boardinghouse on Madison Street. She could not face going home.

The feeling of personal betrayal was unbearable. From the time she was a little girl her father's desire for money had become her own.

Now he had turned on her, betrayed her, his own child!

Emma had anticipated it. Lizzie's eyes often filled with tears as she listened to her sister's warning voice. Lizzie had barely known her real mother. She had died when Lizzie was two. There was no one she could trust except Emma. Their father would betray them, Emma insisted.

In that small rented room on Madison Street the worst of her nightmares advanced upon her—so many unexpressed feelings, so much fear. She and her sister were to be disinherited, replaced by a woman who meant nothing, who had no place living in their house—an obese, stupid, loathsome woman.

Finally she could stand it no longer. She returned to her room at 92 Second Street, having made a decision that would resolve everything.

As she gazed through the yellow-lace-curtained window she listened to the occasional strident noises from the poplar-lined street in front. Except for her stepmother in the adjoining bedroom, she was alone in the house. Yet she could not close out the incessant hum which circulated around her, the mammoth textile mills on the riverbank below, roaring out miles of cotton grabbed by the eager hands of Portuguese and Irish workmen, who had migrated to the town when she was a child. Her wide blue eyes wandered through the window toward the monstrous dark form which hovered three short blocks from her house.

Standing at the entrance to the Fall River Iron Works, it shot up to the incredible height of three hundred and fifty feet. From the top of its cylindrical mass of soot-caked red brick belched forth a stifling mixture of yellow smoke and vapor onto the eighty-three thousand inhabitants below. It was the tallest chimney in the United States.

Lizzie had never lived anywhere but in Fall River. She was thirty-two, not beautiful, yet attractive, with dark reddish hair parted up the middle and combed back into naturally curling waves. She was five feet four, weighing one hundred and thirty-five pounds. Her hands were large but pale white and delicately formed. Her shoulders were broad and straight, but no amount of lacing or whalebone could hide the fact that her waist was thick.

Since her birth she had watched the town undergo dizzying changes of landscape and atmosphere, which had transformed it into the largest cotton-manufacturing center in America—while through its heart, down the amber-stained Quequechan River, zigzagged the Fall River Steamship Line, which provided transportation for goods and passengers from Boston along inland waterways to New York harbor and the world beyond.

For her thirtieth birthday, two years before, Lizzie had taken a summer tour of Europe with a group of young women from Fall River. She had written back letters describing the museums she had visited, the parks in Paris and her greatest love, the theaters, where she had seen plays performed by the world's most famous actors. She had returned with a suitcase of souvenirs, copies of the paintings of Rembrandt, Michelangelo and Da Vinci and theater programs from plays starring William Gillette, Sarah Bernhardt and Lillie Langtry.

On the trip home she shared a cabin with her cousin Miss Anna Borden, to whom she confided her hatred for her stepmother and the dreaded house to which she was returning. She despised her life in Fall River and longed for the spectacles of the world beyond.

Yet she was unmarried, with no employment other than her involvement with the Central Congregational Church, which was the pinnacle of social activity in the community. She taught a Sunday school class. In addition she was secretary-treasurer of Christian Endeavor and was active in the Ladies' Fruit and Flower Mission and the Woman's Christian Temperance Union.

She was a lonely young woman, made even more so by a community that offered little challenge for personal endeavor. Because of the influx of immigrant labor, the grating roar of the cotton mills and the often dense smoke issuing from the continually smoldering furnaces of the Iron Works, Fall River was an oppressive place.

As a child Lizzie had always felt that she was her father's favorite. She had loved her father and looked up to him. He was the only man she had ever respected. Theirs was a peculiar relationship. He spoiled her, yet withheld the warmth of a parent. In a burst of joy at her high school graduation she had removed a small gold ring from her finger and asked her father to wear it as a bond between them. It would only fit his little finger yet he never took it off. It was the only piece of jewelry, other than a pocket watch, that he owned. Whenever anybody asked about the ring he admitted proudly that it had been given to him by Lizzie.

They had long talks together. They talked about business. They talked about money. And she became his confidant.

When he had the outside of the house redecorated he told the painter to take his orders from Lizzie. "Any color she selects will be fine with me," he said.

But he had betrayed her.

The only man she respected in the world had left her without any hope.

As she slipped out of her room on that warm August morning she apparently felt no remorse for what she was about to do. *He had driven her to it.*

The stairs leading from the second floor to the front parlor wound down into a vast pool of sunlight. Bridget, the maid, had left for the store only a few minutes before.

Lizzie made her way through the parlor and sitting room into the large white kitchen.

Bridget had left the gray iron pot of roast mutton simmering on the coal cookstove.

Lizzie's fingers slid down into the pocket of her frock and removed the tiny, neatly folded paper packet. As she eased it open a flurry of minute sugary clusters fluttered along the creased edges. With a sudden tap she let them all drop into the pungent brown broth bubbling from the sides of the roast.

By eleven o'clock that morning the downtown area was swathed in a thick, moist glaze. The three-foot-long Samuel Thaxter thermometer mounted outside the north-facing windows of the Globe Yarn Mill Company registered ninety-four degrees.

Inside, Andrew Jackson Borden, the mill's most prominent director, strode briskly through the company's offices on his morning run of chores. Noticing him, Martin Blaine, the executive treasurer, asked casually, "Are you going over to Swansea to get out of the heat?"

Borden was stopped dead by the question. Turning, he stared at Blaine as if something had triggered off in his head. In a flat, dry voice, suddenly, strangely, he confessed, "I'm having trouble . . . a lot of trouble at home. I can't talk about Swansea until it's settled."

It was an odd outburst, which left Blaine dismayed.

With that, Borden moved quickly down the hallway.

Leaving by the side entrance, he headed away from the river toward the intersection of streets leading up the hill. As he drew nearer to the heart of town the sweltering heat seemed more intense. In the distance he could hear the rattle of traffic, of whinnying horses and drayage wagons laboring along Main Street.

It had not always been so.

Less than a century before, Fall River had been a beautiful, unspoiled place of fresh-water streams and rock-lined meadows. The town had been formed at the point where the Quequechan River fell one hundred and twenty-seven feet in a space of half a mile. Thus, Andrew's great-grandfather had named it Fall River. The entire area, which ran for four miles across the Taunton River to Swansea and Somerset, Massachusetts, once had all been owned by the Bordens.

John, the first Borden to arrive from England, in 1635, was banished with Anne Hutchinson from the Massachusetts Bay Colony for heresy. Resettling in Portsmouth, he left a substantial estate to his son, also named John, whose refusal to pay taxes on the land he possessed resulted in his arrest and imprisonment. Richard Borden, one of John's two sons, became involved in a dispute over water rights and resolved it by purchasing the entire Fall River area. From that time onward the Borden family achieved riches and power.

Then in one generation they lost it all.

It was Andrew's father, Abraham, who disrupted the pattern. He was not able to measure up to his predecessors and became a fish peddler. His fortunes quickly faded yet he managed to hold on to the water rights which he had inherited. In addition to a slum cottage in which he lived at 12 Ferry Street, these were his sole bequest to his eldest son, Andrew.

Andrew's whole life was a retaliation against his father's mistakes. As a young man he vowed to recover the properties and wealth which had been denied him. With defiance, incredible labor and unbending parsimonious business acumen he forged his way back into the mercantile life of the community.

Beginning as an undertaker, he flamboyantly advertised the remarkable virtues of Crane's Patent Casket Burial Cases, for which he was the exclusive agent. Offering a money-back guarantee, he promised that these superior coffins would preserve and keep intact the remains of a loved one far longer than any other casket.

The undertaking industry was in its infancy and people believed him. An immediate success, Andrew used his earnings to buy property, which he then rented. If he observed that a tenant was prospering, he would raise the rent. With this income he purchased farmland subject to foreclosure, which he resold at a handsome profit.

But his greatest coup involved the family of Horace Brayton. The Braytons had inherited several extremely valuable parcels of real estate and were battling among themselves over the distribution of their bequeathed properties. Andrew presented them with an immediate cash offer far below the recognized market value. He knew that the heirs were jealous of each other and were afraid one would get an advantage over the others. Andrew heatedly pressed his low offer, calling on each of them, warning them that they would have to move quickly as they had only forty-eight hours to decide.

He reasoned well. The heirs were so suspicious of each other that they panicked. Only William Brayton turned down his offer. William threatened court action to prevent acceptance, but he was finally forced to go along. In the years that followed, William Brayton went about Fall River bitterly denouncing Andrew, threatening to get even with him. But Andrew had already resold the property, making a small fortune.

As the stories of Andrew's mercenary methods flourished, so did his wealth. It was rumored that he cut off the feet of corpses so that he could cram them into undersized coffins that he got cheap.

Undaunted by the scurrilous comments of his neighbors, Andrew scraped and saved until he managed to amass a personal fortune of half a million dollars.* Thrift became his obsession, and with it a dread of ever falling into debt. He boasted that he had never signed a promissory note or borrowed a penny. He took over the Union Savings Bank, which gave him an inside track on all imminent foreclosures. His control of the bank brought with it a string of titles: director of the

*This amount of money would be equivalent today to twelve million dollars.

Globe Yarn Mill Company, director of the First National Bank, director of Troy Cotton and Manufacturing Company and director of the Merchants Manufacturing Company. He helped organize the Fall River Street Railway, and when a New York corporation, wishing outright ownership of the streetcar lines, offered a generous bonus above the market value for the outstanding stock, everyone agreed to sell but Andrew. Calmly he waited, driving the other stockholders to the brink of desperation. With chilling ruthlessness he forced the corporation to deal with him separately. Finally they had to pay him double the value of his stock to remove him as a thorn in their side.

As Andrew reached Main Street on this blistering summer morning he stopped to gaze upon the modern gray granite complex which stood at the very heart of the downtown area. Newly completed, it took up an entire city block, where it had replaced several structures demolished in its path. It housed a dozen stores and forty offices, representing the life blood of Fall River's mercantile and professional emergence into the industrial mainstream of America. Yet it was an edifice which represented much more than that to Andrew. It was the pinnacle of his life, the achievement of fifty years of uncompromising toil. A large bronze block imbedded in the southwest corner heralded his triumph: THE A. J. BORDEN BUILDING

Crossing Main Street he headed up the short hill to his home. If his business career could be called successful, in contrast, Andrew's personal life was tumultous and unhappy.

When he was twenty-three he had married a farm girl, Sarah J. Morse. She did not possess a rich dowry, but for the only time in his life he fell impulsively and passionately in love. Four years later their daughter Emma Lenora was born; Alice, a second daughter, died a year after her birth.

Andrew vowed that he would have a son.

And then when he was thirty-eight, Sarah conceived a third time.

Andrew's disappointment became inconsolable with the appearance of yet another daughter.

Never the type of man to lightly abandon his desires, he insisted that the baby's middle name be Andrew. For a first name he called her Lizzie.

The sad, subtle twisting of that family's fate began after Lizzie's birth. Two years later Sarah was dead. Within Andrew what little passion and human affection had existed turned cold and atrophied. Without further aspirations to increase his family, he devoted all his energies to acquiring more wealth. For the next few years he remained a widower, and then, finally, needing someone to care for his household, he married a thirty-eight-year-old spinster, Abby Durfee Gray.

Abby had descended from one of the original families of Fall River. Durfee was a name that bore social prominence, yet Abby was from a lesser class. Her father was a tin-peddler who sold sundries, china, linen and household goods from a pushcart in the Fall River streets.

Andrew had met her at the Central Congregational Church, courted her, and brought her into his house to care for his two daughters. It was a miserable, lonely existence for her, and she often complained to her sister Sarah Whitehead that she felt left out of her husband's family. From the beginning it was Emma who hated her, who treated her with coldness and constant suspicion.

Once she had tried to get close to Lizzie, but Emma was always in the way. The feeling of rejection had preyed upon her mind. There was no reason to be treated so, to be hated so.

But Emma could not forgive her for taking her mother's place. And Andrew was caught in the middle.

The struggle between Abby and his two daughters grew shortly after they moved to 92 Second Street. Emma was twenty-one and Lizzie was twelve.

The house was larger than the cramped wooden frame cottage which his father had left him on Ferry Street, yet it was still a grim, boxlike structure, extremely narrow, with a thin yard around its sides and a small barn in the rear. It was hardly a fitting residence for the wealthiest man in Fall River, yet Andrew could never allow himself the indulgence of living as a wealthy man. He avoided that elite section of the town known as The Hill, a neighborhood of fine homes and lovely views. Instead he chose "the flats," near the business district, so he could be close to his holdings. The only washing facilities were a cold-water faucet just inside the kitchen door and the laundry-room tap in the cellar—Andrew believed that running water on each floor was a luxury.

There was just one toilet, also located in the cellar.

When he purchased it in 1871, the house was made up of two little industrial railroad lofts, one above the other. From this complex maze Andrew created an architectural nightmare.

On the second floor he fashioned a dressing room and four bedrooms. No space was wasted on hallways; the rooms simply opened into one another. One of the bedrooms had three doors leading to three adjacent rooms. There was little privacy. Consequently, Andrew insisted that at all times the bedroom he shared with his wife in the rear of the house be kept locked. Thus, when Mrs. Borden wanted to reach the front guest room from her own room she had to go down the back stairs, walk through the first-floor rooms to the front entry and then climb the front stairs.

On the first floor he constructed a front parlor, a dining room, a sitting room and a kitchen. He installed flowered carpets in all the main rooms and purchased an upright piano for the front parlor. Finally, at the rear, isolated from the rest of the house and accessible by a steep dark narrow-walled staircase, he took an attic with a pitched roof and turned it into maid's quarters.

What made 92 Second Street even more agreeable was the fact that Andrew could save money on fuel. Unlike the other houses in the neighborhood, it was not connected to a gas main. The Borden home was lighted solely by kerosene. And Andrew frequently sat in the dark to save kerosene.

There would be many accounts of this house in the years to come, descriptions of its structure and its furnishings. Attention would be drawn to the fact that the front bedrooms on the second floor were so closely connected to each other that it was virtually impossible to gain access to them without being seen or overheard by the occupant of any one of them.

This was the setting for the horror that would shock America and erupt in headlines throughout the world. The dark, daguerreotype images of Andrew and his penny-pinching habits would soon fade. What would endure in memory was that this was the home of Lizzie Borden of Fall River, Massachusetts.

At dinnertime, noon, on Monday, August 1, 1892, Andrew unlatched the narrow picket gate. Neatly dressed in a long Prince Albert coat, with a white shirt and black bow tie, he was a tall, lean man of seventy with tight cheekbones and thinning white hair. Closely cropped sideburns and chin whiskers framed his black eyes and grimly set mouth.

His counterpart in looks was Emma, while Lizzie resembled her mother.

There was a coldness about him—at least that is all the world had ever known of him. He was considered brusque, dour and tight-fisted, the richest man in Fall River, who could not outlive the bitter, humiliating poverty of his boyhood and thus was compelled to house his family in a makeshift, almost shabby dwelling.

The succulent wafting aura of roasting mutton rushed to his nostrils as he climbed the three porch steps, unlocked the front door and entered.

Abby began vomiting at three a.m. Throughout the afternoon she had felt a flame in her throat, centered on the roof of her mouth. Her gums grew thick; her head rocked with heat.

By evening, slowly, mercilessly, her stomach began to shift, stiffening, then releasing, as an awful sensation of freezing to death shuddered through her body.

At first she was not certain what had caused the antagonistic, unendurable cramps. At Monday's dinner she had eaten some potatoes, a few carrots and a portion of mutton. She had dined alone with her husband, Lizzie remaining upstairs, still fuming from the argument of the week before. There was also some leftover swordfish broken into bits which she had eaten later in the day. Perhaps the swordfish had been spoiled.

She had never experienced such pain.

And then in the middle of the night her stomach seemed to explode. She gagged at the pressure in her abdomen. Crawling from her bed she weakly made her way down the back stairs to the kitchen, where she anxiously consumed four glasses of water. It was then that she began vomiting uncontrollably, as if her insides had suddenly split open. Unable to stop the relentless green bile from surging to her lips, she sank to the floor clutching her arms around herself as tightly as she could.

She was a short woman, and her two-hundred-pound weight made all movements incredibly difficult. She lay on the floor retching pitifully.

At dawn, she closed her eyes.

Finally, at seven a.m., Andrew found her lying on the kitchen floor and helped her back upstairs to bed.

At noon she drank a cup of hot tea and ate a little more of the mutton to fortify herself.

But the pain grew worse. In a fog of agony she vomited again and again. Her skin had turned clammy, moist and cold. She was dying of thirst, but glasses of water made the violence in her stomach even more horrible.

Somewhere in her dreams, in the dim, half-awakening of her mind, a terrible thought intruded—more than a reflective urging; a constricting fear.

In the evening when Andrew awakened her, the burning coal climbing up her throat suddenly tore through her lips. "I've been poisoned," she muttered. "I've got to see Dr. Bowen. I've been poisoned."

Andrew stared at her in anger. No, he did not believe it. And she was not to tell Seabury Bowen or anyone else that she had imagined such a thing.

"I have been . . ." she whispered. But finding no consolation in his eyes she turned on her side, clutching her pillow.

The nausea and unyielding cramps persisted, yet somehow she survived the night. Early Wednesday morning she awoke vowing that she had to do something. While dressing herself she noticed that her skin was inflamed. Her arms and legs had broken out in furrows of ugly red splotches. Her head pounded crazily as she staggered down the narrow stairs to the first floor. Andrew's face was ominous. "Where are you going!" he demanded. He tried to stop her.

She was certain that she had been poisoned. Something was ripping open her insides.

Pushing the door open, she tottered down the front steps as Andrew screamed in her ears, *"My money won't pay for it!"*

Fortunately Dr. Bowen lived in a double house directly across the street. He did not have one of the better practices in town but Abby knew him well.

Breathing heavily she forced herself up his steps, rang the bell and waited for his long thin face to appear. The front door opened wide, and as he stood there with his white whiskers and kind, almost luminous eyes, Dr. Bowen seemed like some saint come to rescue her.

Quickly he ushered Abby inside, sat her down in his front parlor and offered her a cup of herbal tea.

She declined to have anything as she let the story pour out of her. Her husband, she said, had received an anonymous note from someone threatening to poison the whole family. She was now certain that they *had been* poisoned.

Dr. Bowen listened intently as Abby described the insidious cramps, the ceaseless vomiting, the gray feelings of death surrounding her. She unbuttoned her clothing to show him the scarlet blotches ravaging her arms and legs.

The anonymous note was her own invention.

Seabury Bowen rose from his chair and followed her out into the street. He would talk to the other members of the family. As they crossed to her house Andrew's implacable figure emerged from the front doorway. "Bowen! You're not to come in here!" he shouted, wild-eyed with fury. "Don't meddle in my business! Go back where you just came from!"

Bowen hesitated, glancing uneasily at Abby, then back at Andrew's threatening form.

Andrew snarled a final "Go back!"

John Vinnicum Morse was sixty-nine. The eldest brother of Andrew's first wife, Sarah, he had ventured from Fall River as a young man and journeyed to Iowa, where he had become a prosperous farmer. At the age of sixty-six he had sold his holdings and returned to the East. For the past three years he had lived in nearby South Dartmouth.

Although retired, he still dabbled in horse trading, occasionally selling mustangs, which he imported from the West. Because of his background and experience Andrew Borden welcomed his advice on the upkeep of the farmland that Andrew owned north of the city.

Andrew relied on him in other ways as well. When Morse arrived at the Borden house at one-thirty on Wednesday afternoon he found both Abby and Andrew violently ill. The maid, Bridget, also complained of severe stomach cramps. But this did not stop Andrew from inviting him for supper and to spend the night in the second-floor guest room.

Morse could not stay for supper. He had promised to dine with relatives on Weybosset Street in Swansea. However, he did agree to return and spend the night.

But Andrew desperately needed John Morse's advice and led him into the sitting room. Its window, open in the heat, was directly beneath Lizzie's. Here they talked for three hours as Andrew outlined the conditions of the will he was preparing.

Lizzie could hear the voices below, her father carefully explaining the breaking up of his fortune, Morse making an occasional comment or agreeing. And all the while her heart pounded with the knowledge that she was being surreptitiously betrayed.

The arsenic which she had added to the mutton had not worked. In her naïveté she had assumed that the mere addition of poison to her stepmother's and father's food would immediately produce fatal results. But she had been mistaken.

Overhearing the voices below, she felt a drastic urgency weighing upon her. As yet her father had not made a will, but within a day or so there would be one, and then all would be lost. Her father's fortune would be divided, and where would she be?

The terrible mournful moments ebbed on, mingling with the chilling fears which had not let up for over a week. Discouraged, she flipped open the book of household hints which she had brought upstairs from the kitchen. The binding was broken and one of the pages had torn loose. She hesitated over the words before her and then looked at them again.

> PRUSSIC ACID—Hydrogen cyanide. A colorless almond-tasting liquid. Warning: Extremely toxic and usually fatal if taken internally.

From floor to ceiling, the back walls of D. R. Smith's Drugstore were covered with packets of neatly lettered yellow and white prescriptions, reachable by a pushbroom pole with a hook on the end. In long, steep rows they hung from eight-penny blue nails, hundreds of them, records of most of the families living in Fall River.

Eli Bence had worked at D. R. Smith's Drugstore at South Main and Columbia streets for thirteen years. He was forty-four years old with dark, graying hair, heavy-lidded eyes and a thin mustache which protruded over his upper lip. Because of the heavily starched collar and long white dustcoat that he wore behind the counter, his body seemed to stiffen and arch forward from his shoulders as he greeted each customer with an intentionally calming, professional demeanor.

He was well aware that the attractive woman in the dark blue dress was the daughter of the wealthiest banker in Fall River. She had grown up on Ferry Street, less than a block away. And yet he could not serve her, a fact that seemed to make her extremely irritable.

"My good lady," Bence attempted to explain again, with equal emphasis but perhaps more simply, "prussic acid is something we don't sell unless we have a prescription from a doctor."

"But it's for cleaning purposes. Why should I need a doctor?"

"It's deadly poison."

"But all I need is ten cents' worth."

"That's quite a lot."

"But I need it to clean my sealskin cape."

"I'm sorry, Miss Borden. Prussic acid is a very dangerous thing to handle. I can't sell it to you."

With that Lizzie turned and walked back out onto South Main Street.

Eli Bence was puzzled.

On such an uncomfortable wet August afternoon it seemed to him to be impractical that anyone would be involved with the cleaning of a garment as heavy as a sealskin cape.

Lizzie returned to her room and waited until John Morse left at six-thirty. Then she slipped out of the house. It was a stifling, yellow evening and the sunset in the distance cast Fall River in an incredible humid glow. Lizzie hurried down Second Street and turned the corner before she got to the City Hall. She would find the poison she needed even if tomorrow she had to visit every drugstore in Bristol County.

She knew that Alice Russell would believe anything she told her. Alice would become part of her plan.

Alice Russell had lived next door to the Borden home for several years but then moved around the corner to a little house next to a bakery shop tucked between Third and Fourth streets. She was a spinster, a good deal older than Emma and Lizzie, but she remained Emma's closest friend. There was a dignity, a gentility about her, and she treated Lizzie in a special way. She listened, sympathized and understood.

She was not an attractive woman. High-collared lace blouses partially hid an awkwardly long, thin neck. Her thick eyebrows arched above a sharply pointed nose and two staring, constantly intrigued dark eyes.

At seven p.m. when Lizzie arrived, Alice invited her into the tiny front room just off the kitchen. The heat was intolerable and Lizzie was perspiring. Her auburn hair was pulled back into a single thick braid that fell over one shoulder. She seemed all charged up yet uneasy about everything. "I'm going away," Lizzie immediately announced. "I've taken your advice and have written to my friends in Marion that I will be coming to visit them."

Alice had known all along of the trouble which Lizzie and Emma had been experiencing. Lizzie had promised to attend the Endeavor Society roll call on Friday, but Alice had recommended that she go to Marion, on Buzzard's Bay, before then, in order to get away from Fall River for a while. "I'm glad you're going," Alice smiled, but she could see that Lizzie was bitterly disturbed.

Suddenly tears filled Lizzie's eyes. "I don't know . . . I feel depressed . . . I feel as if somethingis hanging over me and I can't throw it off. . . . It comes over me at times . . . no matter where I am. The other day when I was with some friends this feeling came over me and somebody said, 'Lizzie, why don't you talk?' But I couldn't . . . *I couldn't.*"

"What do you think it is?"

Lizzie bowed her head. "Father has so much trouble. . . . Last night he and Abby were so sick . . ."

"Was it something they'd eaten?"

"We were all sick . . . all but Maggie."

Alice was aware that "Maggie" was Lizzie's name for Bridget, the family maid. Before Bridget, the Bordens had employed a maid named Maggie, who had been with them for years. Lizzie had continued to call Bridget "Maggie" out of habit.

Alice asked again, "Was it something you all might have eaten?"

Lizzie shook her head. "I don't know. We had some bread from the bakery. . . . Everyone ate some but Maggie . . . and Maggie didn't get sick."

"Well, it couldn't have been the bread. If it had come from the bakery other people would probably be sick and I haven't heard of anybody."

Lizzie nodded. "That is so." She silently hesitated a long moment. Then quickly shot out, "Sometimes I think our milk might be poisoned."

Alice looked at her anxiously. "How do you get your milk? How could it be poisoned?"

"It comes in a can. They set it on the steps overnight . . . and the next morning when they bring more milk they take the empty can."

"But if they put anything in the can the farmer would see it."

Once again Lizzie nodded, but Alice was eager now to resolve the problem. "What time does the milk come?"

At that moment Lizzie realized that she could tell Alice anything and it would be remembered. "I think about four o'clock."

"It's light at four o'clock. . . . I don't think anybody would tamper with the cans . . . somebody might see them."

Lizzie's lips tightened. "I shouldn't think so. It's just that Father and Abby were so awfully sick. . . . I heard them vomiting all night. . . . I knocked on their door and asked if I could do anything and they said no. Sometimes . . . sometimes I feel afraid that Father has an enemy. . . . He has so much trouble with the men who come to see him. . . . There was one man who came . . . I didn't see his face but he and Father had a terrible argument over some property. . . . Father got so mad that he ordered him out of the house. And the barn has been broken into twice. . . ."

"But there's nothing for them to go after in there but the pigeons."

"I know . . . but they've even broken into the house in broad daylight with Emma and Maggie and me there."

Alice was startled by the admission. "I never heard that before."

"Father forbids us to tell anyone. . . ." Suddenly the words rushed out of her. "They took a watch and chain and money and car tickets and something else that I can't remember and there was a nail left in the keyhole . . . maybe that's how they got in—"

"Did your father do anything about it?"

"He went to the police but they didn't find out anything. Father expected they would catch the thief by the tickets." She laughed nervously. "Just as if anybody would use those tickets." And then, in a quivering voice, she added, "I feel as if I should sleep with my eyes half open. . . . They're liable to burn the house down over us. . . . Father is so rude. . . . Abby thought she had been poisoned and told Father that she was going to see Dr. Bowen and he told her, 'My money won't pay for it!' But she went to Dr. Bowen's anyway . . . and then when Dr. Bowen came over . . . I was so ashamed the way Father treated him . . . I was so mortified. . . ." Lizzie's body shivered as she spoke. Alice reached for her hand to comfort her. "I don't know what we're going to do," Lizzie murmured, shaking her head in confusion. She clutched Alice's hand hard. "I'm afraid somebody will do something. . . ."

2

RAGE

Prosecutor:	Do you say that the relations between your stepmother and sister Lizzie were cordial?
Emma:	The last two or three years they were very.
Prosecutor:	Notwithstanding that she never used the term "Mother"?
Emma:	Yes, sir.
Prosecutor:	They remained cordial?
Emma:	For the last three years they were.
Prosecutor:	Were the relations between you and your stepmother cordial?
Emma:	I don't know how to answer that. We always spoke.

—From Emma Borden's testimony at the murder trial of her sister, June 5, 1893

THERE WOULD NEVER BE A PHOTOGRAPH of Emma Borden. She remains an enigmatic, mysterious creature, virtually anonymous in the glare of her sister's notoriety.

There would be only a single pencil drawing: with her sharp shoulders pulled in, she sits quietly on a bench beside Lizzie, her black-gloved hand clutching at her eyes.

One encounters a pristeen blankness, an ominous, puzzling vacancy about Emma. The few details that are known of her suggest that she possessed no personality at all, that she was devoid of emotion. But in looking further there appears a darker, more tenacious element that even her own verbal reticence could not fully conceal.

Is it more than imagination which causes us to focus so on this Victorian lady?

Neighbors in the town of Fall River remembered Emma as a small, plain-looking woman who appeared to desire nothing so much as to be overlooked. Their accounts of her agree that she was prim-looking, extremely quiet, retiring, that she was thin-faced with bony, pale features.

Her few friends seemed to find something flattering in her friendship, as if gaining the confidence of a shy, wild animal. She was timid and invariably evasive. She was never known to have a special talent. She did not long to travel, as did so many ladies of her day. She never married, never had a beau and took no part in the social life of that industrious Massachusetts community on the banks of the Quequechan River twelve miles northwest of New Bedford.

We do know that to Emma, raised by her natural parents for the first eleven years of her life, the intrusion of another woman when she was sixteen was shattering, especially someone who might eventually pose a threat to her and her younger sister's relationship with their father. Later, Emma would make a simple, discreet comment about Abby Durfee: "We never felt that she was much interested in us." It would seem that the reverse was even more true.

When she was instructed to call the new Mrs. Borden "Mother," Emma refused. Despite their difference in age and the respect children are expected to show their elders in the era of 1870, she persisted in referring to Abby as an equal, on a first-name basis. Emma's father was becoming the wealthiest man in Fall River. Another child of sixteen might not have been so enthralled with such matters, but as far back as she could remember, her father's relentless example had instilled within Emma, as in Lizzie, the conviction that money was the very essence of life, but that it could be foolishly lost, as her grandfather had lost it. The prestige of the name Borden might have been regained, but Abby Durfee's intentions, at least to Emma, were devastatingly obvious. By marriage, Abby had become a Borden, able to lay claim to Andrew's growing fortune.

There is no question that Emma idolized Lizzie. Lizzie was everything that Emma could never be: socially outgoing, fashionable, eager to travel and experience life. She was quick-witted and at times arrogant, yet she had the kind of guileless appeal that made both men and woman want to go to great lengths to do things for her. Lizzie had been the darling of the family since she was two years old. It was then that their mother died and it became Emma's role to care for her.

Emma loved Lizzie and wanted to protect her. She was the only female presence that Lizzie could look to for guidance as she grew into womanhood.

But Emma's devotion to Lizzie was a bond more potent than sisterly affection. It was fueled by the overwhelming hatred and suspicion for the woman their father had chosen to marry. The bitterness between Emma and Abby erupted with terrible force as the years went on. How they managed to live together under the same roof for three decades defies conjecture. They hardly spoke to each other. They did not eat together. Emma was constantly antagonistic in her stepmother's company.

Two warring camps separated the Borden household and as Emma and Lizzie grew older, remained unmarried and became more dependent on their father's fortune, Emma's rage against her stepmother intensified and spread through the rooms of 92 Second Street like a cancer.

Her stepmother was not an equal. Yet because she had married their father, she was in charge, able to order about the whole maddening household.

When the family first moved into the house on Second Street Lizzie was still a child of twelve and Emma was given the larger bedroom. But later, an odd circumstance occurred. When Lizzie was thirty, Emma suddenly gave up her room and changed with Lizzie. It was often suggested that Emma was now an old maid of forty and that the still-eligible Lizzie should have the choice room.

Just as no one ever stared closely at Emma, the real motivation for what she did has been completely overlooked. It had to do with Abby Borden.

Originally Emma's bedroom led directly into the room shared by Andrew and her stepmother. At one point Andrew piled furniture in front of the locked door which cut off his and Abbey's bedroom from the rest of the top floor of the house. Yet by now, Emma's hatred for her stepmother had become so intense that she could no longer even stand to sleep in the next room near her. Abruptly, without giving a reason, she moved toward the front of the house and gave Lizzie her room.

During the last week of July, Emma had traveled with Lizzie to Fairhaven, and then had stayed on with her friends the Brownells, but all the while the frenzy within her grew. She had not heard from Lizzie, but she knew that in one more day the title to the family's farm in Swansea would be officially registered in her stepmother's name.

The outrage, the indignity of having her stepmother win after all these years were unbearable.

There never would be a photograph of Emma Borden. No glass-plate camera would ever catch the persistent loathing in her eyes or the icy coldness of her lips and mouth on that dawn morning as she hitched a horse to the black carriage and headed into the woodshed adjacent to the Brownell house to get an axe, her mind ravaged by a fury that she could no longer live with.

It was Thursday, August 4, 1892, a day that would not be forgotten.

In Fall River, temperatures were hotter than anyone remembered—well over one hundred degrees.

Sharp earthquakes were reported in Mexico. . . .

Professor Asaph Hull of the National Observatory announced that he had been making nightly observations of the planet Mars, which was closer to the earth than it had been for centuries. . . .

At dawn an incredible incident had occurred. The eight-hundred-and-odd-ton bark *Alice* barely avoided collision with a line of gigantic amethyst blue icebergs which unexpectedly appeared before her as she rounded Cape Horn. The peril caused the *Alice* and her ashen-faced crew to move ahead under all the canvas she could carry until she was able to pass through a break in the ice field and into open water.

General Adlai E. Stevenson, Democratic candidate for Vice-President, arrived in Louisville, Kentucky, for a public demonstration at the Liederkranz Hall to promote the Grover Cleveland–Stevenson ticket for the November elections.

In London, following his victory over Lord Salisbury's Conservative Party, Prime Minister Gladstone presented his new government to the House of Commons, which greeted him with great enthusiasm. The Irish members shrieked and waved their hats, wildly cheering, and they were joined in these demonstrations by the Liberals. The ovation for the Liberal leader lasted several minutes.

At the Exchange Building in Kansas City the new corn crop was declared a disaster, with less than one half the growth able to be harvested. . . .

The steamer *Mariposa* arrived from Australia bringing intelligence that the British had seized Pago Pago in the Johnston Islands to be used as a coaling station for the English government. . . .

Governor William McKinley of Ohio heartily praised the platform of his Republican party demanding the establishment of a protective tariff. "Free trade gives to the foreign producer equal privileges with us," he told fifteen thousand persons at the Chautauqua Grounds in Beatrice, Nebraska. "We cannot have free trade in this country without free trade restrictions."

In Tashkent, Russia, bloody riots broke out as the epidemic of Asiatic cholera reached its height. Several thousand people fled from the city and tried to cross the province of Syr-Daria in Forghana. At the German border the issuance of passports from Breslau and other frontier places to Russian Poland was restricted . . .

Prince Otto von Bismarck arrived in Jena, where he was greeted by the fervent enthusiasm of thousands of visitors. Later, a choir assembled under the windows of the Prince's rooms and sang Luther's hymn "Ein' Feste Burg."

But a more memorable event than all of these was about to take place in Fall River, Massachusetts. . . .

There were five people in the Borden house that August morning: Lizzie, Andrew, Abby, John Vinnicum Morse and the maid, Bridget Sullivan.*

John Vinnicum Morse was the first one up. He dressed himself and left the second-floor guest room, located in the front of the house, at six a.m. Only four feet from each other, both his and Lizzie's doors led into the second-floor landing (except for a dress closet, their rooms were, in fact, the only ones leading into the landing), and Morse noticed that Lizzie's door was closed when he passed it to go downstairs. Reaching the first floor, he walked through the front entry and into the sitting room, where he waited for the others.

At six-fifteen, in her hot attic room at the head of the rear stairs in the back of the house, Bridget awakened violently ill. Her head throbbed and her stomach reeled with queasy anguish yet she managed

*It may be helpful at this point to consult the floor plans of the Borden house on the accompanying pages. The entire house was only twenty-two feet wide and thirty-nine feet long, congested and boxlike, with little space for privacy.

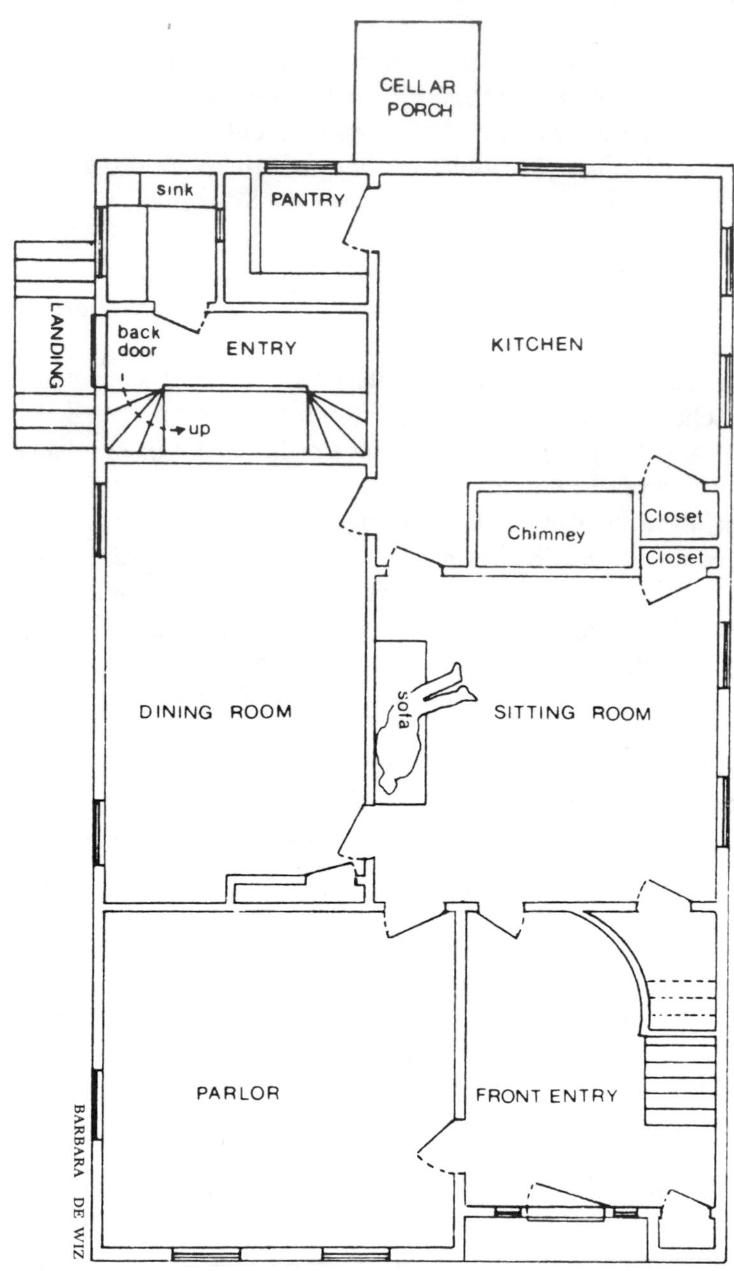

92 SECOND STREET

FIRST FLOOR

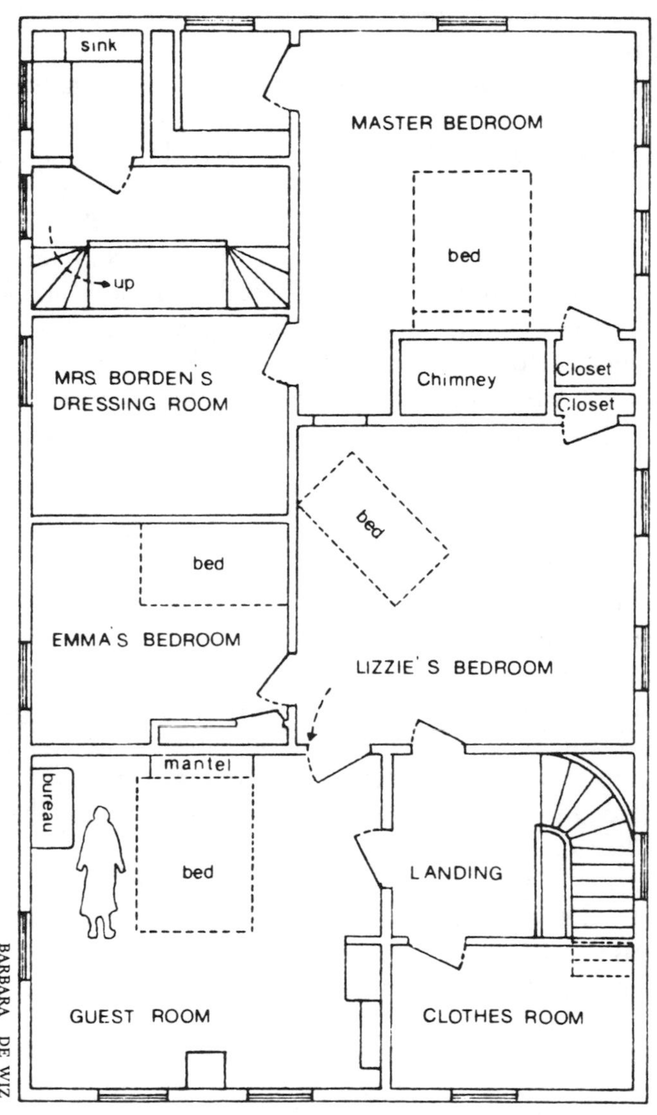

SECOND FLOOR

to struggle down the narrow flight of steps. Unlocking the back door and the screen door, she took in the milk can and set out a pan for the iceman. Then she headed down into the cellar, returned with an armful of kindling for the kitchen stove and made a second trip down for a hod of coal. By the time she got the fire going Abby, wearing a green cotton housedress, was in the kitchen instructing her what to prepare for breakfast.

By six-thirty Abby had joined John Morse in the sitting room and five minutes later her husband came down.

Andrew Borden, fully clothed for business in a white shirt, black bow tie and suit vest, carried a slop pitcher in one hand and the key to his bedroom (which he kept locked in the daytime) in the other. He went first into the sitting room, where he placed the bedroom key on the mantel. Hesitating in the kitchen, he slipped on a cardigan and proceeding out into the backyard, emptied the contents of the slop pitcher onto the ground. He then unlocked the barn door.

Adjacent to the barn were several pear trees, and Andrew paused to pick some fallen pears off the ground. Bringing them back into the house, he stopped to wash his face and hands in the kitchen sink, the one source of running water in the house except for the laundry room in the cellar. Andrew then joined Abby and John Morse in his dining room for breakfast.

Lizzie did not come down.

At seven a.m. the temperature was already eighty-nine degrees, yet the menu Abby had Bridget prepare was enormous. There were johnnycakes with butter, fresh-baked wheat bread, ginger and oatmeal cookies with raisins and the remainder of the mutton, which included hot mutton soup. This was washed down with coffee and thick cream, complemented by a bowl of fresh oranges, pears, apples and bananas.

Breakfast lasted for almost an hour.

Bridget ate hers in the kitchen, and while Andrew and John Morse were still seated in the dining room, Abby left them to instruct Bridget to begin washing the windows.

At eight a.m. Andrew and John Morse adjourned to the sitting room, where both of them relaxed on the long horsehair couch facing the windows, while Abby, armed with a feather duster, began cleaning the first floor.

At eight-forty John Morse prepared to leave the house. He intended to head for the post office and then to walk back to Weybosset Street, about a mile and a half away, for a second visit with his niece and nephew, who had arrived from Excelsior, Minnesota. Abby reminded him to be back by noon for dinner.

Morse agreed.

Andrew accompanied him to the back door by the kitchen entry. Bridget was in the sink room just beside it, drying the dishes. Andrew unlocked the latch and both men stepped out into the yard and talked for a minute or two in lowered voices; Bridget could not hear what they said. Then Andrew called out, "Come back to dinner, John."

Returning, Andrew relocked the screen door and entered the kitchen, where Bridget had begun to clean the stove. Standing over the kitchen sink he brushed his teeth. He then took his bedroom key from the sitting-room mantel, drew a basin of water for his washstand and disappeared with it up the back stairs.

At nine a.m. Lizzie came down the front stairs for the first time that morning. She stopped in the dining room to speak with Abby, admitting that she was sorry that she had missed her uncle. She then went into the kitchen and commented to Bridget that she wanted no breakfast but would make herself a cup of coffee. At that moment Andrew came down and Lizzie gave him a letter she had written to Emma, asking him to mail it.

Suddenly Bridget's throbbing head, combined with the staggering breakfast she had eaten, overpowered her. She fled to the backyard, retching and vomiting. It was several moments before she was able to return to the house.

By the time she did, Lizzie was gone, presumably back upstairs, and Andrew had left the house to go downtown.

Abby Borden was waiting for her in the dining room. Despite the paleness of Bridget's features and the fact that she had just vomited in the backyard, Abby reminded her that she should start washing the windows.

They spoke no more. Abby walked off toward the front of the house, flicking the feather duster along the backs of the chairs and the corners of the moldings. She then ascended the front stairs to the second floor.

It was nine-thirty a.m.

Bridget would never see her alive again.

There were five people who slept and ate in the Borden house on the morning of August 4, 1892. All five would gain worldwide attention. Their movements would be scrutinized by reporters, police, jurors, prosecutors, attorneys and a vast reading public for years to come.

Yet despite the plethora of testimony, the statements of witnesses and the investigatory procedures of countless policemen, no one would suspect what was still about to happen on that tragic, sweltering morning.

3

THE SLAUGHTER

Prosecutor:	Were you always cordial with your stepmother?
Lizzie:	That depends upon one's idea of cordiality.
Prosecutor:	Was it cordial according to your idea of cordiality?
Lizzie:	Yes. I did not regard her as my mother, though she came there when I was young. I decline to say whether my relations between her and myself were those of mother and daughter or not. I called her Mrs. Borden and sometimes mother.
Prosecutor:	Why did you leave off calling her mother?
Lizzie:	Because I wanted to.
Prosecutor:	Have you any other answer to give?
Lizzie:	No, sir. I always went to my sister. She was older than I was.

—From the inquest transcript,
August 10, 1892

EMMA'S ONE CONCERN was that either Bridget or Mrs. Churchill might see her. The street was quiet. It must have been almost ten. She had heard the church bell strike seven times as she was leaving Fairhaven. Yet already the morning was miserably hot.

She eased the reins at the corner and slowly circled around onto Spring Street, up Third and across Rodman so that when she returned down Second Street she would be hidden by the back of the carriage.

The long row of poplars and elms lining Second Street did not sway as she passed them. There was no breeze. It would be a long, sunny day, dull and quiet. The air felt thick and uncomfortable.

She passed the yellow cottage, drawing into the darkness of the carriage so that Mrs. Churchill would not make her out. Then she pulled in on the reins as she neared the gate and walkway leading to the brown two-story wooden frame structure.

She must not hesitate. She must hurry.

As the carriage stopped she tied up the reins and started down. Wrapping the axe in the folds of her black gossamer cape, she tucked the ends up over the blade.

Lizzie was alone in her room. She had waited for her uncle and father to leave the house. Hurriedly, she pulled the light blue dress with the dark diamond pattern over her head, its woven Bengaline linen texture falling down over her knees and ankles. She would find a pharmacist who would sell her the poison that she needed. With only a small amount she would be able to stop her father from signing anything over to her stepmother.

A frenzy overtook her as she started across the second-floor landing and noticed that the door to the guest room was ajar. Inside she could glimpse Abby's hulking shape bent in half, tucking in the sheets of the bed her uncle had slept on. Pushing the image out of her mind, Lizzie had hastened down the stairs when the front door opened.

The figure before her was unexpected.

"Emma . . . ," Lizzie gasped. But it was the look in Emma's eyes that made her stare into the face that she had known so long, as if she were seeing it for the first time.

As the door opened, Lizzie's huge eyes gaped out at her. Lizzie's face was white and her thick chestnut hair was tied back with a gold ribbon in a bun. Emma quickly put her finger to her lips, cautioning Lizzie to be silent. Then she slipped into the front entry, shutting the door behind her.

Immediately Emma locked the door's three locks.

No one must disturb them.

Then Lizzie noticed the axe and her face became deathly pale. It was as if out of their dreams the two sisters had now discovered that their entire fate, their lives centered upon it.

Emma smiled. She rarely smiled anymore, so much feeling had been drained out of her. Years of frustration and bitterness had made her feel very old. Lizzie bloomed in front of her with innocence and beauty, like a child. She always had been a child. Yet she was all that Emma lived for. She wanted so much to make Lizzie happy.

Lizzie led her up the stairs. Through the crack in the guest-room door they saw Abby's short, fat figure bent over a small foot trunk beside the large four-poster bed, her hands pulling and tucking at the sheets and pillow cases.

She seemed so insignificant, despite her enormous size, such a tiny little lady to hold so much power over them.

Emma edged open the door, holding firmly to the handle of the axe. The moment her stepmother saw her she would rush across the room and crack open her face.

Emma crept slowly up behind her. The thick flower-printed carpet muffled the sound of her feet.

It was a long distance but she moved silently. Abby did not seem to sense her presence. She did not whirl around or utter a sound.

Emma raised the handle, suddenly feeling the heaviness of the axe-head as she hoisted it. Even at the last second her stepmother did not turn. Emma swung the blade down with all her might.

It was a bad angle. The axe was even more unwieldy than she had expected. The blade glanced off the side of Abby's head. Abby slipped forward to her knees. At the same time her arms reached out, up, to her side, flailing at whatever it was. Emma struck her again, the edge of the axe impaling itself in Abby's neck.

Abby was on the floor, her arms clutching the rug. The axe came down again.

It was at that moment that Emma noticed Lizzie backing up, to get away from the blood. Her stepmother was moving, trying to get up on her knees.

Emma swung the axe, hacking her twice on the side of the head. Again Abby went down. Emma hit her until the blood poured over the blade.

Again Emma swung the axe.

Abby did not cry out. She couldn't as each time the blade jammed into the cut, which was growing deeper and bloodier, spurting down the back of her dress.

The axe hit her again and again, each time Emma wielding it with all her might, the blood from Abby's neck and head spraying across the floor, hanging like a fog in the air near the edge of the bed as Emma kept hitting her, hitting her, hitting her. . . .

And then she stopped, as Abby's head toppled off, held on only by a thin sinew of flesh.

Emma hit her again.

Neither heat nor illness could keep Andrew Borden from his business; and he *was* ill. Because of Abby's emotional outburst, he had concealed the pains in his stomach and the resultant nausea he had experienced over the past forty-eight hours, but at last they were taking their toll. But still, a morning's work lay ahead of him and the routine he had fashioned for himself for well over fifty years was not to be put aside.

At the National Union Bank he met with John Burrill, the cashier, and a Negro landowner about a loan. Whether or not Andrew would have given him the loan was never resolved, but the meeting lasted for ten minutes. Andrew then crossed the street to the First National Bank of Fall River, where he conferred with Everett Cook, the cashier there. His final visit was to the A. J. Borden Building, where a carpenter, Joseph Shirtsleeves, and his assistant, James Mather, were lowering the front window into one of the new stores to meet the specifications of Jonathan Clegg, a hatter. Clegg had met with Borden earlier that week and had pointed out exactly what work he needed done in the shop he was leasing from him.

As Andrew inspected the work that Shirtsleeves and Mather were doing he noticed a discarded lock on the floor. It had been removed from an old door and was broken into pieces. Andrew picked up the lock, examined it a second and dropped it again on the floor. He then went upstairs to check out the work being done on the second floor. When he came back down he re-entered the store and without a comment, in front of Joseph Shirtsleeves, picked up the broken lock and slipped it into his pocket.

It was Andrew's final act of thrift.

Exhausted by ten-fifteen a.m., he crossed Main Street and headed back home.

Bridget had begun by washing the sitting-room windows on the south side of the house. The sudsing was done with a long-handled mop, followed by rinsing them with water flung up from a bucket. It was an awkward job, demanding repeated trips to the faucet in the barn. She had to climb the stepladder twice, to wash and rinse the top of each tall pane of glass, and while doing it she could see into the house. At no time did she notice anyone on the first floor, neither Lizzie nor Mrs. Borden.

She had been hired by Andrew Borden to wash, iron, cook and sweep. Her duties as housemaid did not include taking care of the bedrooms, except her own. In fact, she never set foot on the second floor. Lizzie and Emma took care of their own rooms and Abby cleaned the guest room.

Bridget was twenty-five. She had a pretty face with dark Irish eyes and a full, well-developed figure. She was trusting and pleasant, with a soft brogue when she spoke.

For a few moments on that hot morning she stopped to chat with Dr. Kelly's servant girl in the house next door. Then she continued with the three parlor windows in the front of the house.

As she headed back toward the barn with her empty pail she slumped on the back porch, her feet dangling over the steps. She still had the insides of all seven double windows to wash, but between the relentless heat and the terrible sick feeling in her stomach, she had to allow herself time to rest.

She knew that she had not much hope of finishing the windows that morning, but the thought of continuing her chores throughout the blazing afternoon was not pleasant. Soon she would have to begin preparing the noon meal.

It was a strange, dour house in which she had given her services for the past two and a half years. She had never understood what went on between these people.

She was aware that the two daughters, Emma and Lizzie, felt great contempt for Mrs. Borden. And she had heard the two girls arguing with Mr. Borden on numerous occasions, their shouts resounding from the parlor through the upstairs. But Bridget kept to herself. She did not want to be involved in the family disruptions.

She had worked in two other homes since leaving Ireland six years before. How and why she chose Fall River was the question. It was a small town like the one she had come from. But the people in New England were strange and different.

Bridget was Catholic. Not that the Bordens were not God-fearing people in their way. Lizzie was a member of the Woman's Christian Temperance Union and she taught a Sunday school class at the Mission Church five blocks away.

But Mr. and Mrs. Borden seldom went to church. In fact Mrs. Borden hardly ever left the house except to visit her sister Mrs. Whitehead. Friends occasionally stopped by, but Mr. Borden did not like to entertain outsiders.

It was just as well, Bridget reflected as she sat motionless looking out over the steaming garden. There was less work for her to do.

Then the thought recurred to her that she still had the insides of seven double windows to wash. She did not like the idea. She would have preferred to lie down for the rest of the day until her spirits revived.

But Mrs. Borden had left specific instructions that on Thursday all the windows *had* to be washed.

Finally, Bridget got up and ambled inside the house, latching the screen door after her. She filled her pail with water from the faucet in the sink room and set up her ladder in front of the two windows in the sitting room. She glanced at Andrew's couch opposite the windows. It was brown leather, mahogany-framed and upholstered with horsehair, with tufted, well-padded arms, and several decorative pillows piled at each end. It looked so inviting. Yet if she stopped again she would never finish with the windows.

She had begun scrubbing the insides of the glass panes when she heard a scratching sound at the front door. And yet she did not hear the bell ring.

Alarmed, Bridget climbed down off the ladder and walked through the front entry.

All three door locks were fastened and Bridget cursed as her wet hands struggled to open them. At that moment she heard Lizzie laugh. She would testify later that it had come from upstairs, from the front landing leading to the guest room.

Finally the locks gave and Bridget swung open the door.

Andrew Borden stood on the doorstep with a key in his hand. He did not say a word. Under his arm he carried a small package.

Bridget went back into the sitting room to finish washing the windows as Andrew walked into the dining room and sat down at the table.

As Emma hid behind the closet door on the front landing so that she could hear what was going on below, Lizzie quickly came down the stairs.

Bridget heard Lizzie ask Andrew how he was feeling.

Andrew replied, "No better, no worse." His muffled voice told Lizzie there was no mail for her. All the letters he had picked up at the post office were his. He had, of course, mailed her letter to Emma.

He then asked about Mrs. Borden. Bridget heard Lizzie tell him that Mrs. Borden had received a note and gone out.

Andrew made no reply. Getting up from his chair in the dining room, he came into the sitting room, where Bridget was still at work. Taking the key from the mantelpiece, he climbed the back stairs to his bedroom. At this point Bridget moved her ladder and pail into the dining room. She had begun washing the two windows there when Andrew came back, returned to the sitting room and lay down on the horsehair couch.

Lizzie emerged from the front entry and walking into the dining room asked Bridget, "Maggie, are you going out this afternoon?"

Stopping her work, Bridget replied, "I don't know. I might and I might not. I don't feel well."

"Well, be sure and lock the door," Lizzie continued. "Mrs. Borden has gone out on a sick call and I might go out too."

"Miss Lizzie, who is sick?" Bridget asked.

Lizzie shook her head. "I don't know. She got a note this morning. It must be in town."

After several minutes Bridget finished the two windows and was about to leave the dining room, where Lizzie was ironing handkerchiefs. Suddenly Lizzie's face beamed. "There is a cheap sale of dress goods at Sargent's this afternoon at eight cents a yard."

This was all the temptation Bridget needed to end her chores. "I'm going to have one!" she exclaimed.

Climbing the back stairs, Bridget felt the heat seize her body. She would lie down for a while, rest, and then go downtown. She stretched out on the top of the bed without removing her shoes.

The next sound she heard was the City Hall bell ringing eleven times.

Andrew could not put his feet up—the couch was not long enough. A white haze from the windows had settled over the papers on his desk, the deeds, the mortgages, the accounts that he could not bear to look at. Still dressed in his suit, white shirt and tie, he dozed off, letting the heat of the afternoon become more distant amid the shades of sleep. He would lie there until John Morse returned, until Abby returned, until it was time for dinner. . . .

As his body began to relax, he turned his arms and legs slightly in toward the crevice in which he buried his head.

His thoughts grew deeper into slumber. He did not hear Emma come down the stairs and slip through the door from the front entry.

Just before he felt the air swirl above his face, his eyes opened to slits.

The thin tall figure of Emma stood above him. Her face was a hideous glare.

He tried to shield his eyes but before his fingers got there the axe hit him.

His body twitched with the blow, yet he could not wince. It had crunched his nose in half.

Blood spit through his teeth. He tried to scream a second before the blade cut him across the cheek.

4

THE BODIES

Inside the house where the bodies lay the rooms were in perfect order. Mrs. Borden had smoothed out the last fold in the snow-white counterpane, and placed the pillows on the bed with the utmost care of a tidy housewife. The author of the hideous slaughter had come and gone as gently as the south wind, but had fulfilled his mission as terrifically as a cyclone. No more cunning plan had ever been hatched in a madman's brain, and no more thorough work was ever done by the guillotine. Mystery sombre and absolute hung in impenetrable folds over the Borden house, and not one ray of light existed to penetrate its blackness.

—*The Fall River Tragedy**

MARK CHASE WAS THE PROPRIETOR of Hall's Livery Stable on the west side of Second Street just south of the City Hall. He had sat out front of his stable in a large wicker chair all morning, positioning

**The Fall River Tragedy* by Edwin H. Porter, printed privately in 1893, was the first book published about the murders. Only four copies are known to exist. A copy which was originally in the Library of Congress has vanished, one is kept at the State House in Boston, one is in the archives of the Fall River Historical Society and one is in my possession. Lizzie bought off the printer and had all the other copies destroyed before they reached the bookshops. Her reasons for doing so will be explored later.

himself in the shade of a large, luxuriant elm as a shield from the torrid burning blaze above. Thursdays, as a rule, were not busy, and this particular day was not turning out to be an exception.

It was just as well. Because of the relentless heat it was not the kind of morning when he felt like doing much.

He had settled himself in his wicker chair at half past nine. That was when he first noticed the black carriage in front of Andrew Borden's house. There were other carriages parked along Second Street but what drew Mark Chase's attention was the horse. Mark Chase knew horses and this one was of an exceptional breed.

What intrigued him was that he had never before seen this particular horse in the neighborhood and he wondered whom it belonged to.

All morning long he waited to see.

But shortly after eleven a.m. he left his spot in the shade and went around to the back of the stable. It seemed as if he were gone only a moment or two.

When he returned, the horse and carriage were gone.

At eleven-ten a.m. Bridget was still lying on top of the bed in her attic room. Suddenly she was startled to her feet by Lizzie's voice booming up the back stairwell: "Maggie, come down!"

Bridget stumbled forward. "What's the matter?"

"Come down quick! Father's dead! Somebody came in and killed him!"

Hurriedly Bridget tottered down the flight of narrow stairs, her heart pounding wildly.

Lizzie stood at the back door, her eyes staring, her face deathly pale.

Bridget tore for the sitting room, but Lizzie quickly blocked her way, fiercely grabbing her arm. "Don't go in there. Go over and get the doctor. I've got to have the doctor! Run!"

Hurtling through the screen door, Bridget raced up the drive and out the front gate. Crossing Second Street, she ran up the front walkway and banged with all her might on Dr. Bowen's door.

It was his wife who answered. "What is it?"—she barely was able to mouth the words.

"Where's the doctor?" Bridget blurted out.

"He's not in . . . not in . . ."

"It's terrible! Terrible! Mr. Borden has just been murdered!"

Without waiting for her reaction, Bridget turned and flew back across the street to tell Lizzie.

Lizzie was waiting, standing in the same spot at the rear entry.

Bridget conveyed her helplessness, her inability to locate Dr. Bowen. But for an instant she was confused. She was almost certain she had latched the screen door. "Miss Lizzie, where were you!" she suddenly wailed. "Didn't I leave the screen door locked?"

"I was in the yard," Lizzie answered, her watery blue eyes centering on Bridget's flushed face. "I heard a groan and came in and the screen door was open. Go get Mrs. Russell!" Lizzie suddenly ordered. "Do you know where she lives?"

"Yes."

"Get her! Run! *Run!* I don't want to be alone in the house!"

At eleven a.m. Adelaide Churchill had walked to M. T. Hudner's Market on South Main Street to buy groceries for her dinner. It was a short walk, no more than three blocks.

Mrs. Churchill was a widow whose household consisted of her mother, her sister, her son, her niece and a hired man. For forty-three years of her life she had lived next door to 92 Second Street.

The property on which the Borden house rested had once been owned by her family, but it had all been divided up when she was a child. She knew the Bordens well—not intimately, but she was on calling terms with them.

After purchasing an armload of staples she walked back up Third Street, turned the corner and continued along Second Street toward her home. Midway down the block she saw Bridget rush across the street from Dr. Bowen's back to the Borden house, her face as pale as a ghost. What immediately occurred to Mrs. Churchill was that someone was sick.

Hurrying her groceries through the back door of her house, Mrs. Churchill put down her packages and peered through her kitchen window. She could see Lizzie on the inside of her screen door, appearing as though she were leaning on the casing of the door, her hand to her head. She watched her for several seconds but Lizzie did not move. They were a short distance, perhaps only ten yards, away from each other. It was the strange look on Lizzie's face that was puzzling. She looked excited and agitated.

Finally, Mrs. Churchill called across, "Lizzie, what is the matter?"

Lizzie quickly turned, stunned by her voice. "Oh, Mrs. Churchill, please come over! Someone has killed Father!"

A four-foot-high board fence separated the two properties, so that Mrs. Churchill had to go out into the street to reach the nearby side entry. She opened the Borden's gate and hurried up the drive. She

1. The Borden house
2. The Borden barn
3. Side entrance to Borden kitchen
4. Adelaide Churchill's house.
5. Dr. Seabury Bowen's house
6. Dr. Chagnon's house
7. The Kelly house

found Lizzie slumped on the lowest step of the back stairway, her face empty and white.

Mrs. Churchill bent down, her fingers touching Lizzie's arm. "Lizzie?"

But Lizzie did not respond.

"Where is your father, Lizzie?"

It took a moment or so before Lizzie murmured, "In the sitting room."

Mrs. Churchill moved past Lizzie through the kitchen and pushed open the door of the sitting room. Stifling a gasp, she glanced at the bloody carnage that was Andrew Borden. Quickly she returned. Trembling with anxiety, she prodded Lizzie, "Where were you when it happened?"

"I was in the barn . . . I went there to get a piece of iron."

"Where is your mother?"

Lizzie's voice grew very quiet. "I don't know . . . she got a note to go see someone who is sick. . . ." Hesitantly, Lizzie added, "Father must have an enemy. . . . We've all been sick. . . . We think the milk has been poisoned. I tried to find Dr. Bowen but he isn't home. I must have a doctor."

"Shall I try to get someone to get a doctor?"

"Yes—"

Mrs. Churchill left Lizzie on the steps and hastened back up the driveway, through the front gate. Crossing the street to Hall's Livery Stable, where Tom, her hired man, had taken the carriage, she told him to find a doctor. The nearest physician was Dr. Chagnon. She ordered Tom to hurry.

John Cunningham, the local newsdealer, who was lounging at the stable, overheard Mrs. Churchill giving urgent instructions to her hired man. Briskly Cunningham left the stable and crossed to a store where there was a telephone. He immediately telephoned the Fall River *Globe*, giving them an exclusive story that something terrible involving a knife slashing had occurred at the Borden house.

Cunningham then called the police.

When Mrs. Churchill arrived back at the Borden house she found Bridget standing with Lizzie. Lizzie had not moved from the rear entry. She was still clutching the screen door, her face pale and tense.

Mrs. Churchill heard a sudden noise behind her, which turned out to be Dr. Bowen passing through the kitchen. "He's been murdered! Addy!" Bowen gesticulated. "Come in and see Mr. Borden!"

"Oh, no," Mrs. Churchill gasped, drawing back, "I don't want to see him. I saw him already . . . I don't want to see him."

Bowen turned to Lizzie. "Have you seen anybody around the place?"

"I have not," Lizzie replied.

"Where have you been?"

"I was in the barn looking for iron."

The doctor asked for a sheet to cover the body.

To carry out Dr. Bowen's request Bridget asked him to get her the keys from the mantel as she had no desire to view Mr. Borden's body. She then announced that she was terrified to go up the back strairs alone. Finally Mrs. Churchill agreed to accompany her to Andrew and Abby's bedroom, where the linens were kept.

Dr. Bowen returned to the sitting room. Andrew Borden was

stretched out on the sofa, his head on a pillow, his long legs resting on floor. There was blood everywhere, on the flowered carpet, on the wall over the sofa and even splattered on a picture hanging from the wall. Andrew's head was bent slightly to the right, but his face was unrecognizable as human. There were eleven distinct cuts across the forehead between the ears and above the mouth, slicing the flesh into a grotesque, seething patchwork. Fresh blood still seeped from the wounds. One eye had been cut in half and dangled from its socket. The nose had been severed, lopped loose from the upper jaw. It was obvious to Bowen that the wounds had been inflicted by a sharp heavy weapon and Andrew had been struck from above with blows crashing vertically down while his head rested on the pillows of the couch.

Mrs. Churchill returned with the sheet and Bowen covered the body. When he came back into the kitchen he found Lizzie seated in a rocker. Alice Russell had arrived and both she and Bridget were fanning Lizzie, rubbing her hands and applying cold cloths to her head. When Alice attempted to loosen her dress, Lizzie remarked flatly, "I don't feel faint." She then asked Bowen to send a telegram to Emma letting her know what had happened.

Dr. Bowen left the house.

Mrs. Churchill again asked Lizzie the whereabouts of her stepmother.

"I wish someone would try to find her. I thought I heard her come in," Lizzie announced.

But Bridget was still too afraid to explore the upstairs on her own. Mrs. Churchill again said she would go with her.

Both ladies went through the dining room, avoiding the sitting room, where Andrew's corpse lay bleeding. Proceeding through the front entry, they started up the front stairs.

As the door to the guest room caught Mrs. Churchill's eyes she noticed that it was ajar. She drew back, clutching the banister. The lower part of a woman's body sprawled on the floor on the far side of the bed.

Hurriedly Mrs. Churchill and Bridget came back down the stairs and returned to the kitchen.

Mrs. Churchill sank down on a chair beside the kitchen table, her hands shaking. The second corpse was too much for her.

At last, Alice Russell asked, "Is there another?"

Mrs. Churchill nodded, tears filling her eyes. "Yes, she's up there."

It was then that Lizzie, sitting quietly through it all, abruptly spoke up. "I will have to get right over to Oak Grove Cemetery to see about things."

Mrs. Churchill stared at her. With alarm in her voice, she finally murmured, "Oh, no . . . the undertaker will see to everything for you."

5

THE POLICEMEN'S PICNIC

Andrew J. Borden and wife, two of the eldest, wealthiest and most highly respected persons in the city, were brutally murdered with an axe at 11 o'clock this morning in their home on Second Street within a few minutes walk of the City Hall. The Borden family consisted of the father, mother, two daughters and a servant. The elder daughter has been in Fairhaven for some days. The rest of the family have been ill for three or four days and Dr. Bowen, the attending physician, thought they had been poisoned.

Miss Lizzie Borden, the youngest daughter, was in the barn when she heard a cry of distress coming apparently from the house and she ran in. Going directly to a sitting room leading from the main hallway in the house she saw the father lying back on the sofa, lifeless and covered with blood.

She ran out again shrieking and her cries attracted the servant and a neighbor. They made a hasty search for the mother and found her upstairs in a spare room lying dead, face downward, on the floor. The women ran downstairs terrified and summoned Dr. Bowen who lives opposite. He found both of the victims dead. Then the daughter and servant fainted.

The city is thoroughly excited over the murders and about a dozen different theories have been advanced by the police who have as yet not the slightest clue to the murderer. The stomachs of both victims were removed and placed in alcohol. They will be sent to Boston tomorrow for analysis to determine whether milk poisoning was attempted. The police are suspicious of John V. Morse, brother-in-law of Mr. Borden by his first marriage.

—*The New York Times,* Friday, August 5, 1892

NEITHER LIZZIE NOR BRIDGET HAD FAINTED following the discovery of the bodies, but already the press had begun suggestively coloring the facts. The story of the murders was to enflame the national curiosity. It would become a melodramatic sensation. The fable, the myth of "the unsolvable axe murders," was beginning.

When local newsdealer John Cunningham telephoned the Central Police Station to report "the knife slashing" which had taken place in the Borden house, he spoke directly to Rufus B. Hilliard, the City Marshal. Most of the force were attending the department's annual picnic and clambake at Rocky Point, Rhode Island. Consequently Hilliard was compelled to send an inexperienced young officer, George W. Allen, to 92 Second Street to investigate.

Officer Allen ran the four hundred yards in record time but found the front door to the Borden house bolted and locked.

He raced around to the rear and entered through the screen door. Without hesitation he sprang through the kitchen into the sitting room, where he was confronted by the hideous spectre of Andrew Borden's face.

Allen had a sensitive nature. He took one look at Andrew, let out a scream and fled from the house.

On his way through the front gate he almost knocked down a very large man who was passing by, a housepainter named Charles S. Sawyer. In a daze, Allen ordered Sawyer to stand before the side door and to admit nobody but the police or doctors until officers returned to investigate.*

Completely unhinged by the incident, Allen tore off down the street as if pursued by demons. Racing into the police station he was able only to gibber, "He's dead! He's dead!" without being able to articulate who was dead.

*It was not until six p.m., when Sawyer complained that he was getting hungry, that the police realized he had been doing guard duty all day and replaced him with a uniformed officer.

Meanwhile Dr. Bowen had sent the telegram to Emma and returned to the house to learn of Abby Borden's body on the second floor.

Climbing the front stairs, he found the body lying face down in a pool of blood. Her head and the nape of her neck were a bloody nightmare. Examining closer, he discovered that Abby's head had been almost lopped off. In addition there was one wound on the back of the neck, and a misdirected or poorly aimed blow had sliced a grotesque flap from the back of the scalp.

But the most telling element was the blood which surrounded her face and hair. It was dark and congealed, indicating that she had died some time before her husband.

As in the case of Andrew, there were no signs of a struggle. The bed was completely made, even the fringed spread was smooth and in place. Obviously the murderer had struck swiftly, creeping up on her from behind and taking her by surprise.

Bowen walked back down the stairs into the kitchen, where Mrs. Churchill, Bridget, Alice Russell and Lizzie were waiting. He announced that Mrs. Borden was dead, that she had been murdered. For a moment his attention fixed on Lizzie. "You were lucky you weren't in the house when it happened. You might have been murdered as well."

Lizzie looked away without replying.

Bowen noticed that she had changed into a different dress. The one she had worn before was pale blue. This one was pink.

And then he noticed the book on the side counter, its pages bent back, one of them broken loose from the binding. Looking closer he saw that it was a volume of household hints and on the page broken loose was an entry:

> PRUSSIC ACID—Hydrogen cyanide. A colorless almond-tasting liquid. Warning: Extremely toxic and usually fatal if taken internally.

City Marshal Rufus B. Hilliard had his hands full. With much of his staff depleted as a result of the police department's annual picnic and clambake and now Officer George Allen too frightened to return to the Borden house, he had to quickly round up some force members to go to the scene and investigate.

At that moment Deputy Marshal John Fleet arrived from across town with Patrolman William H. Medley and Officer Charles Wilson. Dispatching them to 92 Second Street, Marshal Hilliard ordered three other young officers, Wixon, Mullaly and Devine, to hurry after them.

The six policemen vigorously descended on the house.

Coincidentally, Dr. William A. Dolan, Medical Examiner for Bristol County, was passing 92 Second Street when he saw the flurry of activity. After hitching his horse, he went inside to inquire what was going on. He found all six policemen intently staring at the two bodies: Andrew's in the sitting room and Abby's upstairs. As Dr. Bowen began recounting to Dolan what had occurred, the youthful officer Mullaly took the initiative and tore himself loose from the two groups.

He announced to Adelaide Churchill that he wished to see the lady of the house, needlessly adding, "The City Marshal sent me." Mrs. Churchill took Mullaly with her into the dining room, where Lizzie was resting on the sofa.

Mullaly immediately demanded from Lizzie if there were any axes or hatchets in the house.

Lizzie, coolly eyeing him from the sofa, commented, "Yes. They are everywhere."

She then instructed Bridget to give him a tour of the cellar.

Bridget and Mullaly descended the back stairs. Near the washtubs Bridget produced an axe which had dried blood and hairs on it—a cow's, as it eventually turned out. She led Mullaly into the warm, damp fruit cellar, where they located a claw-headed hatchet, also bearing brown stains, which proved to be rust. Then she reached up into the chimney and lifted down a box which contained two dusty hatchets that had obviously not been used for a long time. One of the hatchets was handleless, its head covered with ashes. The handle had been broken off near the head, but the broken wood appeared new.*

Beside the head of the hatchet lay its broken handle.

Officer Mullaly's investigative powers were at an end. He carried the hatchets into the laundry room and stalwartly stood guard over them, waiting for orders from his superiors.

Meanwhile upstairs, it had dawned on Officer James Wixon that since Andrew's blood still ran freely and Abby's was coagulated, their assailant must have hidden in the house for some time.

The front door was bolted. How had the killer managed to get away?

The solution seized him.

Racing through the house, Wixon tore out the rear screen door and

*This hatchet would later be introduced as evidence.

headed for the back lot. Peering through the pear trees he caught a glimpse of a man's straw hat behind the high fence. Jumping up on the woodpile, Wixon tore his hands on the barbed wire as he hurtled over the fence.

The straw hat covered the head of a man sawing wood in the company of two other astonished laborers. Under heated questioning, one of them guiltily admitted that he had stood on a sawhorse earlier that morning and pilfered a pear from an overhanging bough.

Embarrassed, Wixon sauntered back around the block and quietly returned to the kitchen, his palms lacerated and bleeding.

In the midst of policemen and doctors coming and going, John Vinnicum Morse strolled in from the street. He stopped in the backyard and picked up some ripe fruit from under the pear trees and began eating it. He seemed to be in no hurry to enter the house.

Patrolman Medley and Sergeant Philip Harrington, who had just arrived, were also in the backyard. Lizzie had told them, as she had Dr. Bowen, that she was in the barn loft looking for iron. The iron was to be used to make sinkers for a fishing trip she had planned. She was an excellent angler, she explained, a fact that could be verified by all who knew her.

The two policemen entered the unbearably hot barn loft. The floor was thickly covered with hay dust, which they found absolutely free of footprints or marks of any kind. Medley and Harrington placed their hands in the dust, leaving two clearly distinct impressions. From that moment on both men were certain that Lizzie was lying.

At three p.m. Andrew's and Abby's mutilated bodies were carried into the dining room so that Dr. Dolan could perform autopsies. The gruesome task was performed on the same dining-room table on which Bridget had served breakfast only eight hours before. The stomach of each of the victims was removed and tied at either end to retain the contents of the organ, and was then placed in an individual container. These containers, together with the axe and three hatchets discovered by Officer Mullaly, were rushed by special messenger to Edward S. Wood, M.D., professor of chemistry at Harvard Medical School.

Upstairs Deputy Marshal John Fleet was questioning Lizzie. They were alone in her bedroom. Fleet was a handsome, youngish-looking man, with intent, patient eyes. He was well educated and well bred. Those who knew him felt that he could easily have been a doctor or a lawyer, so far was he from the common notion of a small-town policeman. Yet of all the officers present, he was the most experienced. Truly, the investigation was in his hands.

Lizzie rested on her bed. Her two windows were open to the noises of the police searching the yard below.

Fleet asked Lizzie if she knew anything about the murders.

She insisted that she did not. All she knew was that her father had come home at about ten-thirty or ten forty-five a.m. looking weak and exhausted. He had retreated into the sitting room, where he settled into the large chair. He took out some papers and began studying them.

She was in the adjacent dining room, ironing some handkerchiefs on the dining-room table.

But his appearance, the fact that he looked so ill, bothered her greatly. Eventually, in about five or ten minutes, she went to him and helped him lie down on the sofa, propping the pillows up under his head. Leaving him to doze, she went outside to the barn.

Fleet asked her exactly where she had gone to in the barn.

Lizzie replied that she had climbed up to the barn loft. After she had been up there half an hour she came down again, went into the house and found her father on the couch in the position she had left him. His face had been crushed and he was covered with blood.

In terror, she called Maggie.

Fleet stopped her. Who was Maggie?

Lizzie explained that it was the servant girl.

"Who was in the house this morning and last night?" Fleet continued.

"No one but my father, Mrs. Borden, Maggie and Mr. Morse," Lizzie replied.

"Who is Mr. Morse?"

"My uncle. He arrived here yesterday. Last night he slept in the guest room . . . where Mrs. Borden was found."

"Do you think Mr. Morse had anything to do with the killing of your parents?"

"No," Lizzie answered. "He left the house this morning before nine o'clock and did not return until after the bodies were found."

"Do you think that Maggie could be the murderer?"

Lizzie shook her head. "Maggie was upstairs when my father lay down on the couch. When I came back from the barn she was still upstairs."

"Are you certain she couldn't have done it?" For a moment, Lizzie fell silent. Instantly Fleet prodded, "Well, who do you think could have killed your father and mother?"

"She's not my mother," Lizzie suddenly snapped back at him. "She is my stepmother. My mother died when I was a child."

Fleet was taken aback by the biting emphasis in her voice. At that moment Alice Russell entered the room. "Lizzie, tell him what you told me," she pleaded.

Lizzie gave Alice a long, searching look. Slowly she began relating the story of a man who had come to see her father two weeks before. "He came to the front door and he was angry . . . and Father stood there talking with him . . ."

"What were they talking about?"

"He was talking about a store. . . . Father said to him, 'I can't let you have the store for that purpose.' I was coming down the stairs. . . . I heard the man start to shout . . . he was very angry. . . ." As she spoke, Lizzie's face grew ashen. Alice moved across the room and took her hand for support.

Dr. Bowen had entered the room and was standing just inside the door.

Fleet glanced at him, then at Alice, and back at Lizzie's face. There was no point in pushing her, he decided. Later there would be time.

Fleet rose and, excusing himself, left the room.

Lizzie suddenly clutched Alice's hand as Dr. Bowen sat down on the bed beside her. "Why didn't you tell him about the house being broken into—about the things that were taken?" Alice asked anxiously.

Lizzie shivered. "It wouldn't have mattered."

Bowen nodded to Alice for her to leave them alone.

Alice went out and shut the door behind her.

"He thinks I murdered them!" Lizzie suddenly blurted out.

"No . . . no, he doesn't think that. . . ." Bowen attempted to calm her.

"But I told him the truth . . . I told him the truth!"

"I know you did . . . I know. . . ."

Bowen reached for the empty glass on the table beside her. Sprinkling the bottom with a mild dose of Bromo-caffeine he filled it half full with water.

Lizzie sipped it down and lay back against the pillow, closing her eyes.

6

THE VIGIL

> A leading physician said that he was fully convinced that the act was not done by a man, as all authorities agreed in saying that hacking is almost a positive sign of the deed of a woman who is unconscious of what she is doing.
>
> —The Fall River *Herald*

WHEN EMMA ARRIVED AT 92 SECOND STREET it was almost seven p.m. The sky was a golden yellow blur, although the tops of the stately poplars and elms extending like fingers toward the center of town were splattered with rushes of crimson. Throughout the day it had not cooled. And yet it was a tranquil summer evening, torpid and mellow, with a sense of timelessness and peace—everywhere, perhaps, but inside the brown two-story wooden frame house where the corpses of Andrew and Abby still lay exposed on the dining-room table awaiting the undertaker. Here a residue of inexplicable violence and revolting butchery permeated the humid air with a thick, dull rancidness, attracting multitudes of hungry flies circling through the open windows and buzzing over the traces of blood tracked from room to room.

The plaster, papered walls and hardwood floors visibly trembled as dozens of police circulated through the house from cellar to attic, searching every room, every closet, every trunk, suitcase and drawer.

Frustrated, they could not uncover the note which Abby supposedly had received, telling her of the sick friend in town. And they could not find the murder weapon.

John Vinnicum Morse had been questioned shortly after he entered the house from the backyard.

He had left the Bordens at approximately eight forty-five a.m. and walked first to the post office and then to 4 Weybosset Street, about a mile and a half away, to visit his niece and nephew from Excelsior, Minnesota. He had talked with them and returned to the Borden house three hours later.

Bridget went to pieces. She became so agitated that she hysterically blurted out to the police that all morning long she had been washing windows on the *third* floor.

In her upstairs bedroom, Lizzie's interrogation became unceasing. At first she had been composed and cooperative, responding clearly and directly to everything that was asked of her. But finally she began to weary of hearing the same questions—*Where were you? What were you doing when?— Did you? Didn't you? Why didn't you?*—repeated over and over. Arrogantly she began rebuffing them. She complained that she was getting tired and demanded that they be brief. As she felt the pressure against her building she became so nauseous that Dr. Bowen had to give her more sedatives.

She closed her eyes for several moments. When she opened them the blue-uniformed presence of a man in his early forties stood at the foot of her bed. Sergeant Philip Harrington's thin Irish face intently peered down at her.

"What is it?" she asked, irritated by the intrusion.

She noticed his jaw harden.

"Tell me what you know about all this?" he demanded.

What she saw in his eyes was cold, implacable distrust. She sensed immediately that he would be more aggressive than the others, that he felt cocksure he was on to something. "I can tell you nothing about it," she murmured.

Harrington was poised, his voice reeking of suspicion. He was prepared to fire the next question—the next—the next. "When did you last see your father?"

"When he came back from the post office."

"Tell me about it."

"He had some mail. I asked him if he had any for me but he said no."

"Then what?"

"He sat down to read the paper—I went out to the barn. . . ."

The iciness in Harrington's voice suddenly cut through her. *"How long were you in the barn?"*

"About twenty minutes," she mumbled. Lizzie looked up at him with almost a plea in her voice. "When I came back . . . I found him dead."

He did not believe her. She was certain of it.

"When you were going to or coming from the barn did you see anyone in the yard or going up or down the street?"

She shook her head quickly.

"While you were in the barn . . . did you hear any noise . . . did you hear anybody walking through the yard?"

"No."

"Not even the opening or closing of the screen door?"

"No, sir."

"But you must have . . . you were only a short distance . . . you must have heard the screen door open and close."

Lizzie hesitated. And then quickly snapped. "I was in the loft."

Harrington shifted his feet, looking pleased with himself. "What do you think was the motive?"

"I don't know."

"Was it robbery?"

"I don't think so."

"Why not?"

"Nothing appears to have been taken."

Harrington smiled. "That's true."

"But a few weeks ago Father had angry words with a man about something."

"What was it about?"

"I don't know, but they were both angry. And then the man went away."

"Did you see this man?"

"No. They were in another room."

"Did your father say anything about him afterward?"

"No. But about two weeks later the same man came back again and I heard them arguing and Father said, 'No! I will not let my store for such a business!' "

"But you never saw the man?"

"No, sir."

At this point Lizzie felt queasy. The strain of the day was taking its toll. Yet she had to get through this.

Harrington smiled coolly. "Perhaps you're not in a mental condition to give me a clear statement of the facts . . . perhaps you'll feel differently tomorrow. . . . You might remember the man's name . . . you might even remember what he looked like. . . ."

"No," she replied strongly. "I can tell you all I know now just as well as any other time!"

"I have one more question. . . ."

"Yes?"

"Exactly how long did you say you were out of the house?"

"I already told you . . . twenty minutes."

With that Harrington left her. Later he would recall that Lizzie was wearing a plain house wrap with an alternating pink and light stripe.

He went down the stairs to the kitchen, where he passed Dr. Bowen. Bowen was shuffling several sheets of notepaper in his hands. "What are those?" Harrington asked.

"Oh, they're nothing," Bowen replied.

Harrington noticed the word "Emma" in the left-hand corner of one of the pages.

Immediately Bowen turned slightly, and before Harrington could stop him, lifted the lid from the stove and threw the pages into the fire.

Harrington noticed that there were other scraps of paper with writing on them already burning. Among them was a thin, rolled-up paper about twelve inches long.

When Emma found Lizzie in her room she was still lying on her bed.

Emma embraced her, holding her for several moments.

Lizzie did not cry. At no time during the day had she broken down. The pact between the two sisters was so fervent that they could withstand the questioning and the wave of intrusion into their lives.

The secret of what had occurred was theirs alone, to be cherished as a grim possession, communicable to no one but each other. Stronger than a bond of love, the secret wedded them forever.

Emma would stand by, and Lizzie would protect her. By her silence, she would shield Emma's deed from the world. Without a murder weapon there was no evidence. No power on earth would be able to prove that either of them was responsible for the deaths of Abby and Andrew.

Only they knew of their responsibility.

And it would haunt them.

As it grew dark, cordons of police were stationed around 92 Second Street to guard it from the curious who had begun to gather in front of the house. Bridget, trembling with terror that the unknown murderer would seek further victims, was taken to the home of a neighbor.

No lights were lit in the guest room, still stained with Abby's blood.

Yet John Vinnicum Morse agreed to sleep there.

Alice Russell remained, staying in the rear bedroom, close by Lizzie and Emma.

The sight of Andrew and Abby on the dining-room table was horrifying. The undertaker had not come. In that dim kerosene-lighted room they lay on their backs, naked, their blood-drenched clothes having been rolled up and placed in the cellar washroom.

7

AN AWAKENING MOB

> "Lizzie is of a repellant disposition, and, after an unsuccessful passage with her father, would become sulky and refuse to speak to him for days at a time. She moved in the best society in Fall River, was a member of the Congregational Church and is a brilliant conversationalist. She thought she ought to entertain as others did, and felt that with her father's wealth she was expected to hold her end up with others of her set. Her father's constant refusal to allow her to entertain lavishly angered her. I have heard many bitter things she has said of her father, and know she was deeply resentful of her father's maintained stand in the matter. . . . I am positive that Emma knows nothing of the murder."
>
> —Hiram C. Harrington, from an interview in the Fall River *Globe,* August 5, 1892

IRONICALLY, Lizzie's two initial adversaries had the same last name.

Hiram C. Harrington was a blacksmith who had married Andrew Borden's only sister, Luana. His tantalizing interview in the Fall River *Globe,* which arrived in households less than twenty-four hours after the killings, helped kindle the epic onslaught of excitement soon to follow.

He maintained that he had spent part of the previous evening with Lizzie, an incredible fabrication, as City Marshal Hilliard had issued strict orders to allow no one into the house except Dr. Bowen and the medical examiner. But in the *Globe* interview Harrington insisted: "Last evening I had a long interview with Miss Lizzie who has refused to see anyone." He then went on to relate Lizzie's private comments to him about her father's departure and arrival back at the house on the morning of August 4—that she had assisted him to remove his coat and put on his dressing gown and then had volunteered to adjust the windows so he could take a nap. Harrington remarked that Lizzie "was very composed, showed no signs of any emotion, nor were there any traces of grief upon her countenance. This did not surprise me as she is not naturally emotional."*

The *Globe* was a Democratic-run newspaper determined to go to any lengths to increase its circulation over its two rivals, the *Herald* and the *News*. As a result of the telephone call from the newsdealer, John Cunningham, it had learned of the killings even before the police and had quickly seized the advantage. It boasted in its initial headline that one of its reporters had been the first person on the scene.

On that same Friday morning, while Fall River's residents were poring over Hiram C. Harrington's fictitious interview, Sergeant Philip Harrington (no relation to Hiram), convinced that Lizzie was his prime suspect, was interrogating Eli Bence, the clerk at D. R. Smith's Drugstore at the corner of South Main and Columbia streets.

Bence recounted that on that hot Wednesday morning prior to the murders Lizzie had entered the shop and asked for ten cents' worth of prussic acid in order to clean a sealskin cape. Bence had found it a startling request, since they were in the midst of a heat wave. He had refused Lizzie's money, although Lizzie protested that she had *often* bought ten cents' worth of prussic acid to clean her sealskins.

Bence explained that he finally told her flatly, "My good lady, it is something we don't sell except by prescription as it is a very dangerous thing to handle."

Meanwhile the town of Fall River, located less than twenty miles from Providence and fifty miles south of Boston, was becoming the focus of millions. Stories of the homicides were being flashed by scores of telegraphers to the front pages of newspapers throughout the world. More than a grisly act of butchery, in an age of Victorian mores the

*Neither Lizzie nor her father had spoken to Harrington in years and he chose the most volatile moment possible to avenge the rebuff. Emma, however, had remained friendly with Luana Harrington, visiting her often. Consequently, Harrington did not implicate her as an accomplice.

Borden killings expressed an uncommon ferocity: the murder of an extremely wealthy man and his wife senselessly hacked to death in the privacy of their own home.

Twenty-five major dailies dispatched staff members to cover the story first-hand, while others wired requests asking local reporters to serve as correspondents. The sordid double murders were being discussed with fascination in New York, Boston, Chicago, London, Paris.

But the effect on Fall River was eerie and chilling.

Saloons flourished, not from jovial conviviality, but because of mounting panic. Most of the town's businesses were shut down. Gripped by tension and fear, workmen abandoned their machines and left the factories. Thousands of tightly packed, hot, sweating, stony-faced spectators jammed Second Street in front of the Borden house. They gaped at the closed front door through which Andrew Borden had passed the morning before, realizing how vulnerable and defenseless they had become. If such a thing could happen to Andrew and Abby Borden, it could happen to them. The wake of the crimes had fostered a sense of inescapable dread. In their midst a demented monster was loose, an axe-wielding maniac capable of striking down whole families without provocation.

Attempting to quell the symptoms of runaway hysteria, Marshal Hilliard announced that an arrest would be made by Friday evening. Under his supervision, with the help of Deputy Marshal Fleet, State Detective George Seaver, Medical Examiner Dolan and Captain Dennis Desmond, his men began tearing the Borden house and yard apart.

The afternoon was spent ransacking rooms, bureaus, beds, boxes, trunks and everything else where something might be hidden. An old well by the barn was emptied and several piles of lumber against the back fence were moved board by board.

Medical Examiner Dolan and Sergeant Harrington emptied the closets and inspected every article of clothing in the house for possible bloodstains. At one point Lizzie appeared from a doorway and asked Dolan and Harrington, "Is there anything I can do or show you, gentlemen?" Harrington later commented to the *Globe* on her "cool and steady" behavior throughout the search. From this the *Globe* editorialized on Lizzie's demeanor: "In temperament she is extremely phlegmatic and is never easily excited or disturbed. She is extremely matter-of-fact and not given to betraying her emotions."

While Dolan and Harrington were scrutinizing Lizzie's belongings Emma summoned the family attorney, Andrew J. Jennings.

Jennings was a short, balding man in his late fifties with heavy eyebrows and dark piercing eyes. He was extremely able and fiercely intelligent, with a quicksilver cleverness. He knew how to handle the press and the police and did so with the polished familiarity of a high-priced professional. Jennings maintained that he was there unofficially and stayed out of the way of the police. Yet he had brought with him a Mr. O. M. Hanscom, a top Pinkerton detective who had arrived that morning from Boston. Jennings had engaged Hanscom to observe the methods of Marshal Hilliard, Harrington and the others, so that no new evidence could be surreptitiously planted.

Under O. M. Hanscom's watchful eye the frantic search lasted for three hours. When Jennings emerged from the house late in the afternoon he was surrounded by reporters. He insisted that he had no particular desire to talk about the murders, but admitted that, as far as he knew, Andrew Borden left no will.

"I have read many cases in books, in newspapers and in fiction—in novels—and I never heard of a case as remarkable as this," Jennings mused, obviously aware that his every word would be quoted. "A most outrageous, brutal crime, perpetrated in mid-day in an open house on a prominent thoroughfare, and *absolutely motiveless.*"

When a reporter asked as to what he thought about the possibility of the murder being committed by a member of the family, Jennings stared back at him coldly. "There are but two women of the household and this man Morse," he replied, obviously warming toward a conclusive statement. "Morse accounts so satisfactorily for every hour of that morning, showing him to be out of the house, that there seems to be no ground to base a reasonable suspicion. Further than that, he appeared on the scene almost immediately after the discovery from the outside, and in the same clothes that he had worn in the morning. Now it is almost impossible that this frightful work could have been done without the clothes of the person who did it being spattered with blood."

Saving his best thrust for last, Jennings coolly added, "Then came Lizzie Borden, dressed in the same clothes she wore before the killing. This, together with the improbability that any woman could do such a piece of work, makes the suspicion seem almost irrational."

Jennings had talked with Lizzie and Emma while inside the house, and the three of them had devised a strategy that would momentarily divert the focus from Lizzie as a suspect. The result of their conversation appeared that same afternoon in the Fall River *News,* the oldest and largest paper in the city.

$5,000

REWARD!

The above Reward will be paid to any one who may secure the

Arrest and Conviction

of the person or persons, who occasioned the death of

Mr. Andrew J. Borden and Wife.

EMMA J. BORDEN,
LIZZIE A. BORDEN.

Ultimately the search of the house proved fruitless. At the end of the day Medical Examiner Dolan remarked, "We examined everything down to the slightest bump in the wallpaper."

City Marshal Hilliard had hoped to discover the evidence which would have enabled him to make his promised arrest, but by six p.m. he hopelessly admitted defeat. Officers Harrington and Fleet prodded him to arrest Lizzie, but Hilliard refused to act without some physical evidence, such as a bloodstained dress or the murder weapon, neither of which had been found.

And there was still the question of the note which Lizzie said her stepmother had received, requesting her to visit a sick friend on the morning of the murders. According to Lizzie's story, the note had led her to believe that Abby had left the house.

The question of the note had excited public interest, and its disappearance plagued Hilliard. His men had found other letters and fragments of letters in the wastepaper baskets and had put them together piece by piece.

In its Friday afternoon edition the Fall River *News* had implored its readers "to unite in one effort in the cause of justice: to find the note and deliver it into the editor's hands," and in New York City the

Journal was offering a reward of five hundred dollars to the writer of the note if she should step forward.

Finally Lizzie admitted that she feared she might have burned the note in the stove.

Rufus Hilliard was round-faced with a crimson handlebar mustache. He had been the City Marshal of Fall River for thirteen years. He was a quiet man, faced with a monumental dilemma. He knew there was no way he could make an arrest.

That evening he vowed to the press that he would examine "every clue, every trace of evidence," yet the complexity of unanswered details had become overwhelming. His office was already deluged with letters suggesting who the murderer might be and how the crime was accomplished.

If only he knew.

Within minutes after returning to the Central Police Station he was notified that John Vinnicum Morse had slipped out through the crowd milling in front of the Borden house. It was dark and Morse had somehow gotten by the police guard. Apparently his sole intention had been to mail a letter at the post office, but his timing could not have been worse.

He actually reached the post office unobserved but was recognized when he emerged through its lighted archway.

As a result of the various news stories throughout the day Morse, in the minds of the crowd, was the suspected killer. When they glimpsed him they began chasing him up the street.

Morse raced away in terror as a screaming mob, estimated by the police as a thousand in number, angrily tried to run him down.

There was no question that if they had caught him they would have torn him apart, but he was saved by Officer John Devine and a squad of men who had been quietly following him the whole time.

The ugliness of the incident suggested what was to come if no arrest was made.

In desperation Marshal Hilliard began threading through the conclusions he had drawn from the statements of witnesses and the mountain of accumulated, unconnected data which lay before him. There had to be some detail, perhaps a chance observation, that might give him a place to work from.

Not a scream nor a groan was heard coming from the Borden house on the morning of the murders.

> Mrs. Churchill's kitchen windows looked over the Borden's yard directly opposite and were exactly twenty-eight feet from the rear screen door.
>
> Living with Mrs. Churchill was a Miss Addie Cheetham, who claimed that she had been sitting by the kitchen window writing a letter from ten a.m. until ten fifty-five a.m. and at no time did she see anyone enter or leave the Borden house.
>
> Mrs. Churchill reported that she had seen Andrew leave the back of the house at nine a.m.
>
> Mrs. Churchill's hired man, Tom Bowles, saw Bridget cleaning windows on the north and west sides of the house early in the forenoon, but she was gone when he returned at eleven-twenty.

No hint of a stranger entering or leaving the house after nine a.m. *And the front door was locked.* If the killer got in, he would have had to have been noticed.

The most significant incongruity was the time span separating the murders.

> At ten-thirty a.m. Andrew Borden had been seen on Main Street by persons on the Chace Hill streetcar, which left the City Hall for Bedford and Quarry streets exactly at that time.
>
> Between ten forty-five and ten-fifty, Bridget let him through the locked front door of his home.
>
> The report of the "knifing" at 92 Second Street was clocked in at the Central Police Station at eleven-fifteen a.m., only twenty minutes after Andrew was known to have been alive.
>
> But more important was the fact that Abby's brutally hacked body lay for more than an hour in the upstairs guest room.

The enigma in Hilliard's mind resolved itself into a simple question: Could there have been a dead body and an assassin in the house for over an hour without the knowledge of either Lizzie or Bridget?

. . .

The feverish clamor which had seized Fall River would not subside. People who a few days before had been concerned only with their jobs and their families were now obsessed with the killings. It was all they could think about.

Had the murderer become a phantom? When would he strike again?

On Saturday morning the Fall River *Globe,* charging the police with gross incompetence, sneered, "It may seem strange that no arrest has been made up to ten o'clock this morning."

On that same day two significant events would occur, the first of which would have a fateful effect on Lizzie.

Badly shaken and fearful of continuing any further on his own, Marshal Hilliard telegraphed an appeal for assistance to Bristol County District Attorney Hosea Knowlton.

Later that morning a funeral service was held for Andrew and Abby.

In the first-floor sitting room where Andrew had been butchered, two black caskets were placed side by side. The lid on Andrew's casket was shut but Abby's was half-open so that her face and upper body could be viewed by guests. There were no flowers. On Andrew's casket was placed a sheaf of wheat, on Abby's an olive branch.

The gathering was sparse and private, attended only by Abby's two sisters, Dr. Bowen and his wife, Mr. and Mrs. Charles J. Holmes, Frank Almy, publisher of the Fall River *News,* Mrs. Churchill, Alice Russell, Emma, Lizzie and John Vinnicum Morse.

Andrew's sister, Luana Harrington, and her husband, Hiram (who had given the damning interview to the *Globe*), were, for obvious reasons, absent.

Two clergymen arrived, the Reverend Edwin A. Buck of Central Congregational Church, to which Lizzie belonged, and Dr. Adams of the rival First Congregational Church, in which Andrew was a nonattending pew holder. A compromise was quickly reached. Both ministers would conduct the services.

Four thousand people had gotten as close to the house as possible. Shortly before eleven, as the crowd waited anxiously on the street, Lizzie emerged, her face pale. She seemed hesitant and overwrought with fatigue as she clutched the arm of Undertaker Winward.

Several steps behind her came Emma, described later by the press as looking "entirely calm." She walked quickly behind her sister to the waiting carriage.

It was noted by the press that both Lizzie and Emma seemed to have broken with convention: They wore no veils.

The last person to leave the house was John Vinnicum Morse, who rode in the carriage with the Reverend Buck and Dr. Adams.

The procession consisted of eleven carriages and two hearses. As if honoring a national hero, immense throngs of people lined the sidewalks eager for a glimpse of the mourners as the funeral party made its way past City Hall and up Rock Street toward the Oak Grove Cemetery, a distance of a mile.

The awaiting pallbearers were the blue-ribbon aristocrats of Fall River's business and social establishment: Abraham G. Hart, cashier of the Union Savings Bank; George W. Dean, a retired industrial magnate; two cousins—Richard B. Borden, treasurer of the Troy Mills, and Andrew Borden, treasurer of the Merchants Mill; and financiers and property owners James C. Eddy, Henry Buffington, J. Henry Wells, Simon B. Chase and John H. Boone.

On that humid, cloudless morning the mourners made their way through the rows of polished limestone and veined granite monuments.

By two open graves the coffins were set down.

The Reverend Buck began reading: "*I am the resurrection, and the life . . . he that believeth in me, though he were dead, yet shall he live . . . and whosoever liveth and believeth in me shall never die. . . .* "

Then Dr. Adams prayed for the spiritual guidance of all and the inclination of all to submit to divine control. He besought that justice should overtake the wrong that had been done and that all those seeking to serve the ends of justice "be delivered from mistake . . . and be helped to possess mercifullness and righteousness."

At times it seemed as if he were no longer addressing a higher power but were speaking directly to those temporal powers symbolized by the heavy police guard encircling the area.

Suddenly an elderly lady broke from the crowd and rushed toward Abby's casket. She was about to kneel before it when she was shunted away by an officer and jostled to the fence beside the grounds, where, with her back to the crowd, she buried her head in tears.

Lizzie had recognized her. It was Maggie, the maid who had once worked for them.

And then the silence became interminable. The carriages kept their places and no one stirred, waiting for the burial.

But the caskets were not lowered into the graves. The police at the gravesite suddenly had received a telegram from Harvard Medical School ordering that the bodies be returned to their hearses and deposited in a receiving tomb. Professor Wood wanted to perform another autopsy.

. . .

The newly completed Mellen House at the corner of Franklin and South Main streets was the pride of Fall River. Since its construction in 1887, its modern sixty-eight rooms, each with running water and a bathroom, and its mahogany-walled, white-marble-floored lobby had elegantly accommodated a continuous stream of Cape Cod and New York tourists, including such celebrities as Lillian Russell and Jenny Lind.

After the abortive funeral, while the startled mourners were still making their way back to 92 Second Street, Hosea Knowlton met in a third-floor suite of the Mellen House with Marshal Hilliard and Medical Examiner Dolan. Locking themselves in, they began probing the theories and evidence accumulated in the past forty-eight hours.

Knowlton, a graduate of Harvard Law School, had served in both branches of the state legislature prior to his election as district attorney of Bristol County. He was forty-two, a stocky, intense little man who moved swiftly and impatiently.

Step by step Hilliard reconstructed the summoning of Dr. Bowen and his discovery of the carnage on the second floor, Lizzie's demeanor during her interviews with the police and John Morse's alibi as to his whereabouts.

Immediately acting as devil's advocate, Knowlton rationalized the instances where Lizzie's credibility might be challenged.

She said that she had gone into the barn to search for metal in order to fashion sinkers for fishing, Hilliard pointed out, yet when Patrolman Medley and Sergeant Harrington had examined the dust on the floor of both the barn and the loft, why had they discovered no footprints?

Knowlton quickly interjected a possible answer. Following the awful discovery of her father's body, perhaps she was in such a state of emotional panic that she had forgotten precisely where she had gone for the lead.

Hilliard went on to the note from the sick friend which Lizzie claimed her stepmother had received the morning of the murders. It was that note which had led her to believe that her stepmother had left the house. Yet in their search the police had not found the note, and Lizzie finally admitted that she probably burned it in the kitchen stove.

But wasn't it peculiar, Hilliard pointed out, that with all the furor that had been raised over the note, the articles in the newspapers, and the various rewards posted, that the woman who wrote it had not come forward and cleared up the mystery?

Knowlton countered: What if the sick woman feared the notoriety which would come to her if she disclosed her identity?

Hilliard became exasperated. To each theory, each puzzling bit of evidence, Knowlton offered a pat solution. He seemed hesitant, however, regarding the final question: Who could have committed the crime?

Realizing that this was the most politically explosive problem any of them had ever encountered, the three elected officials fell silent.

They would have to delay. No arrest could be made.

The only two people known to have been in the house were Lizzie and Bridget. If Bridget were the killer, how could she have committed the murder of Mrs. Borden without Lizzie, present in the adjoining bedroom, being aware of it. And even if Bridget had wielded the bloody axe, would she then have nonchalantly gone back outdoors and continued washing windows?

No, it must have been Lizzie. In the end they would have to arrest her. There was no one else. But without the murder weapon, a bloodstained dress or a witness, was such an arrest possible?

Knowlton, Hilliard and Dolan were so involved in the chaotic details before them that one possibility never entered their minds: Why not check with the Brownell family, who lived in Fairhaven, as to Emma's whereabouts on that morning?

John W. Coughlin was the mayor of Fall River. He was also a physician and a surgeon.

On Saturday evening he confided to Marshal Hilliard that he was disturbed over the plight of the city, but specifically he was extremely worried about the danger to those living in the Borden household. He suggested that they both drive to 92 Second Street and tactfully request that everyone stay safely indoors.

To Marshal Hilliard, it was an opportune move. There would be no suggestion of a house arrest, merely a diplomatic warning, and with it, the mayor's promise of continuing protection by the police.

Yet when Hilliard and the mayor turned into Second Street they found it blocked with traffic. Both Hilliard and the mayor were recognized but no one would let them through. Angrily Hilliard sent for a detail of police to force back the hostile mob so that they could get up the street.

It took twenty minutes for their carriage to forge its way to the front steps of the house. Emma met them at the door and showed them into the parlor, the one room in the house reserved for special guests.

She left them alone for several moments and then returned with Lizzie and John Vinnicum Morse.

It was seven forty-five p.m., and as the five of them sat in the glow of Andrew Borden's kerosene lamps, Mayor Coughlin cautiously suggested that it would be "better for all concerned" if members of the family remained inside for the next few days.

Emma nodded, acknowledging Coughlin's concern, but Lizzie reacted with immediate distrust. "Why? Is there anybody in this house suspected?"

Finally Coughlin remarked, "Perhaps Mr. Morse can answer that better than I . . . his experience last night would justify the inference that somebody in this house was suspected."

But Lizzie would not be put off. She sensed what was coming. Coldly she stared into Coughlin's eyes. "I want to know the truth."

The mayor cleared his throat, twisting for a moment in his chair.

"I want to know the truth," she demanded again, her voice like ice, her temples and cheeks turning crimson with indignation.

Finally Coughlin replied faintly, "Well, Miss Borden, I regret to answer but I must answer—yes, you are suspected."

It was the first time that she had heard her fears confirmed by an official source, and yet she had expected it all along. She had known it was coming. But the bitter waiting, the terrible uncertainty had torn at her unmercifully.

At last it had come, and as it did, all tension vanished from her mind. Her voice was flat and quiet: "I am ready to go now."

At that moment Emma interjected, "We have tried to keep it from her as long as we could."

It was a strange remark and Lizzie glared at Emma uncertainly. What did she mean, *We have tried to keep it from her as long as we could?*

No, Mayor Coughlin struggled to insist, nobody wanted Lizzie to go anywhere.

John Morse abruptly interrupted: "How will we get our mail?"

It was the distraction Coughlin sorely desired. It would be brought to the house, he promised, as he rose from his chair. Once again he assured them that if there was any annoyance from the crowds, they had only to report it to the policemen on duty to receive all the protection the force could provide.

Hilliard hastened to back him up. "We want to do everything we can in this matter."

Lizzie made no further comment but sat rigidly in her chair.

Emma led Coughlin and Hilliard to the door, thanked them both for coming and showed them out.

But there was to be no rest in the Borden house that night.

There was something Lizzie sensed, the possibility of betrayal.

That night Emma asked Alice Russell to change beds with her, to separate her from Lizzie's room.

The overflowing crowds pouring into Central Congregational Church on Sunday morning anticipated a fiery sermon by the Reverend W. Walker Jubb on the crimes committed during the past week. They had been joined by the rival First Church congregation of Dr. Adams for a united service at the stone church on Main Street.

It was this church to which Lizzie belonged. And the Reverend Jubb was her pastor.

The Reverend Jubb left no one disappointed.

He began with the Gospel of St. Matthew, reading the significant words "*. . . for there is nothing covered, that shall not be revealed; and hid, that shall not be known.*"

Invoking the divine blessing on the community, he then briefly mentioned the murders. Embarking on a flaming defense of Lizzie, he shouted: "While we hope for the triumph of justice, let our acts be tempered with mercy! Help us to refrain from giving voice to those insinuations which we have no right to utter! Save us from blasting a life, innocent and blameless!"

As sunlight filtered down through the stained-glass windows above he quoted from Ecclesiastes: "*The thing that hath been, it is that which shall be; and that which is done is that which shall be done; and there is no new thing under the sun.*"

Stepping to the side of the pulpit, he solemnly stared into the hearts of his listeners: "I cannot close my sermon this morning without speaking of the horrible crime that has startled our beloved city this week. A more brutal, cunning, daring and fiendish murder I never heard of in all my life. What must have been the person who could have been guilty of such a revolting crime? One to commit such a murder must have been without heart, without soul, a fiend incarnate, the very vilest of degraded and depraved humanity, or he must have been a maniac. This city cannot afford to have in its midst such an inhuman brute as the murderer of Andrew J. Borden and his wife. Why, a man who would conceive and execute such a murder as that would not hesitate to burn down the city!"

Exhorting the police to do their duty and capture the criminal, he warned that "they should not say too much and thus assist in defeating the ends of justice." He cautioned the press to be aware of its enormous power and to "use discretion in disseminating its theories and conclusions" so that their pens "may be guided by consideration and charity."

And finally he charged the congregation sitting before him: "Let us ourselves curb our tongues and preserve a blameless life from undeserved suspicions."

He then alluded, first to Lizzie, then to Emma and Lizzie: "A daughter now stands in the same relation to each one of you, as you, as church members, do to each other. God help and comfort her. Poor stricken girls, may they both be comforted, and may they both realize how fully God is their refuge."

Within the wooden frame house five blocks away on Second Street, the ever-vigilant O. M. Hanscom was somewhere roaming about and John Morse was still upstairs. In the kitchen Alice Russell was preparing breakfast for Lizzie, Emma and herself.

Alice had dressed to go out but changed her mind about attending church. She had no desire to meet people and become involved in conversations about Lizzie, Emma and the murders.

Instead she visited her cottage on the next block and returned within an hour.

The crowd in front of the house had not subsided, yet she had no difficulty slipping through the police guard. As she walked back into the kitchen she saw Lizzie standing between the stove and the open door of the coal closet with a blue dress in her hands.

Emma, who was at the sink washing the breakfast dishes, turned. "What are you going to do with that?" she asked, referring to the dress.

"I am going to burn this old thing up, it's all covered with paint," Lizzie answered.

The image of the dress nagged at Alice as she went upstairs to the room in which she was staying.

When she returned a few moments later, Lizzie was tearing the dress to pieces.

Dr. B. J. Handy's revelation on Monday morning quickly created an uproar that aroused the nation and sent the police combing Fall River. Handy, one of the best-known physicians in the city, reported that on the day of the murders he had seen a strange-looking man on Second Street at about ten-thirty a.m. He had looked twice at the passerby and even turned in his carriage to inspect him more closely.

The man was approximately thirty, five feet five inches in height, and looked as if he weighed about one hundred and thirty pounds. His clothes were light gray but the doctor could not recollect whether the man's hat was felt or straw.

What most attracted him were the man's features, which were pale, almost white. He had the appearance of someone who had never been touched by the sun's rays, who might have spent years in confinement or whose work was of such nature as to keep him constantly in a cellar. And he appeared to be in a state of intense nervousness.

Through pure intuition Dr. Handy concluded that this queer-looking stranger knew something about the murders. He communicated his suspicions to the police, giving them a complete description of the man, and the police were soon attacked for not being able to identify and arrest the suspect immediately.

Eager reporters, running up expense bills, with their editors prodding them for ever more sensational details of the murders, cabled the news of the frantic search. Column after column of the country's leading newspapers contained voluminous discussions of the mysterious stranger known only as "Dr. Handy's Wild Eyed Man."

There were other theories. That afternoon John Beattie, an alderman of Fall River, stated in the Fall River *News:*

> "My theory—and it is mine alone—is one formed from the circumstances of the case. The brain which devised this crime was cunning enough to devise beforehand the means to escape detection. Supposing it was a woman, she was cunning enough to wear a loose wrapper which would have covered her clothes, and gloves which would have protected her hands from the stains of blood. If so, there was time to burn both wrapper and gloves in the hot fire, which was known to have been burning in the kitchen stove at the time of the tragedy."

Meanwhile, the one private operative on the case, Pinkerton Detective O. M. Hanscom, was unable to locate the dress Lizzie wore at the time of the killings. Cornering Alice Russell, he interrogated her about the dress.

Alice ran to Lizzie. "Where is the dress?"

"What dress?"

"The one you were tearing to pieces?"

"I burned it."

Stricken, Alice blurted, "The worst thing you could have done was to burn that dress! I've just been questioned about it!"

Lizzie, staring back at her in alarm, finally muttered, "Why did you let me do it! Why didn't you tell me!"

By evening a messenger had arrived at the Borden house with a summons issued by District Attorney Hosea Knowlton. An immediate inquest had been called for the next morning, Tuesday, at ten, before

Judge J. C. Blaisdell in the Second District Court of Bristol County.

Knowlton could wait no longer. He had conferred with Massachusetts Attorney General Arthur Pillsbury, who had advised him to take over the investigation. The inquest was to be conducted privately, with just the witnesses present.

Since the only people known to have been in the house between nine and eleven on the morning of November fourth were Lizzie and Bridget, Knowlton was convinced they concealed the secret of the murders. Behind closed doors he planned to ruthlessly break them down until one of them admitted the truth.

8

MURDERESS

"If Lizzie had done that deed, she could never have hidden the instrument of death so the police could never find it."

—Emma Borden, from an interview in the Boston *Sunday Post*, April 13, 1913

BRIDGET SULLIVAN FELT CERTAIN she was to be arrested for the murders.

Still, she bravely put on her new green-patterned gown with hat to match and her white linen gloves.

But when Officer Patrick Doherty came in the carriage to fetch her to the Central Police Station she broke down sobbing as soon as she saw his handsome face.

Nothing Doherty could say would assuage her fears. As the carriage left the friend's house at 95 Division Street, where she was staying, and the horse galloped onto South Main, Doherty insisted that his only intention was to have her talk to the district attorney.

Bridget's tears rolled from her brown eyes. She had already given all the information in her power to give to the police. She could tell them nothing more than she had already told them.

Things were not always rosy in the Borden house, she admitted, and she had threatened to return to Ireland several times in the past two years, but, she explained, "Mrs. Borden was a lovely woman and I remained there because she wanted me to."

Doherty felt strong compassion for this frightened young woman who huddled beside him as she told him more about herself. She was one of fourteen children and had come to America six years before, when she was nineteen. She had worked for two other families in the three years before she was engaged by the Bordens. She had become very close to Mrs. Borden and actually felt sorry for her. Whenever she mentioned returning to Ireland, Mrs. Borden would say that she would be desperately lonely without her. It was as if Mrs. Borden had no friends at all. She hardly left the house. And the two girls were terrible to her, always treating her as if she were an outsider.

Finally, as the carriage turned up Spring Street, Bridget managed to compose herself, aided by Doherty's kind words of reassurance. But when she saw the crowd milling in front of the Central Police Station she sank back in terror.

Throughout the downtown thoroughfares people hung along the curbing for blocks. Again businesses were suspended. Crowds surged toward the Central Police Station awaiting the outcome of the closed hearing to be conducted by District Attorney Knowlton. There had been no arrests and the murderer was still at large. Amid the furor even the ubiquitous O. M. Hanscom was besieged by reporters as he attempted to steal away from the house on Second Street. He declined to be interviewed but was credited with saying with a smile that Marshal Hilliard was doing good work.

Shortly after ten a.m. the doors of the Second District Courtroom were shut as Hosea Knowlton began his examination. From the moment Bridget took the stand she was in distress. Knowlton immediately tore into her about her whereabouts on the Thursday morning of the murders.

Carefully Bridget attempted to answer his questions. After serving breakfast she had washed the breakfast dishes. She had then begun washing windows. The only break she had taken from her work was when she chatted for a few moments with the servant girl who worked for the Kelly family next door. She had seen no one leave the house except Mr. Borden and Mr. Morse, until Mr. Borden returned at about ten forty-five a.m. and she had to unlock the front door to let him in.

Knowlton could not believe that she was unaware of the violence occurring within the house, but Bridget insisted that while she was doing her chores she had heard no noise at all.

When he questioned her about the note Mrs. Borden had received she insisted that she knew nothing about it.

As the hours dragged on and Bridget repeated her story her voice faltered and she began to cry.

Finally, Knowlton released her from the stand.

Lizzie arrived at two p.m. accompanied by Andrew Jennings.

Jennings asked permission from Judge Blaisdell to be present at the hearing in order to look after the interests of the witness, but he was refused. He argued at length with the judge that he should be permitted to stay, but Blaisdell would not yield.

Jennings was forced to withdraw.*

Alone in the room with Knowlton, Judge Blaisdell and court reporter Annie White, Lizzie took the witness stand.

Knowlton was ready for her.

What followed was a battle of egos. At forty-two, Knowlton, vigorous and Harvard trained, was intent on becoming the next attorney general of the State of Massachusetts. Eager for a confession, he planned to use every means to batter and intimidate Lizzie. It was as if she had been accused and was already being tried for the murder of her parents.

Faced with a legal mind whose future rested on her conviction, Lizzie retaliated with the performance of her life.

"Give me your full name."

"Lizzie Andrew Borden."

"You were so christened?"

"I was."

"What is your age?"

"Thirty-two."

"Your mother is not living?"

"She died when I was two years of age."

Knowlton went immediately to Andrew Borden's wealth.

"I have no idea how much my father was worth."

"Did you know something about the real estate he owned?"

"Yes."

"How did you know?"

"He told me."

"Did he ever deed you any property?"

*Under Massachusetts law a prosecutor could elect to hold an inquiry before a judge with no one present except an official court stenographer. Witnesses were sworn and both the judge and the prosecutor had the right to question them. A suspect did not have the right to be represented by counsel.

"He gave Emma and I some land, but then he bought it back."

"For how much?"

"He paid us five thousand dollars."

"What about his will?"

"I never knew he had made one until my uncle, John Morse, told me he had."*

"Did you know of anybody your father had trouble with?"

Lizzie then related the story about the man who had come to the house a few weeks before and argued with her father. "I heard them talk about a store. My father told him he could not have the store. The man said: "I thought with your liking for money you would let anybody in.' I heard my father order him out of the house."

Knowlton attempted to pin down her antipathy toward Abby. "Did you ever have any trouble with your stepmother?"

"No," she replied quickly.

"Never?"

It was a sensitive area and Lizzie became guarded. "Not recently."

"Within a year?"

"No."

"Within three years?"

"No."

"Well how long!"

"About five years ago."

"What was it about?"

"About my stepmother's sister Mrs. George Whitehead."

"Was it a violent expression of feeling?"

"It was simply a difference of opinion."

Knowlton moved in closer for the kill. "Were you always cordial with your stepmother?"

"That depends upon one's idea of cordiality."

"Was it cordial according to your idea of cordiality?"

"Yes. I did not regard her as my mother, though she came there when I was young. I decline to say whether my relations between her and myself were those of mother and daughter or not."

"But what did you call her?"

"I called her Mrs. Borden, and sometimes mother."

Knowlton felt that he had her. "Why did you leave off calling her mother?"

Defiantly Lizzie snapped back. "Because I wanted to!"

*In fact, Andrew Borden's will was never discovered.

With anger in his voice, he prodded, "Have you any other answer to give me?"

Lizzie quieted. "No, sir. I always went to my sister. She was older than I was."

Knowlton unloosed a barrage of questions, jumping from subject to subject. "Were your father and mother happily united?"

"So far as I had any opportunity of judging."

"What were you wearing on the morning of the murders?"

"A blue dress."

"You wore it all day?"

"In the afternoon I put on a pink dress."

Skipping quickly to John Morse, he asked about when he first came to the house to visit.

"I do not know. I am away so much myself."*

Knowlton restated the question.

Lizzie answered, "Do you mean this time that he came and stayed all night?"

Sarcastically Knowlton countered, "Not *this time.* Was this *his first visit* to your house?"

"He has been in the East a year or so now."

"Had he ever visited before he came back East and stayed?"

"Once he did—in the winter when the river was frozen over, some fourteen years ago, was it not?"

Knowlton crisply kept command. "I am not answering questions but asking them."

Immediately coming back to the present, he asked her to recall what time her uncle had arrived on the day before the murders.

For the first time Lizzie lost track. "He stayed all night, Wednesday night."

"My question is, *when* he came there?"

"I don't know. I was not at home when he came. *I was out.*" She quickly explained that John Morse had been there, but she did not see him. She had gone to pay a call on Alice Russell. She returned home and went to bed without glancing into the sitting room. When she came down in the morning Morse was already gone.

Abruptly Knowlton repeated the question.

*There was a peculiar airiness to Lizzie, born of small-town loneliness. She would have liked to have envisioned herself as constantly traveling the world. In fact, except for a weekend visit to New Bedford, she had not been away from home since her trip to Europe two years before.

Just as abruptly Lizzie changed her story. She had *not* been out when her uncle arrived. "I was in my room all day, not feeling well."

"Why didn't you stop into the sitting room to say goodnight when you came in from your call on Alice Russell?"

"I had no reason except that I was not feeling well and did not come down all day."

"But you were down. You came in from outside."

Knowlton repeated the question a third time. "When did your uncle come there?"

Lizzie answered that she did not know. She had *only heard* Morse's voice. Her door was open because of the hot weather. It was open but she shut it because she wanted to take a nap and the voices of her uncle and father "annoyed her." She had not come down to eat, and then hastily she remembered that she had come down to both dinner and supper with her parents.

Knowlton had her rattled. Egging her on to the more profound matter, he hurried to the morning of the murders.

Lizzie had first seen her father in the sitting room reading the Providence *Journal.* Abby was in the dining room. Maggie (Bridget), with a long-handled mop in her hand, was on her way out to begin washing the windows. She had not felt up to having coffee but thought she might have eaten half a banana.

Her father had left for town shortly after nine o'clock.

"Where were you when he returned?" Knowlton asked suddenly.

"In the kitchen, reading."

Quickly she stumbled through an explanation that she had not been able to finish ironing handkerchiefs because the iron was not right. "I am not sure that I was in the kitchen when my father returned. I stayed in my room long enough to sew a piece of lace on a garment. That was before he came back."

She had fallen into the trap. The front door was locked. Maggie had gone out the back door. Her stepmother was lying dead in the upstairs guest room. And she was alone in the kitchen.

Knowlton jumped on the opportunity. "Where was Maggie when the bell rang?"

"I don't know, sir."

"Where were you when the bell rang?"

"I think in my room upstairs."

"Then you were *upstairs* when the bell rang?"

Again he put her upstairs, where the murderer was obviously hiding. She replied in confusion, "I don't know for sure, but I think I was. . . . as I say, I took up these clean clothes and basted a little piece of tape on a garment."

"Did you come down before your father came in?"

Suddenly she blurted, "I was on the stairs coming down when she let him in."

At this point Lizzie's voice rose nervously.

Knowlton would not stop. "You remember. Miss Borden—I will call your attention to it to see if I have any misunderstanding, not for the purpose of confusing you—you remember that you told me several times that you were downstairs and not upstairs when your father came home? You have forgotten that, perhaps?"

"I don't know what I have said. I have answered so many questions and am so confused that I don't know one thing from another."

The hammering continued. He wanted to know about Abby. He wanted to know what Abby had been doing in the guest room between nine-thirty a.m. and eleven. He wanted to know why Lizzie had not seen her.

"I last saw my stepmother when I was downstairs. She was dusting the dining room. She said she had been upstairs and made the bed, and was going upstairs to put on the pillow slips. She had some cotton cloth pillows up there, and she said she was going to work on them. If she had remained downstairs I should have seen her. She would have gone up the back way to go to her room. If she had gone to the kitchen I would have seen her. There is no reason to suppose I would not have seen her when she was downstairs or in her room, except when I went downstairs once for two or three minutes."

Knowlton was not to be put off by the vagueness of her answer. "I ask you again what you suppose she was doing from the time you saw her till eleven o'clock?"

"I don't know, unless she was making the bed."

"She would have had to pass your room. You would have seen her, wouldn't you?"

"Yes, unless I was in my room or down in the cellar. I suppose she had gone away because she told me she was going and we talked about dinner."

"Did you hear her go or come?"

"No."

It was five-thirty. Lizzie's interrogation had lasted two and a half hours, and she was exhausted.

Knowlton announced they would commence again the following morning at ten.

Shortly after six p.m., Lizzie returned home in a closed police carriage, accompanied by Marshal Hilliard and her friend Mary Brigham.

Meanwhile the police were conducting an all-out search for the murder weapon, the one crucial bit of evidence Knowlton needed. Despite the inquest, Marshal Hilliard, in response to public pressure, had heightened his investigation. The Board of Aldermen met that evening and adopted a measure: "Inasmuch as a terrible crime has been committed in this city requiring an unusually large number of men to do police duty, it is hereby ordered that the City Marshal be and he is hereby directed to employ such extra constables as he may deem necessary for the detection of the criminals, the expense to be charged to the appropriation for police."

One of the investigators hired that evening was an unfortunate choice. Edwin D. McHenry, a private detective from Providence, Rhode Island, would ultimately have a devastating effect on the fateful events to follow.

The following morning there was a public outcry. Sensational news had leaked out that Knowlton had targeted Lizzie as the killer. An editorial in the Springfield *Daily Republican* was an indication of national feeling:

> All through the investigation carried on by the Fall River police, a lack of ability has been shown seldom equalled, and causes they assign for connecting the daughter with the murder are on a par with their other exhibitions of lack of wisdom. Because someone, unknown to them and too smart for them to catch, butchered two people in the daytime on a principal street of the city, using brute force, far in excess of that possessed by this girl, they conclude that there is probable reason to believe that she is the murderess. Because they found no one walking along the street with his hands and clothes reeking with blood, they conclude that it is probable, after swinging the axe with the precision and effect of a butcher, she washed the blood from her hands and clothes.

Massachusetts Attorney General Arthur Pillsbury was cornered by newsmen with the charge that all the evidence amassed by the police against Lizzie was circumstantial. Defensively, Pillsbury replied, "Police officers do not always tell what they know."

At ten a.m. the inquest resumed, with Knowlton questioning Dr. Bowen, Adelaide Churchill, Hiram Harrington, John Morse and Emma. Present in the courtroom was Professor Edward Wood of

Harvard, to whom the stomachs of the murdered couple had been sent for analysis.

While the inquest was progressing, a carpenter, Maurice Daly, armed with his tools, was accompanied by Marshal Hilliard and Sergeant Philip Harrington to the Borden house. After half an hour they left carrying three bundles, which contained chunks of woodwork gouged from the areas near the doors and windows which had been splattered with blood.

Lizzie was recalled to the stand at one o'clock. The news rippled heatedly through the vast crowd milling outside in Court Square. All of Fall River waited anxiously.

Behind the court's closed doors Knowlton surveyed the attractively attired lady with the watery blue eyes, full lips and reddish wavy hair who stood before him. Once more both of them were poised to continue their fascinating struggle with its inevitable goal: he had to crack her.

Court reporter Annie White's fingers swiftly began jotting down the words as Judge Blaisdell intently watched the untrained, inexperienced young woman, seemingly at the prosecutor's mercy, unemotionally parting with vague scraps of information—inexplicably and defiantly reversing her testimony from the day before.

"I call your attention to the fact you said twice yesterday that you first saw your father after he came in when you were standing on the stairs."

"I did not. I was in the kitchen when he came in, or in one of the three rooms, the dining room, kitchen and sitting room."

Taken by surprise, Knowlton stared at her. Apparently deciding to play her game, he rushed on as if accepting this new version of her whereabouts. "Could anyone have passed by you?"

"It would have been difficult for anybody to pass through those rooms unless they passed through while I was in the dining room."

"Yet a portion of the time Bridget was out of doors, wasn't she?"

"Yes. So far as I know. I was alone in the house the larger part of the time while my father was away. I was eating a pear when he came in. I had put a stick of wood into the fire to see if I could start it. After my father came in I did no more ironing."

"What time was that?"

"I don't know. When I went out to the barn I left him on the sofa. The last thing I said was to ask him if he wanted the window left open. Then I went to the barn to get some lead."

"Where did you go in the barn?"

"I went upstairs. There was a bench which contained some lead."

"Did you unhook the screen door when you left the house?"

"Yes."

"Had Bridget finished washing windows?"

"I don't know when she got through washing the windows inside. I knew she washed the windows outside. I knew she didn't wash the kitchen windows, but I didn't know whether she washed the sitting-room windows or not."

If she had been busy sewing and ironing how had she known exactly which windows Bridget had washed? Unless it was essential for her to be aware of Bridget's whereabouts every moment.

"Why did you go into the barn?"

"I had no fishing apparatus, but there was some at the farm at Swansea. It is five years since I used the fish line and I didn't remember if there was any sinker on my line."

"What! Did you think you would find sinkers in the barn?"

"My father once told me that there was some lead and nails in the barn."

"How long do you think you were occupied in looking for sinkers?"

"About fifteen or twenty minutes."

"Did you do anything besides look for sinkers in the twenty minutes?"

"Yes, sir. I ate some pears."

"Would it take you all that time to eat a few pears?"

"I do not do things in a hurry."

"Was Bridget washing the dining-room windows and the sitting-room windows?"

"I do not know. I did not see her."

"Where was she when your father came home?"

"Maggie had come in and gone upstairs."

"But she opened the front door for your father."

"I did not see her."

"But she had been washing the windows inside."

At this point Lizzie's answers became preposterous. "She might have been in one room and I in another."

It made no sense. In the cramped railroad-flat structure of the downstairs Andrew had been at the front door, Bridget had let him in, Lizzie had been downstairs in the kitchen, Bridget had come in and out washing the windows—yet neither Lizzie nor Bridget saw the other!

Was there a complicity between Bridget and Lizzie? Knowlton was certain of it, as others have been ever since.

But what once again was overlooked is the subtle confusion which can result from a detail *left out.* Bridget was telling the truth. She had performed her chores and had never seen Lizzie. During the entire time Lizzie was upstairs in the guest room with Emma.

Knowlton became enraged. "Miss Borden, I have been trying to get the story of that morning from yourself and Miss Sullivan and I have not succeeded. Do you desire to give me information or not?"

"I am telling you exactly what occurred. I never saw Maggie."

"About what time did you go out into the barn?"

"About as near as I can recollect, ten o'clock."

Ten o'clock. It was not an error or a miscalculation.

Contrary to the statements of all other witnesses, she was now insisting that her father was lying on the couch in the sitting room at "about as near as I can recollect, ten o'clock" when she left to go to the barn.

It was an ingenious fabrication since it meant that she was not in the house when either her stepmother or father was murdered. *And why shouldn't she be telling the truth, and all others be mistaken?* Earlier Knowlton had asked, "Did you unhook the screen door when you left the house?"

Lizzie had cleverly replied, "Yes."

It was her one hope for an alibi. The unknown murderer had slipped in and out of the house through the screen door while she was in the barn.

From this point on her testimony became dizzying in complexity as Knowlton struggled to keep up with her.

"What did you go into the barn for?"

"To find some sinkers."

"How many pears did you eat in that twenty minutes?"

"Three."

"Is that all you did?"

"No, I went over to the window and opened it."

"I don't suppose you stayed there any longer than was necessary?"

"No, sir, because it was very close."

"I suppose the hottest place on the premises?"

"I suppose so."

"Could you, while standing looking out of that window, see anybody enter the kitchen?"

"No, sir."

"I thought you said you could see people from the barn?"

"Not after you pass a jog in the barn. It obstructs the view of the back door."

Knowlton's next question was obvious. Having got her up a tree, he simply shook the tree. "I ask you why you should select that place, which was the only place which would put you out of sight of the house, to eat those three pears in?"

Wide-eyed, Lizzie gaped back at him. "I cannot give you any reason."

"But why did you go to that place to eat pears which happened to be out of sight of the house—"

"For only about two minutes—"

"I ask you again, why you took those pears from the pear tree."

"I did not take them from the pear tree."

At this point in their game of cat and mouse they had switched roles. Knowlton grumbled, "From the ground. *Wherever* you took them from. I thank you for correcting me. Going upstairs to the rear of the barn, the hottest place, and standing there, eating those pears that morning?"

But Lizzie was her father's child. She was not about to let him off the hook. "I *beg* your pardon. I was not at the *rear* of the barn, I was at the other end that faced the street."

Knowlton stared at her in dismay. "Where you could see anybody coming into the house?"

"Yes, sir."

Her twisting of stories was too much for him to handle. Stumbling on, he ventured, "What kind of lead were you looking for, for sinkers? Hard lead?"

"No, sir. Soft lead."

"Did you expect to find the sinkers already made?"

"Well, no, I thought I might find one with a hole through it."

"When were you going fishing?"

"Monday."

"Had you lines all ready?"

"No, sir."

"Did you have a line?"

"Yes, sir."

"Where was your line?"

"Down to the farm."

"Do you know whether there were any sinkers on the line you left at the farm?"

"I think there were none."

"Did you have any hooks?"

"No, sir."

"Then you were making all this preparation without either hook or line. Why did you go into the barn after sinkers?"

"Because I was going downtown to buy some hooks and line and I thought it would save me from buying them."

His line of questioning was getting nowhere, yet he rushed forward. "Do you not think I could go into the barn and do the same as you in a few minutes?"

Calmly she replied, "I do not do things in a hurry."

Regaining the advantage, firing question after question, he dramatically led her back into the house—to the sight of her father lying on the sofa.

"Describe anything you noticed at the time."

"I did not notice anything, I was so frightened and horrified. I ran to the foot of the stairs and called Maggie . . . I said, 'Go for Dr. Bowen, I think father is hurt.' "

"Did you know he was dead?"

"No, sir."

Knowlton was certain she was lying. Of course she knew he was dead. In photographs Knowlton had studied what she must have seen—the mutilated face . . . the neck. "You saw him?"

"No, sir."

"You went into the room?"

"No, sir."

"You looked in at the door?"

"No, sir."

"Saw his face?"

"No, sir."

No, sir. No, sir. But "No, sir," was all Lizzie could reply as she attempted to block out the images.

Mercilessly Knowlton lashed at her. "You saw where his face was bleeding?"

"No, sir."

"Did you see the blood on the floor?"

"No, sir."

"You saw his face covered with blood?"

"No, sir."

"Did you see his eyeball hanging out?"

"No, sir."

"See the gashes where his face was laid open?"

Suddenly Lizzie covered her face and became silent.

Instinctively, Knowlton backed off.

After a moment Judge Blaisdell asked Knowlton to find out what effort Lizzie had made to notify her mother of her father's death.

Quickly Lizzie denied suggesting to Mrs. Churchill that her step-mother might be upstairs. And then, just as quickly, she changed her story. "I did not do anything except what I said to Mrs. Churchill. I said to her, 'I don't know where Mrs. Borden is, but I wish you would look.' "

"Where did you intend her to look?" Knowlton asked.

"In Mrs. Borden's room."

At that moment Knowlton slipped in, "Why did you go to Smith's Drugstore to buy prussic acid?"

"I did not."

"Smith's Drugstore is at the corner of South Main and Columbia. Do you know where that is?"

"I do not."

"I now ask if you can furnish any other suspicion concerning any person who might have committed the crime?"

"Yes. One night as I was coming home not long ago I saw the shadow of a man on the house at the east end. I thought it was a man because I could not see any skirts. I hurried in the front door. It was about eight forty-five, not later than nine. I saw somebody run around the house last winter. The last time I saw anybody after my sister went to Fairhaven. I told Mr. Jennings and I may have also told Mr. Hanscom."

"Who suggested the reward offered? You or your sister?"

"I don't know. I may have."

Knowlton had more questions. About the house on Ferry Street. About the hatchets found in the basement. About the screen door—she had closed it when she left, yet it was open when she returned—about the dress she had worn that morning . . .

When Lizzie left the court at five p.m. and got into her carriage the crowd outside realized that the cloud of suspicion had lifted. She had been let go and soon the authorities would publicly admit that they were unable to connect her with the murders.

But there was to be no relief for anyone.

The crowds surrounding the Central Police Station began muttering and grumbling as the hours dragged by. The community was losing its patience. For days it had been informed that the end was near, and now nothing.

Throughout the long night that followed not a word emanated from Knowlton and Hilliard.

When the inquest was resumed Thursday morning there was near hysteria in the streets of Fall River. Throngs surged against the doorways of the court and fighting broke out. A double guard of patrolmen positioned themselves in the hallways leading to Judge Blaisdell's courtroom.

Eli Bence was questioned, as was his fellow employee, Fred Hart. And then Bridget arrived.

The day wore on.

At four-thirty p.m. the closed carriage, which had become as familiar a sight as the police patrol wagon, rattled over the rough pavement and across the cobblestones. Hundreds of men, women and children pressed toward it. There were cries and shouts as Marshal Hilliard and Mary Brigham, with the help of the police, struggled to get out, followed by Lizzie and Emma. Emma appeared extremely agitated as the four of them disappeared into the building.

The excitement grew as the hour passed.

At five p.m. Bridget emerged and, accompanied by a police officer, hurried down the street.

Within the building, Lizzie, Emma and Mary Brigham, her friend, had been escorted by a police guard from the courtroom to the matron's room on the second floor.

Andrew Jennings arrived, hastening up the stairs to join them.

There was silence in the room.

Marshal Hilliard entered, holding a sheet of paper in his hand. He asked Mary Brigham to leave. And then, he spoke to Lizzie. "I have here a warrant for your arrest—issued by the judge of the District Court. I shall read it to you if you desire, but you have the right to waive the reading of it."

"Waive the reading," Jennings snapped.

Hilliard glanced at Lizzie. She glared back at him icily. "You need not read it."

Emma sank to the floor, sobbing violently.

Lizzie stood rigidly, unflinching.

A carriage was ordered and within seconds Andrew Jennings and Mary Brigham were guiding Emma along the hallway and down the stairs. By the time they emerged through the front entrance of the building, Emma was grasping Jennings's arm for support.

The crowd rushed them. With handsticks, fists and shoulders the police fought back. Emma was suffering intensely. To many who saw her she looked lost, bewildered. She was staggering, barely able to walk. Mary Brigham and Jennings got her into the carriage. As they climbed in beside her the horses suddenly swept off toward Second Street.

Lizzie sat alone upstairs in the matron's room, frozen, unable to feel anything but numbness. She could not cry.

She was led to another room as if she were in a daze. Again the door closed and she was alone.

Suddenly she began to fall apart inside. In the week since the murders she had felt little emotion.

Tears rushed from her eyes, her throat throbbed with bitter pain. She began to cough, her fingernails jabbed at her hands, tearing at her clothing, attempting to tear away her skin. She choked, sobbing—as if wanting to rip her throat and chest from her body.

Then she began to vomit.

The matrons rushed in but they could not stop the vomiting.

In panic someone ran for Dr. Bowen, but by the time he got there Lizzie's swollen face and neck had turned purple.

Her fit of vomiting was now uncontrollable. She bent over the bare wooden floor, pathetically clutching her stomach.

Bowen administered a sedative.

At the same moment, two miles away, within the gas-lighted receiving vault of Oak Grove Cemetery, a second autopsy was being performed on the bodies of Andrew and Abby. A wound was discovered in Abby's back, between the shoulder blades. It was a deep cut made by an axe wielded with such force that it had penetrated the flesh and bone clear up to the helve.

It alone would have produced instant death.

The mutilated heads were severed from both bodies and were carried by Medical Examiner Dolan into another chamber, where they underwent a surgical operation. The flesh and blood were scaled from the bones, revealing the glaring white skulls with great rents where the murder axe had crushed them.

The skulls were photographed.

9

IMPRISONED

LOCKED UP. LIZZIE BORDEN AT LAST IN CUSTODY.

—Headline from the Fall River *Globe*, August 11, 1892

SHOCKING PARRICIDE IN AMERICA . . . a terrible crime is believed to have been committed in Fall River, Massachusetts, involving a young woman, Miss L. A. Borden, who was arrested last evening.

—*The Evening Echo*, London (England), August 12, 1892

"She still retains the same Christian spirit of resignation as at the onset, and her calmness is the calmness of innocence."

—Reverend E. A. Buck, from an interview in the Providence *Journal*, August 12, 1892

ON FRIDAY MORNING, AUGUST 12TH, a vast crowd huddled in the drenching rain outside the Second District Court in Fall River. Shortly after nine a.m. Emma, John Morse and Andrew Jennings arrived and hurried inside.

As they entered the courtroom on the second floor, Marshal Hilliard, who awaited them, motioned to Jennings.

Jennings nodded that the prisoner could be brought in.

Lizzie, apparently recovered from her nausea of the night before, entered on the arm of Reverend Buck. She was wearing a dark blue suit and a black hat with flowers on the front. A reporter who was present described her: "The prisoner was not crying, but her features were far from firm. She has a face betokening strength of character, but a rather sensitive mouth. She was constantly moving her lips as she sat in the courtroom to show that she was not altogether unemotional."

As Knowlton and Judge Blaisdell entered, Clerk Leonard stood at his desk and called the case of the Commonwealth of Massachusetts against Lizzie Borden on complaint of murder, but Jennings waved to him that he needed a few more moments to complete a document he was preparing. He then walked over to Lizzie with a piece of paper and asked her to sign it. It stated that Judge Blaisdell was not qualified to hear the complaint and that she objected to his doing so.

Knowlton arose and asked the judge if the paper was intended to delay the prisoner's plea. Blaisdell replied that it must not and ordered the clerk to read the warrant.

"You need not read it," Jennings interjected, "the prisoner pleads not guilty."

Blaisdell snapped back at him, "The prisoner must plead in person."

Marshal Hilliard pointed toward Lizzie and she stood up.

"What is your plea?" asked the clerk.

"Not guilty," Lizzie murmured.

Apparently unable to hear her, Clerk Leonard repeated the question.

Lizzie's voice became piercing. "*Not* guilty."

With that Jennings arose. "It seems to me, Your Honor, that this proceeding is most extraordinary. This girl is called to plead to a complaint brought in spite of the fact that she was not allowed to be represented by counsel in the hearing before the inquest. Your Honor sits here to hear this case, which is returnable before you, when you have already been sitting in another capacity. By all the laws of human nature you cannot help being prejudiced from the character of the evidence which has already been submitted to you. You might look at things differently from what you do if certain questions that have been asked in the inquest had been excluded. The Constitution does not allow a judge to sit in such a double capacity; it guarantees a defendant from a prejudicial hearing."

It was a stunning challenge and Knowlton came right back at him. "My brother is entirely in error. I must respectfully submit that it is not a compliment to Your Honor's conception of duty to suggest that you cannot faithfully or impartially perform your duties in this case. The inquest was against no one. It was to ascertain who committed these murders. It is Your Honor's duty to hear this complaint and you must not be deterred."

But Jennings, still smarting from being excluded when Lizzie was questioned, hammered his objection home. "Perhaps the District Attorney did not comprehend my point. The police determined whom they thought the guilty person was, then they had a secret inquest to examine her without anybody to defend her."

Blaisdell quickly ruled. "I think Mr. Jennings is mistaken. His motion is overruled."

"Then, Your Honor, we are ready for trial."

Knowlton unexpectedly asked for a delay. "The evidence in this case cannot be completed at once."

Jennings came back at him. "We are very anxious to proceed at once. We ask for a trial at the earliest possible moment."

Finally Blaisdell settled it. The preliminary hearing would be held within ten days, on Monday, August 22nd.

The prisoner spent that night in the matron's room of Central Police Station.*

The following morning news leaked out that since Fall River had no house of detention, she would be taken to the Taunton Jail.

Shortly after three p.m. Marshal Hilliard, State Detective Seaver and Reverend Buck slipped Lizzie out through the side entrance. There was a direct road from the police station to the depot, but Hilliard planned to disappoint the morbid curiosity seekers, lining it, who were eager for the first glimpse of Lizzie following her arrest. The carriage took a zigzag route from Purchase Street, up the hills, skirting the river, until it arrived moments before the train's departure. When they pulled up to the station Lizzie got out, attractively attired in a high-style blue dress with a short blue veil. On the railway platform she turned white and tottered, but Hilliard and Reverend Buck helped her onto the train. She took her seat, surrounded by a few friends, who remained silent. She stared vacantly out the window. Finally Emma slammed down the window shade, shutting out the pushing, jeering crowd on the platform.

The word had spread that Lizzie Borden was on the train, and at the few places where it stopped, clusters of spectators eagerly waited for a glimpse of her.

*In 1892 in Massachusetts murder was not a bailable offense.

Taunton was reached at four-thirty p.m. and a gathering of hundreds swarmed through the station.

To distract the crowds, State Detective Seaver dashed up along the cars to the north end of the platform, as Lizzie, Hilliard and Reverend Buck left from the south end.

Taunton Jail was a series of solid stone structures with slanted roofs and thin, barred windows. If one looked quickly, then glanced away, it might have seemed picturesque, as its outsides were covered with ragged patches of ivy.

Lizzie entered and walked up the three steps to the office of the keeper. Marshal Hilliard had her committed, and she was led down the long corridor toward the women's section.

There were sixty-five cells. Fifty-six were reserved for men and nine for women. Five of the women's cells were occupied by petty offenders.

The jail had never accommodated an accused murderess.

Reverend Buck remained a short while, giving her a few last words of cheer, and then he departed.

The cell door clanged shut.

It was a tiny, narrow room, nine and a half feet long by seven and a half feet wide, furnished with a bed, a chair and a washbowl. Across the corridor, looking through the iron bars, was a blank, whitewashed wall. For Lizzie the first few hours were the most terrifying. She had never been so helplessly confined in her life.

Yet no person in Taunton experienced a greater shock that afternoon than the prison matron, Mrs. Wright. She had once been a resident of Fall River and her husband, Sheriff Andrew J. Wright, had been marshal of the city, in the same position held by Marshal Hilliard. She had had a close acquaintance many years before with a Borden family who lived on Ferry Street. Mr. Borden was then a struggling, impoverished tradesman. His first name had slipped her memory. She had read about the murders but simply never associated the victims with the people she had known.

Seeing Lizzie, she immediately noticed something familiar about her large, pale blue eyes. Waiting for the Reverend Buck to leave, she began questioning the new prisoner. Finally, hesitantly, she asked, "You are not the Lizzie Borden who used as a child to play with my daughter, Isabel?"

Lizzie nodded.

The matron left. When she appeared in the keeper's office moments later, Mrs. Wright was weeping.

. . .

The press, siding with Andrew Jennings, relentlessly castigated Judge Blaisdell for not disqualifying himself from the preliminary hearing, citing the fact that he had already heard the same testimony at the closed inquest. When Blaisdell refused to step down, Reverend Jubb called Blaisdell's behavior "indecent and not to be tolerated in any civilized country."

Blaisdell resolutely fought back against the stinging attacks. When he was shown an editorial which criticized the harsh words used in the complaint accusing Lizzie of murdering her father, scornfully Blaisdell pointed out that the form of the complaint had been decided upon at least a hundred and fifty years before Lizzie was born and had been adapted to fit capital crimes.

People were predicting that Lizzie would soon collapse mentally and physically under the pressure. At a meeting of the women's auxiliary of the Young Men's Christian Association of Fall River prayers were offered for her. Reverend Dr. Mason of Bowdoin College Church, Brunswick, Maine, stood up in the pulpit of the Central Congregational Church in Fall River and proclaimed: "A great, dark cloud has settled upon one of our families. But God is in that cloud. He is with that poor, tried tempest-tossed girl . . . he will give her strength and peace . . . he will make her glad. It is impossible for a wrong to be done in this world that eternity will not undo. Good is coming . . . good out of evil . . . light out of darkness. The Father is over all. He will vindicate and raise and glorify!"

The public was not reconciled to Lizzie's arrest. Suspects were still being interrogated. On August 18, Charles Peckham turned himself in to the Fall River police and made a full confession. He explained that he had gotten away by leaping over the barbed-wire fence behind the Borden house. He had been wearing the clothes in which he now turned himself in, but they were not stained because Andrew Borden's blood had stagnated.

Joseph Lemay went to the police with a more credible story. Eight days after the murders he had seen the killer with his bloody axe weeping for Mrs. Borden on the edge of a scrub of maples.

Even Emma was amused by the letter she received.

Waltham, Mass., August 17, 1982

Miss Emma Borden:

Dear Madam—You must excuse that I take the liberty in sending you these few lines. I ought to have written to you before this, as I was unable to do so, as I was travelling every day. My name is Samuel Robinsky. I

> am a Jewish peddler. When the fatal murder in Fall River occurred I was only a few miles from Fall River. That day, while sitting on the roadside, towards New Bedford, I met a man who was covered with blood . . .

The letter described the man as medium height, weighing about one hundred thirty-five pounds, with dark brown hair and reddish whiskers, clothed in a gray suit and a brown derby hat. The letter continued:

> I read last Sunday's Boston *Globe* and thought that I might have seen the murderer. I kept quiet as I had no license and feared to be arrested. My stranger was very much afraid. . . . If I come again to Fall River next week I shall call on you, if you think it is necessary, but all I can swear he is the stranger which I have seen that afternoon. Will close now. Will go to Fitchburg tomorrow morning and return to Boston Saturday night. Please do not say anything to the police. I would be arrested. If I had known about the murder the time I met my stranger it would have been different, as I would have followed him up and perhaps got the reward.
>
> I remain very respectfully,
> Samuel Robinsky
>
> P.S. Please excuse paper and mistakes as I am a foreigner.*

Lizzie told Mrs. Wright that she did not want to see the daily newspapers. She began to dread all accounts regarding the case.

Andrew Jennings had been her father's attorney. As long as he trusted in her innocence, he was her one hope.

With her fears mounting, Lizzie was returned to Fall River after ten days in the Taunton Jail.

When Lizzie stepped off the train she was clad in the dress she had worn when she departed, with her face partly covered by the same blue veil. Her return set off such a fever of excitement and attracted such teeming crowds that a riot ensued.

The police gained control as Lizzie was spirited to a private room on the second floor of the Central Police Station, where she was placed in the custody of police matron Hannah Reagan.

There Emma came to her.

Mrs. Reagan had been tidying up the room, but when Emma arrived she left the two sisters alone.

Within minutes Mrs. Reagan heard loud shouting and peered back

*Andrew Jennings sent a telegram to George L. Mayberry, Mayor of Waltham, and to the police in Boston, but Robinsky could not be found.

inside. Lizzie was lying on the couch. As Emma bent over her, according to Mrs. Reagan, Lizzie yelled, "Emma, you have given me away, haven't you."

"No, Lizzie!" Heatedly Emma shook her head. "I have not! I only told Mr. Jennings what I thought he ought to know!"

Lizzie turned toward the window and shut her eyes. She did not speak to Emma again.

Emma remained in the room, silently sitting in a chair beside Lizzie's bed.

That afternoon Hannah Regan told what she had heard to reporter Edwin H. Porter. When it appeared on the front page of the Fall River *Globe,* Andrew Jennings was beside himself. Quickly he drew up a document for Mrs. Reagan's signature which read:

> This is to certify that my attention has been called to a report said to have been made by me in regard to a quarrel between Lizzie and her sister Emma, in which Lizzie said, "Emma, you have given me away, etc." and that I expressly and positively deny that any such conversation ever took place and that I further deny that I ever heard anything that could be construed as a quarrel between the sisters.

Jennings had the Reverend Jubb hurry with it to the matron's room.

Getting her alone, Jubb implored Mrs. Reagan, "If you sign this paper, it will make everything all right between Miss Lizzie Borden and her sister."

It was an amazing statement and whether it was his own invention or quoted from the words of Andrew Jennings, the implication was obvious. Even if its cause was hidden, bitter warfare had erupted between the two sisters.

Hannah Reagan was unmoved by Reverend Jubb's plea. She refused to sign the statement.

How had Emma given Lizzie away? What had she told Andrew Jennings that "he ought to know"?

These questions puzzled the nation's readers as the story spread across the country.

But contrary to Lizzie's fears, Emma had not betrayed her, not even to shield herself. Lizzie was high-strung, impulsive and under a terrible strain. Emma loved Lizzie and in her passion had told Jennings what he wanted to hear, precisely what she thought "he ought to know"—that Lizzie never had a motive—*that she must be innocent.*

Consequently, Jennings dedicated himself to saving Lizzie with greater fervor than ever.

The following morning Fall River was again charged with excitement. An immense delegation of mill girls swelled the throngs converging at the courthouse entrances. Squads of extra police were stationed throughout the corridors and along the stairways.

The courtroom, seating three hundred, rapidly filled. There were forty reporters from out-of-town newspapers present as Prosecutor Knowlton began examining witnesses. A commotion arose when Medical Examiner Dolan stated that on one of the hatchets found in the basement he had discovered two gray hairs.

More witnesses appeared as the preliminary hearing continued.

Professor Edward Wood took the stand. He mentioned first that he had examined the stomach of the victims for evidence of prussic acid and found none. And then he added: "I did not test them for any other poison."*

In his laboratory in Bostón he had run tests on the axes and hatches from the basement and found no evidence of blood on any of them. He had also analyzed the gray hairs discovered on one of them; they had come from a cow.

There were more witnesses.

Finally Andrew Jennings arose and prepared the stage for Lizzie's most emotional moment. "We have heard a description of the injuries, and I suggest that even the learned District Attorney cannot imagine that any person could have committed this crime unless his heart was as black as hell."

With every eye in the room on her, Lizzie's mouth shook. Her whole body shuddered with sudden, convulsive sobbing. She spread her hand over her face, struggling to hide the tears that poured over it.

Jennings went on, steadily describing the victims. "Blow after blow was showered upon them . . ."

Lizzie's body trembled with tension as her hands sought desperately to cover her distorted mouth and streaming eyes. She bit her lips fiercely to control herself.

Jennings's voice rose: "I have no doubt that every person with a feeling of sympathy for that girl felt their hearts leap with joy as Professor Wood gave his testimony. If I could have had my way I would have shouted with joy. That was the deliverance of Lizzie Borden. If that hatchet had been lost on the way to Professor Wood's laboratory

*It is unfortunate that Professor Wood did not test the stomachs for arsenic.

by a railroad accident, Lizzie Borden would have been a condemned woman upon the testimony of Dr. Dolan regarding the description of that hatchet. Lizzie Borden's life was in Dr. Dolan's hands and by the goodness of God's providence Professor Wood came, and like that shot at Concord, which rang round the world, his story went like a song of joy from Maine to Mexico and from the Atlantic to the Pacific. They haven't proved that this girl had anything to do with the murder. They can't find any blood on her dress, on her hair, on her shoes. They can't find any motive. *They can't find the axe,* and so I demand this woman's release."

Focusing on Judge Blaisdell, he cautioned: "The great public is going to take your decision as they took the arrest upon the strength of Mr. Knowlton's experience. They can't find a motive, no blood, no poison and so I say that this woman shan't be deprived of her liberty and her good name."

His conclusion was resounding: "Don't, Your Honor, put the stigma of guilt upon this woman, reared as she has been with a past character beyond reproach. Don't let it go out in the world as the decision of a just judge that she is probably guilty. God grant Your Honor wisdom to decide, and, while you do your duty, do it as God tells you to do it, giving to the accused the benefit of the doubt."

As they watched Lizzie the spectators were torn by emotion. The case had dragged on for over two weeks under the gaze of the world. When Jennings finished speaking there were tears in the eyes of the majority of the three hundred people present. Melvin Adams, the associate counsel, was deeply affected and Jennings's young assistant, Arthur Philipps, was weeping.

Lizzie's lips were still trembling but the tears in her eyes were finally hidden by her gloved hand.

Mayor Coughlin, Dr. Dolan and other prominent persons stepped forward to grasp Jennings's hand. A ripple of applause started, which spontaneously exploded into a thunderous ovation.

But Judge Blaisdell was not moved either by Jennings's impassioned words or Lizzie's tears. On the following morning he pushed the point that Lizzie should not expect leniency merely because she was a woman: "Suppose for a single moment *a man* was standing there. He was found close by the guest chamber which to Mrs. Borden was a chamber of death. Suppose *a man* had been found in the vicinity of Mrs. Borden—was the first to find the body—and the only account he could give was the unreasonable one that he was out in the barn looking for sinkers—then he was out in the yard—then he was out for something else—would there be any question in the minds of men what should be done with such *a man?*"

Overlooking the absence of a murder weapon, Blaisdell held that Lizzie was "probably guilty," giving her into the hands of the Grand Jury, which would not convene until November.

Her imprisonment would continue.

That night she was returned to her lonely cell in Taunton.

10

AN EXPOSÉ

Hart:	A woman came in and said she wanted ten cents worth of prussic acid to put around the edges of a seal skin cape. She did not speak to me, though she was very close to me.
Prosecutor:	Is the defendant the woman?
Hart:	Yes, sir.

—Frederick E. Hart, a clerk at D. R. Smith's Drugstore, from his testimony at the preliminary hearing, August 30, 1892

Kilroy:	I was a customer in Smith's Drug Store at the time. I saw this lady come in. She went to the counter and asked for prussic acid. Mr. Bence said: "I can't sell prussic acid without a prescription." The only other thing I heard was the woman use the words "seal skin cape." She left the store then. That was all I heard.
Prosecutor:	Are you sure this is the woman *(pointing to Lizzie)*?
Kilroy:	Yes, sir.

—Frank H. Kilroy, from his testimony at the preliminary hearing, August 30, 1892

ON THE EVE OF LIZZIE'S ARREST, one of the additional detectives hired by Marshal Hilliard was Edwin D. McHenry, a freelance investigator from Providence, Rhode Island. Hilliard entrusted him with a single task: to "take care" of Pinkerton operative O. M. Hanscom.

Hanscom worried the police because he seemed to be everywhere they were. Ostensibly he had been employed by Andrew Jennings to search for evidence, but his actual occupation was to keep an eye on Hilliard and his men.

After dark, on the day McHenry was hired, he spotted Hanscom eavesdropping outside the rear window of Marshal Hilliard's residence while Hilliard and Detective Seaver were in conference. Surprising him, McHenry chased Hanscom around the building.

When Hilliard was alerted, he became furious. The thought of being spied upon himself by Hanscom, while Hanscom was being spied upon by McHenry, was more than he could bear. He roared, "I intend to probe this affair to the bottom, no matter who it hits. Outside detectives must not interfere with the work of my men."

With Detective McHenry present, a reporter from the Boston *Globe* interviewed Attorney General Pillsbury in front of the Borden house the following morning. Later, the reporter would embarrass the Attorney General by commenting: "O. M. Hanscom will prevent the Fall River police from hanging Lizzie Borden."

The reporter was Henry Trickey.

The liaison between Detective McHenry and reporter Trickey, which occurred that morning in front of the Borden home, would have a telling effect on Lizzie's defense.

Both Trickey and McHenry were ruthless men. Trickey was slim, dark-haired with a thin-line mustache. At twenty-four, he was already the top crime reporter on the Boston *Globe,* having built his reputation by unearthing evidence in a series of celebrated murder trials. On that morning, when Detective McHenry approached him with an explosive, untold story about Lizzie, Trickey candidly replied, "The *Globe* will pay as much for it as any other paper."

But it's worth a great deal more to somebody else."

Trickey was fascinated. "Who?" he inquired.

"The defense."

McHenry explained that since being employed on the case he had obtained copies of Prosecutor Knowlton's most crucial evidence, which would ultimately damn Lizzie to death.

What he required was a thousand dollars and the Boston *Globe*'s promise that they would notify him twenty-four hours before they published the story so that he could quietly leave town before it was revealed that he had betrayed his employers, the Fall River police.

Trickey was so excited that he gave McHenry the thirty dollars he had in his pocket and rushed back to Boston for more money. When they met again on October 9, McHenry furnished him with copies of signed affidavits of twenty-five witnesses who had been located since the inquest. But Trickey had failed to come up with the thousand dollars McHenry had wanted. He could give him only five hundred.

Fearful that McHenry might attempt to make a similar deal with the rival Boston *Herald* in exchange for an additional five hundred, Trickey rushed the affidavits to his office in Boston without verifying the existence of the witnesses who signed them.

On October 10th, the Boston *Globe*'s front page erupted with the story.

Thirteen columns of devastating admissions were supported by an editorial in bold type:

> The *Globe* is enabled to lay before its readers not only every fact of importance now in the government's possession, but as well to describe how and by whom the information was secured by the patient and unceasing toil of the police. The evidence is forthcoming from twenty-five people, all of whom stand high in the community. Every statement of importance in the twenty-odd affidavits now held by the government, which the *Globe* today publishes substantially in detail, is corroborated in a most convincing manner.

A neighbor was quoted as saying he saw Mr. Borden enter the house and at the same time saw a blind cautiously opened by a young woman in the bedroom where Mrs. Borden's body was later found. "The window was so situated that she must have been standing over the mutilated remains of her mother at the very time her father was about to enter the house."

A neighboring couple had visited the Bordens the night before the murders and overheard Lizzie admitting to her father that she was pregnant. Andrew was in a fury. Threatening to throw her out, he gave her one day to "name the man who got you in trouble."

Bridget was quoted as saying that Lizzie told her she could have all the money she wanted if she did not talk to the police. There were statements by attorneys, by John Morse, by others . . .

The resultant uproar was immediate.

Telegrams poured in from the Fall River police, from John Morse

Daily Globe.

DAILY GLOBE:
Sept. '92 - - 200,143
Sept. '91 - - - - - - - 154,178
GAIN - - - 45,965

OCTOBER 10, 1892—TEN PAGES. PRICE TWO CENTS.

LATEST!

For Other Evening News See Second, Fourth, Fifth and Eighth Pages.

ASTOUNDED.

All New England Read Story.

Globes Were Bought by Thousands.

Lizzie Borden Appears in New Light.

Belief in Her Innocence Sadly Shaken.

Excitement Runs High in Fall River.

Police Think the Scoop is a Corker.

Lawyer Jennings Says Lies Have Been Told.

Doesn't Believe There is Any Secret.

Opinions on That Spying by Detective McHenry.

FALL RIVER, Mass., Oct. 10.—Doubts of Lizzie A. Borden's guilt; hopes that in the government's weakness she might receive exoneration; belief that her past life might be a powerful factor in making the world give assent to her plea, "I am innocent" all were shaken this morning. Facts, appalling in themselves, tremendous in their significance, have thrown Fall River, where the sentiment for and against has been so intense, into a condition of excitement, amazement and horror.

During the entire history of the Borden tragedy a shadow so profound had never fallen across Lizzie Borden's path, and all Fall River saw it. What it meant and what on Main st., a man rushed out on to the sidewalk, having a GLOBE above his head, and shouted:

"For heaven's sake have you seen THE GLOBE?"

The headlines were soon seen, and then there was a furious rush for the news stand. Men trampled on each other in their eagerness to secure a paper, and in a short time the sidewalk was crowded with an excited mob, reading the startling news.

It fairly electrified the crowd.

Meantime a boy fought his way through the crowd and put a flaming bulletin out upon the sidewalk. The crowd became denser and denser, and excitement raged. Passers by stopped, read and dove into the news depot, some returning with two or three papers. Three men stood behind the counter working to satisfy the demand for GLOBES. Men threw down their money, grabbed the paper and became absorbed in the story without waiting for their change. Some could not contain themselves, and fairly shouted in amazement as they read.

Boys with huge bundles were rushing about Main st., shouting, and together with

The Excited Readers

made the centre of Fall River a regular pandemonium.

Inside of 10 minutes several thousand people were gathered about Main st., from Pleasant to Franklin sts., reading and discussing.

And still the demand for GLOBES had not been half met.

There were corner gatherings and animated discussions, but not the expression of diverse opinions.

Mingling among the crowd THE GLOBE correspondent heard such expressions from many lips as this: "This is a sad day for Lizzie Borden. I had asked myself what could have incited her to do it, if she did it, but there is no doubt about a motive now. It is all explained.

"I had hoped she might be proven innocent, but it looks hard for her now, and her past life—why, great Scott, Fall River never knew her, her intimate friends did not know her."

No story ever caused such a furor, because none ever came with such corroboration or so unexpectedly.

Boys carried GLOBES into the mills, where they were eagerly read by the operatives while they tried to work.

Detective McHenry's spying upon Lizzie in some quarters met with condemnation, but it was quickly supported by many who cry: "If the woman is guilty she deserves conviction; any method to serve the ends of justice is right."

THE GLOBE's story caused an awful cloud to settle over the influential part of the city. On the hill, among Lizzie Borden's friends, and around the Central Congregational church, there was a gloom that was pathetic. In that part of the city hopes in her innocence were centred, hopes that aroused to fervent prayer. The GLOBES went there, they were read, but it was a grave matter for them. No outburst of excitement appeared in this quarter, but there was a poignant grief. Many wept for Lizzie Borden, whom hope had buoyed up for weeks. She was their fellow church member, their friend in many cases, life acquaintance, fellow worker in the temperance cause, their respected sister in the church and social world.

At Police Headquarters

the story created a tremendous sensation. Police officers bought copies of THE GLOBE and saw their work minutely outlined. How could THE GLOBE have got it? . . . Still there it was with many things they thought no one could possibly have been informed of outside the small police circle. All hands not on duty hurried to the station house.

City Marshal Hilliard was not in, having gone to New Bedford to consult with District Attorney Knowlton.

Deputy John Fleet was preparing the morning court docket. Mr. Fleet was handed a copy of THE GLOBE. His eyebrows went up half an inch as he comprehended the force of the headline.

"Great heavens," said he, "what does this mean, what is this, anyway?"

"It comes pretty near telling its own story," said the reporter.

"Does it," echoed the deputy, "why, my dear man, it is a corker. It is beyond understanding. Say, now, how did you fellows get all this?"

"Dead right, isn't it?" was asked.

"You must excuse me; give me time to think this thing over. It's the biggest surprise we have had here for some time. Pretty solid stuff, too."

Mr. Fleet read with astonishment.

"There is liable to be some decided criticism of your department on account of allowing McHenry to spy on the defendant," was suggested.

"Well, I have not read it all yet," said Mr. Fleet, "and can't talk upon that. But this means that we will have to do some tall work now that that story is published. Say, how did THE GLOBE get it?"

Special Officer Medley was one of the first to buy a GLOBE, and a reporter saw him immediately after. Said he: "You fellows have

LIZZIE HAD A SECRET.

Mr. Borden Discovered It. Then a Quarrel.

Startling Testimony of 25 New Witnesses.

Seen in Mother's Room With a Hood on Her Head.

Accused Sister of Treachery and Kicked Her in Anger.

Theft of a Watch---Money Offered to Bridget --Story of a Will.

FALL RIVER, Mass., Oct. 9.—Besides those who testified for the government in the preliminary examination of Lizzie A. Borden before Judge Blaisdell fully 25 new witnesses will be called by the State at the trial of the defendant for murder in December.

On the afternoon of September 1 Miss Borden was committed to the county jail at Taunton to await the action of the grand jury at its November sitting.

Judge Blaisdell's jurisdiction not being final his action in thus concluding the examination was justified in two ways. He knew that if he dismissed the defendant she would soon be under arrest on a bench warrant issued by a court higher than his own. Moreover, he knew that the government's case against her was much stronger than was indicated by the testimony developed in open court.

He knew that it was the desire of District Attorney Knowlton to submit the least evidence necessary to hold the prisoner, and therefore, when he heard enough from his seat on the bench to partly substantiate his opinion formed elsewhere by other facts, the government's case was closed, and the defence followed with little testimony and able argument.

Judge Blaisdell said in his decision he was satisfied that the government had not produced enough evidence to warrant the conviction, nor perhaps the finding of an indictment, but he felt satisfied that enough had been shown to warrant holding the defendant for the grand jury, which body could deliberately consider the entire case against her and report upon the evidence.

The public, however, not occupying the position of confidence with the State's officials that Judge Blaisdell possessed by virtue of his office was highly indignant at the decision, and from the Atlantic to the Pacific the finding was denounced and termed "a high-handed outrage."

The situation indicated other facts to those who had without prejudice or opinion followed the case along. The ability and characteristic fairness of the attorney-general, Albert E. Pillsbury, precluded the possibility that he was participating in a persecution of Miss Borden.

Mr. Knowlton has for years borne the one in which he saw Miss Lizzie is so situated that she must have been standing

Over the Mutilated Remains

of her mother at the very time that her father was about to enter the house, between 10.30 and 10.45 o'clock.

The next witness of importance is Mrs. Gustave F. Ronald, whose husband is a well known civil engineer, and whose home during the winter is at Pawtuxet, R. I.

She and her husband were guests at the Wilbur House at the time of the murder.

About 9.30 o'clock on the morning of Aug. 4 she went out with her baby in its carriage for a walk.

She wheeled the little one up 2d st. and stopped under the big trees near the Borden house about 20 minutes of 10 o clock.

A minute later she heard a terrible cry or groan and began looking around to see whence it came.

She looked up at the Borden house and saw in a room through a partially open window a woman whose head was in part covered by a rubber cap or hood, and whose face she saw plainly, as the distance was short.

This window she has designated to the authorities, and it is the one nearest to the murdered woman as she lay in the guest chamber of her home when found by the police.

Mrs. Ronald was almost that minute approached by Mr. Peter Mahany of 103 Pleasant st., Fall River, who is a timekeeper in the Troy mill.

He likewise had heard the groan, seen the woman at the window, who wore the peculiar head covering, and recognized her as the younger daughter of the Borden family, all members of which he knew quite well by sight. The window that he designates as the one in which he saw Miss Lizzie was the same as that pointed out by Mrs. Ronald.

Augustus Gunning, who now resides at 308 Plainfield st., Johnsonville, R. I., near Providence, was at that time a lodger in Mrs. Churchill's house, and he too, about 10 o'clock on the morning of Aug. 4, saw Lizzie Borden in the window of the guest chamber with a dark colored garment on and a hood of similar color covering her head. As he looked across she seemed to be engaged in cleaning, but upon seeing threatening a law suit, from multitudes of Fall River residents connected with the case. Andrew Jennings lashed out that most of the witnesses were fictitious and the addresses given for them were nonexistent. In regard to Lizzie's secret, Dr. Bowen, the Borden family physician, stated that Lizzie had no "secret."

The following morning the *Globe* editors started backtracking in panic:

DETECTIVE MCHENRY TALKS
HE FURNISHED THE GLOBE WITH THE BORDEN STORY
IT HAS BEEN PROVED WRONG IN SOME PARTICULARS

Under pressure McHenry admitted he had used fictitious names but that the statements were true.

However, the damage was irreparable. That afternoon the editors of the newspaper recanted on its front page:

> The *Globe* feels it is its duty as an honest newspaper to state that it has been grievously misled in the Lizzie Borden case. It published on Monday a communication that it believed to be true evidence. Some of this remarkably ingenious and cunningly contrived story undoubtedly was based on true facts. The *Globe* believes however that much of it is false and never should have been published. The *Globe* being thus misled has innocently added to the terrible burdens of Miss Lizzie Borden. We hereby tender our heartfelt apology for the inhuman reflection on her honor as a woman and for any injustice the publication reflected on her.

The outcome was that newspapers everywhere began to rally behind Lizzie's cause. A wave of sympathy was building.

On May 2nd, the Boston *Globe* had celebrated its twentieth anniversary with the largest circulation in New England. Its editor-in-chief, Charles H. Taylor, had affirmed its goal: "My aim has been to make the *Globe* a cheerful, attractive and useful newspaper that would enter the home as a kindly, helpful friend of the family. My disposition has always been to build up rather than to join in tearing down."

Now, only six months later, with its reputation darkened, it faced the possibility of financial ruin.

Taylor steeled himself for the staggering lawsuit to be instituted by Andrew Jennings. But it never came. Wishing to avoid the further exposure of a libel case, Jennings was aiming all his efforts toward the Grand Jury hearing scheduled for November 7th.

. . .

District Attorney Knowlton did an astonishing thing. When the Grand Jury convened he presented his evidence. Then he invited Andrew Jennings to present the case for the defense.

Never before in the history of American jurisprudence had a Grand Jury been asked to weigh both sides of a case to determine guilt or innocence. This had always been the exclusive function of the trial jury. The Grand Jury's sole duty had always been to hear the evidence of the prosecution and determine if it was sufficient to warrant a trial.

It was a clever move, since once again Knowlton wished to create a precedent—just as Lizzie and the other witnesses had been questioned secretly before the same judge who later presided over the preliminary hearing, if the Grand Jury listened to both sides of the case and decided that Lizzie should be indicted, it could weigh heavily on the outcome of her resultant trial.

In fact, she would be tried for murder, but behind closed doors.

The newspapers of the country took issue with Knowlton's inordinate strategy on their front pages, and professionals in the law were amazed.

Jennings refused Knowlton's offer.

On November 7th, the Grand Jury assembled. After two weeks of deliberation it adjourned on November 21st, without issuing any indictments.

And then on December 1st it reconvened to hear one witness: Alice Russell, who revealed, for the first time, that Lizzie burned the dress she had worn on the day of the murders.

The following day three indictments were returned against Lizzie. One charged her with the murder of her father, the second charged her with the murder of her stepmother and the third charged her jointly with the murder of both.

There were twenty-one members of the Grand Jury. Twenty voted yes, one voted no. Twenty men had said, after having heard the evidence, that Lizzie Borden was guilty. It was a triumphant moment for Knowlton, Hilliard and Judge Blaisdell.

That same day Boston *Globe* reporter Henry Trickey was indicted for tampering with witnesses.

Three days later the leading headlines in the *Globe* announced:

HENRY G. TRICKEY DEAD

ALTHOUGH ONLY 24 YEARS OLD, HIS LIFE WAS MOST EVENTFUL

. . .

Trickey had died in Ontario.

Whether he was the victim of a freak accident or a despondent suicide was never disclosed.

The *Globe* maintained that he was on his way to an interview and being late, was attempting to board a west-bound train when he stumbled and fell under the wheels.

11

ROBINSON

"I went in to hang a dress, there was no vacant nail, and I noticed this dress of Lizzie's. Later I said to my sister, 'Lizzie, you have not destroyed that old dress yet. Why don't you?' "

—Emma Borden, from her testimony at the murder trial of her sister, June 16, 1893

THERE HAD BEEN A CHOLERA SCARE in New York and a New York newspaper printed a passionate editorial desiring that the plague would come to Narragansett Bay and destroy every man connected with the prosecution of Lizzie. It exulted in the act of purging Fall River of such men as would dare to insinuate that Lizzie was guilty.

The trial was set for June 5th in New Bedford. As Lizzie waited in her cell in Taunton, people everywhere were poised for the outcome.

Sermons on her innocence were given, and the Woman's Christian Temperance Union, of which Lizzie was a member in good standing, supported her with demonstrations and gatherings in the major cities of the United States. Mrs. Susan S. Fessenden, president of the W.C.T.U., thrilled listeners at their annual meeting in Chicago as she shouted in a frenzy, "Is Lizzie Borden guilty? *No, no, a thousand times no!*" Impassioned feminists saw in Lizzie a symbol of innate moral superiority, and she was applauded in magazine articles by several popular women journalists. Even famed women's rights leader Lucy Stone was moved to praise her unflinching courage.

Meanwhile, as the months dragged on, Lizzie was allowed out of her cell for long walks in the open air and treated almost royally. She received flowers from countless admirers and her meals were catered in a specially designed three-tier steel container from the town's best hotel. Yet nothing could overcome the effects of prolonged isolation.

To a woman reporter who interviewed her in her jail cell at Taunton Lizzie candidly admitted: "I cannot sleep nights now, and nothing they give me will produce sleep. . . . The hardest thing for me to stand here is the night, when there is no light. They will not allow me to have even a candle to read by, and to sit in the dark all the evening is very hard. . . . They say I don't show any grief. Certainly I don't in public. I never did reveal my feelings, and I cannot change my nature now. They say I don't cry. They should see me when I am alone. . . ."

Although it had always been accepted practice that the Attorney General of the State of Massachusetts prosecuted capital cases, as the trial date approached and ever-increasing floods of communications from women's pressure groups, religious organizations and the state's influential textile-manufacturing establishment poured into his office, Attorney General Arthur Pillsbury began to waver. It seemed as if the whole world were clamoring in Lizzie's behalf. Why should he suddenly step in and become the villain when District Attorney Knowlton had already cast himself so well in the role.

Pillsbury's excuse was ill health, and his sudden withdrawal from the case shook Knowlton.

> Hon. A. E. Pillsbury, Attorney General
> My Dear Sir:
>
> I have thought more about the Lizzie Borden case since I talked with you, and think perhaps that it may be well to write to you. . . .
>
> Personally I would like very much to get rid of the trial of the case, and feel that my feelings in that direction may have influenced my better judgement; I feel this all the more upon your not unexpected announcement that the burden of the trial would come upon me.
>
> Yours truly,
> Hosea M. Knowlton

But Pillsbury was not about to let the district attorney off the hook. Publicly announcing that his health would not permit him to participate in a strenuous trial and that he planned to vacation in Florida during the month of June, when the trial would commence, he placed the responsibility solely in Knowlton's hands.

Knowlton was more than wary of the prospect; his whole political future was at stake. Yet he firmly clung to his belief that Lizzie was guilty and that she had to be tried and convicted. He wrote to Pillsbury: "Nothing has developed which satisfies either of us that she is innocent; neither of us can escape the conclusion that she must have some knowledge of the occurrence."

While Knowlton and Pillsbury were testing each other, a panel of judges was named to preside over the trial.

In 1891, an act was passed in the Massachusetts State Legislature stipulating that a panel of three Superior Court judges had to preside over all capital cases. Therefore, Lizzie's was one of the first trials in the state's history over which such a panel was required. It consisted of Judges Albert Mason, Caleb Blodget and Justin Dewey.

Justin Dewey was a graduate of Williams College. He was white-haired, with a thin beard and deep-set, reflective eyes. He had been fairly successful working for a well-known attorney in Alford, Massachusetts, but he was also a strong family man with three unmarried daughters to raise. Consequently, the guaranteed income of a Superior Court judgeship had come as a windfall at a crucial time in his life.

As soon as the judges were named, Andrew Jennings made an audacious move. Admitting that he felt he should not personally conduct Lizzie's defense, he chose the one man who had more influence than anyone else in the state. Once a representative to the Congress of the United States, George D. Robinson had been one of the ablest trial lawyers in Massachusetts. His gentle backwoods manner concealed a polished professionalism. Because of his immense popularity and his ability to reach the common man who lived in the small rural towns he had been elected Governor for three consecutive terms and had returned to private practice only six years before Jennings contacted him. In addition to his spectacular political record and his shrewd Yankee instincts, he possessed one invaluable credential: as Governor, in 1886, he had appointed Justin Dewey to the Superior Court system for life.

At their first meeting, the ex-Governor assured Lizzie, "It's going to be all right, little girl." For the purposes of discretion, he suggested that she should start wearing black.

Jennings was feeling more confident. Aware that Knowlton's forces were no longer spearheaded by Pillsbury, and having replaced himself with the most respected attorney money could buy,* he could only wish for some dramatic event which might cast an indelible question of doubt in Lizzie's favor.

The miracle he hoped for was unexpected and eerie. It occurred on May 31, 1893.

Stephen Manchester operated a dairy farm on the outskirts of Fall River. He had been married twice, but because of his eccentric and tight-fisted ways, both wives had deserted him, leaving him to live alone with his twenty-two-year-old daughter, Bertha.

Bertha ran the farm while Stephen was delivering milk to the city's residents. Conditioned since childhood to do the most strenuous chores, she was tough and hard physically and, taking after her father, extremely difficult to get along with. Although young in years, she was considered as strong as any man and, with a cold eye, could boss any of the farmhands into submission.

On May 31, 1893, exactly five days before the start of Lizzie's trial, Bertha Manchester was butchered to death in her Fall River kitchen by an unknown assassin wielding an axe. She was found stretched out beside her black iron stove, her clothing torn to shreds, as if she had put up a fierce struggle for her life.

The autopsy report of the medical examiner (once again Dr. William Dolan) described "twenty-three distinct and separate axe wounds on the back of the skull and its base." So similar were the injuries to those of the Borden murders that a terrible hush fell over Fall River.

It erupted into hysteria—the axe killer was again on the rampage. The June 1st headlines in the Boston *Globe* screamed: STARTLING PARALLELISMS—MANY POINTS OF RESEMBLANCE FOUND BETWEEN BORDEN AND MANCHESTER MURDERS. Feverish speculation gripped the city as Charles J. Holmes, Lizzie's friend and editor of the Fall River *News*, published a detailed comparison between the Manchester murder and the Borden murders. The similarities were uncanny:

1. As in the case of the Bordens, no items of value were taken by Bertha Manchester's assassin.
2. There was evidence that the unknown murderer had lingered for a considerable period of time in the Manchester farmhouse.
3. The savage wounds on Bertha Manchester's skull were in precisely the same locations as the wounds on Abby Borden's skull.

*Lizzie and Emma paid Robinson $25,000 for his services. By comparison, the annual salary for Superior Court judges in 1893 was $5,000.

4. Both the Borden murders and the Manchester murder suggested incredible audacity on the part of the killer—nine-thirty a.m., when Bertha Manchester was slaughtered, was normally a busy time at the dairy farm.

There was little doubt in anyone's mind that the Fall River axe murderer was still on the loose—even though Lizzie had been in jail in Taunton for ten months!

For Andrew Jennings, the succession of events could not have been more perfectly timed.

When he heard the news, Jennings was in Boston with ex-Governor Robinson going over the last-minute plans for Lizzie's defense. Excitedly he hurried to Fall River, where he was met at the train station by representatives of the press. Smiling happily, he stood jauntily on the station platform. "Well," quipped Jennings to the newsmen, "are they going to claim that Lizzie Borden did this too?"

His stinging and sarcastic question was telegraphed around the world. There was no doubt that it echoed the prevalent feelings of the jurors already selected to hear Lizzie's case.

It was not until June 5th that a twenty-two-year-old itinerant farm worker was arrested for the Manchester murder.

When José Correira, a Portuguese immigrant, had been fired by Stephen Manchester he had bitterly argued with him over severance pay.

Manchester had slapped him.

After brooding for several days, Correira returned to the farm looking for Stephen, but found Bertha. In a frenzy he repeatedly struck her with an axe until her mutilated remains lay on the kitchen floor at his feet.*

But by the time the press publicized the details of José Correira's arrest the Borden jury had already been isolated from the outside world. Their last knowledge was the possibility that the Fall River axe murderer was still at large—and that it was not Lizzie.

The most famous murder trial in American history was about to begin.

*It was later established that José Correira could not have committed the Borden murders. He did not arrive in the United States from the Azores until April 1893, eight months after the Borden killings had occurred. But this information never reached the jury.

II

THE TRIAL

12

THE PROSECUTION

A mighty whale we rush upon
And in our irons throw:
She sinks her monstrous body down
Among the waves below.

And when she rises out again
We soon renew the fight,
Thrust our sharp lances in amain
And all her rage excite.

With joyful hearts we see her die
And on the surface lay;
While all with eager haste apply
To save our deathful prey.
—New Bedford whaling song,
1765

NEW BEDFORD, the historical and prosperous county seat of Bristol County, located fifteen miles from Fall River, was a part of the original Plymouth Colony purchased on November 29, 1652, by William Bradford and Captain Miles Standish from the two Indian chiefs Wesanequen and Wamsutta, for thirty yards of cloth, eight moose-skins, fifteen axes, fifteen hoes, fifteen pair of breeches, eight blankets, eight pairs of stockings, two kettles, one cloak, eight pairs of shoes, one iron pot and ten shillings. Soon after it was settled, the colonists of Plymouth had been joined by Quakers from Rhode Island, comprising a rugged, God-fearing stock. By 1775, scores of whaling vessels were already sailing in the summer months from its shores and returning with great bounties of blubber and oil taken off the capes of Virginia. From the beginning, whaling, considered the most heroic and perilous of maritime pursuits, was its principal industry as its harbor filled with three- and four-masted sloops and schooners.

By 1820, New Bedford had become the leading whaling port in the world.

Lizzie was to be tried only seven blocks from the Seamen's Bethel, made famous in Herman Melville's *Moby Dick*, where from his lofty pulpit, which he reached by climbing a ship's side ladder, Father Mapple, as if praying from the bottom of the sea, had intoned: "*O Father! . . . mortal or immortal, here I die. I have striven to be Thine, more than to be this world's, or mine own. Yet this is nothing: I leave eternity to Thee; for what is man that he should live out the lifetime of his God?*"

Andrew Jennings guided Robinson in picking the jury. He wanted only people from the New Bedford community, none from anywhere near Fall River. In his eyes the residents of New Bedford, with their rock-solid Puritanical-Quaker traditions, were less vulnerable to the small-town pettiness which plagued Fall River. The men he chose were of middle years or older, staunch, conservative tradesmen and farmers who might be less affected by the gossip which everywhere abounded.

His precautions were well-founded. New Bedford was immediately assaulted by an avalanche of dazzling notoriety.

Hotels and lodging houses were crowded to overflowing with correspondents from the world's leading newspapers. The Western Union and Postal Telegraph rushed to install thirty additional lines to serve them as twenty telegraphers were imported to work out of carriage stands set up in the rear of the courthouse. The excitement was spreading to Boston, New York and Chicago, and with ever-increasing rapidity, across the Atlantic.

There was little else to write about. Grover Cleveland and Adlai E. Stevenson had easily defeated Benjamin Harrison and Whitelaw Reid for President and Vice-President of the United States, and the World's Columbian Exposition, which had opened in Chicago, had already become tiresome.

Lizzie's trial was the story of the year.

And then, suddenly, into the heart of this legendary New England whaling town walked a man whose journalistic power was unrivaled. He would become Lizzie's greatest champion—to the very end.

Joseph Howard was born in Brooklyn, where his father had been clerk and treasurer of the Congregational Church on Cranberry Street. He often maintained that as a boy he had been inspired by the fiery oratory of the church's famed pastor, reformer Henry Ward Beecher. Reaching manhood, he set out to achieve prominence by becoming a news reporter. The Civil War was ending and his ambition drove him to concoct a story that plans were being made to establish a universal compulsory military draft. Both Howard and the New York *World*, the newspaper in which the story appeared, were censured by the government, and Howard was imprisoned. But eventually he got even by revealing the Crédit Mobilier scandal of 1873. Howard uncovered explosive data showing that during the building of the Union Pacific Railroad (constructed by a group of wealthy entrepreneurs known as the Crédit Mobilier), several congressmen and cabinet members had been richly paid off. His investigation ravaged President Grant's administration, finally exposing it as one of the most corrupt in history. Consequently, Grant was rendered powerless and the nation's economy almost collapsed.

Flamboyant, in the mode of Richard Harding Davis and Stephen Crane, Howard was the most sensational and disruptive reporter of his day. He became so celebrated that his columns were the first to be syndicated in America's press.

It was only suitable that he should be present for the trial of the century.

Before his arrival in New Bedford he had already been stirred by public sentiment. Intending to hold up a banner so that all might follow, he approached Lizzie's ordeal with a passionate belief in her innocence.

He was not alone. The sympathetic attention of the world had become centered on a two-story brick building with four white Doric columns and a white wooden portico leading from a pristine, maple-lined walkway. Approachable only by a single staircase, which rose through a vast cavity in its center, the courtroom was located on the second floor. In the rear, rows of spoke-backed, wooden spectator benches hunched in tiers facing the judge's bench, to the left of which was the witness stand and jury box. Since the courtroom could seat no more than two hundred, a series of long tables with four-legged wooden stools had been jammed along the white plaster walls. Four large brass chandeliers with gas-burning pots hung from the ceiling.

It was Monday, June 5th, 1893. Temporary barricade fences had been set up all around the building to control the crowds, but the crush of spectators struggling to enter the building proved overwhelming.

By eleven twenty-five a.m. it was insufferably hot when Lizzie was taken from an adjacent detention room and led to the bar to be tried. Her gown was stylish, but black. In her hand she clutched a long black fan, which she kept closed and stiffly upright as if it were a small baton, its tip barely touching her cheek.

It was carefully observed by the reporters present that, for the first time since the murders, Lizzie had gone into mourning.

Joseph Howard would be covering the trial not only for his syndicated column, but also as a news reporter for the front pages of such major dailies as the Chicago *Tribune,* the New York *Recorder,* the Boston *Globe* and the San Francisco *Chronicle.* Red-bearded, with his wide-brimmed straw hat perched at a flippant angle, Howard entered the courtroom accompanied by the unusual presence of a curvacious blonde stenographer. He sat so that he could face the defendant at an angle, his roving eye taking in the large number of women present for his millions of readers: "There were two or three very pretty girls and one especially attractive bride from Boston, but a large majority were vinegar-faced, sharp-nosed, lean-visaged and extremely spare in physique. A precise photograph would show sandwiched in with many reputable-looking and neatly-attired matrons, a host of unkempt and unattractive females."

At eleven twenty-eight, the three judges, Albert Mason, Caleb Blodget and Justin Dewey, entered and took their places upon the bench as the court crier shouted: "Hear ye, hear ye, hear ye! All those having anything to do before the Honorable, the Justices of the Superior Court gather round, give your attention, and you shall be heard. God save the Commonwealth of Massachusetts! Be seated!"

Almost in an echo of Melville's Father Mapple, the Reverend M. C. Julian of New Bedford offered a prayer for divine guidance: "*Almighty and all-wise God, our Father, we look to Thee as the only source of courage. . . . we pray Thee that innocence may be revealed and guilt exposed, to the glory of Thy own great name and the well being of the world. . . .*"

District Attorney Knowlton rose and addressed the Court. Formally he notified the judges that "the Attorney General of the Commonwealth finds himself in such a condition of health that he fears to engage actively in the trial of this cause." He went on to add that William H. Moody, the District Attorney of Essex County, had been assigned as his co-prosecutor.

One hundred and eight jurors were questioned, from which twelve were chosen.* The Court clerk formally read the three indictments: Lizzie Andrew Borden was charged with murder of Andrew Jackson Borden, the murder of Abbey Durfee Borden, and the murders of Abby Durfee Borden and Andrew Jackson Borden. The clerk's reading ended with the words: "To each of these indictments the defendant has pleaded not guilty and has placed herself upon the country, which country you are. Gentlemen of the jury, harken to the evidence."

And then co-prosecutor William Moody solemnly walked across the courtroom floor. He was thirty-nine, the youngest of the legal professionals involved. He was slender and earnest-looking, with neatly trimmed dark whiskers and bright eyes. As he leaned forward upon the rail of the jury box, he began to speak in a conversational tone.

This was to be his first murder case.†

"Upon the fourth day of August of the last year an old man and woman, husband and wife, each without a known enemy in the world, in their own home, upon a frequented street in the most populous city in this County under the light of day and in the midst of its activities, were, first one, then, after an interval of an hour, another, severally killed by unlawful human agency. Today a woman of good social position, of hitherto unquestioned character, a member of a Christian church and active in good works, the own daughter of one of the victims, is at the bar of this Court, accused by the Grand Jury of this County of these crimes.

"There is no language, gentlemen, at my command which can better measure the solemn importance of the inquiry which you are about to begin, than this simple statement of fact. For the sake of these crimes and for the sake of these accusations, every man may well pause at the threshold of this trial and carefully search his understanding and con-

*Thirty-one were excused because they said they had formulated an opinion as to Lizzie's guilt, sixteen because they were against capital punishment, one because he was related to Lizzie, and the rest because of advanced age. It took four hours of examination to select Frank G. Cole, William F. Dean, John C. Finn, Louis B. Hodges, George Potter, Charles I. Richards, Augustus Swift, William Westcot, Frederic C. Wilbar, Lemuel K. Wilber, John Wilbur and Allen H. Wordell. One of the twelve was a blacksmith. The others were farmers and country tradesmen.

†Moody's introduction lasted for two hours. Its major points are given here.

science for any vestige of prejudgment, and, finding it, cast it aside as an unclean thing."

Despite his inexperience, Moody's manner was extremely effective. His voice was sincere and convincing. Factually, intelligently, he began outlining the history of the case as if he alone had mastered the details and was about to reveal them all for the first time. He discussed Andrew's wealth and the relationship of the family. He portrayed Abby, and Lizzie's hatred of her. Progressing to the day of the murders, he described the house, reiterating each human event leading to the discovery of the victims. He claimed that Mrs. Borden's body could be seen as Bridget struggled with the front door locks when Andrew Borden arrived home: "The prisoner from the hall above made some laugh or exclamation. At that time, gentlemen, Mrs. Borden's body lay *within plain view of that hall,* dead probably more than an hour."

Told simply and directly, it made an enthralling tale.

"Now, gentlemen, it will appear that about the two rooms in which the homicides were committed there was blood spattering in various directions, so that it would make it probable that one or more spatters of blood would be upon the person or upon the clothing of the assailant."

He gestured toward the table in the center of the courtroom—to Lizzie's shoes, her stockings, a blue silk dress and a skirt.

"The most rigid examination by the most competent expert in this country fails to disclose any marks of blood upon the dress which is produced as the one she wore on the morning of the homicide and the skirt which she is said to have worn upon that morning produces one minute spot of blood, which I do not think it worthwhile to call to your attention at the present time."

His reference to the blue silk dress and skirt was confusing. According to witnesses, the dress Lizzie had worn on the morning of the murders had been blue, but it was cotton, not silk.

Quickly Moody alluded to the missing dress—the one Lizzie burned—and to Alice Russell's description of it: "Upon being shown that dress [referring to the blue silk] she [Alice Russell] will say that it is not the dress that the prisoner at the bar had on when she came in upon the morning of the homicide. . . . It was a dress which the prisoner had purchased in the spring of that year, a cotton dress and not a silk dress like this [holding dark blue silk dress up to view]."

At first one wonders why Moody introduced any dress at all, as the blue cotton one was missing.

Yet it enabled him to recount its destruction: "As she saw the

Courtesy of Fall River Historical Society

Andrew J. Borden. He could not outlive the bitter, humiliating poverty of his boyhood.

Abby Borden. The feeling of rejection had preyed upon her mind; there was no reason to be hated so.

Courtesy of Fall River Historical Society

Courtesy of Fall River Historical Society

Lizzie as a girl. She had given her father a small gold ring as a bond between them.

Courtesy of Fall River Historical Society

Lizzie as a young woman.

Courtesy of Fall River Historical Society

An unspoiled place of fresh streams and meadows less than a century before, Fall River had become the largest cotton manufacturing center in America.

Courtesy of Fall River Historical Society

A. J. Borden Building. On the morning of the murders, Andrew made a final visit.

Courtesy of Fall River Historical Society

The maid, Bridget Sullivan. "Miss Lizzie, where was you? Didn't I leave the screen door hooked?"

Author's collection

Lizzie's uncle, John Vinnicum Morse. "I saw blood spots on the door leading from the sitting room into the dining room and above Mr. Borden's head. I think that Emma washed them off on Sunday."

Courtesy of Fall River Historical Society

The Borden porch. Lizzie called: "Oh, Mrs. Churchill, do come over. Someone has killed Father."

Courtesy of Fall River Historical Society

The guest room. As Mrs. Churchill climbed the stairs the room looked in perfect order.

From Edwin H. Porter, The Fall River Tragedy

Adelaide Churchill nodded, tears filling her eyes. "Yes, she's up there."

Courtesy of Fall River Historical Society

Mrs. Churchill drew back, clutching the banister. Abby's body sprawled on the floor on the far side of the bed.

From *Edwin H. Porter, The Fall River Tragedy*

92 Second Street. On the night of the murders, 2,000 people mobbed the front of the house.

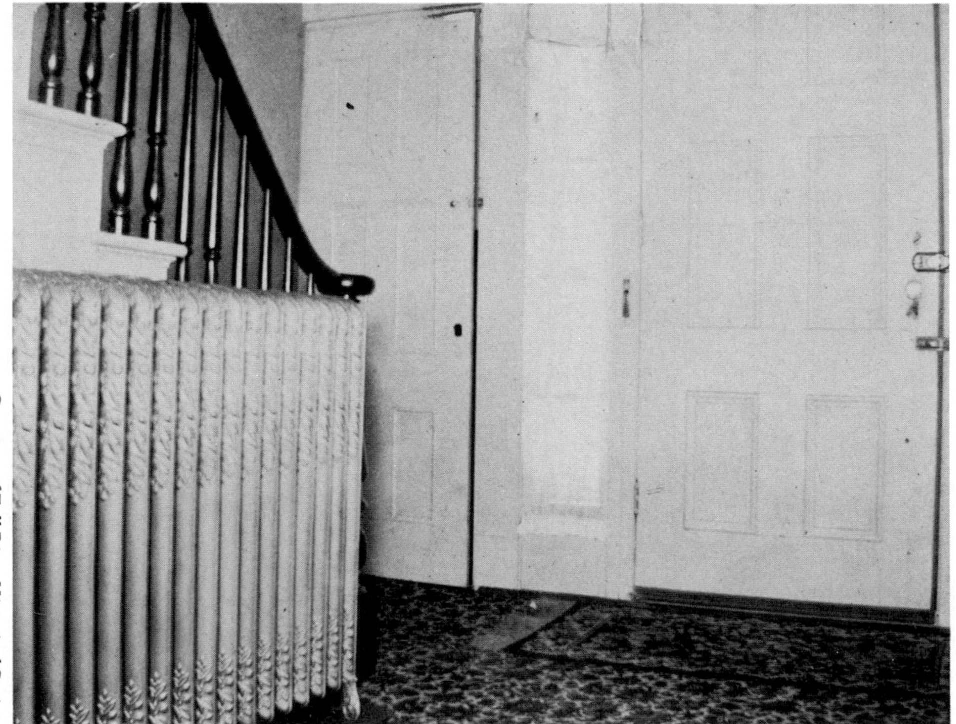

Courtesy of Fall River Historical Society

The Borden's front door (from inside the house). All three locks were fastened.

Courtesy of Fall River Historical Society

"His face was hardly to be recognized by one who knew him," Dr. Bowen testified. "I asked for a sheet to cover up Mr. Borden."

From The Illustrated American

A rare sketch of Emma Borden, with her hand clutching at her eyes, seated next to Lizzie. Reporter Joe Howard saw Emma as "a little, old-fashioned New England maiden."

From Edwin H. Porter, The Fall River Tragedy

Lizzie's attorney, Andrew Jennings. "They can't find any blood on her dress, on her hair, on her shoes. They can't find the axe. . . ."

From Edwin H. Porter, The Fall River Tragedy

Hosea Knowlton, the prosecutor. "Was Lizzie in the passageway when the assassin came in? She alone knows. . . ."

From the New York Recorder

Reporter Joe Howard talking to the mayor of New Bedford during trial recess.

From Edwin H. Porter, The Fall River Tragedy

Hannah Reagan. "I could not hear what Miss Emma said, only 'I did not, Lizzie. I did not give you away, Lizzie.'"

From Edwin H. Porter, The Fall River Tragedy

Alice Russell. "I am afraid, Lizzie, the worst thing you could have done was to burn that dress."

Courtesy of Fall River Historical Society

Second Street at the time of the murders. Mark Chase saw a carriage parked in front of the Borden house on the left.

Courtesy of Fall River Historical Society

Lizzie under arrest. "I cannot sleep nights now, and nothing they give me will produce sleep. . . . The hardest thing for me to stand here is the night, when there is no light."

Courtesy of Fall River Historical Society

Maplecroft. It was everything Lizzie never had. Caterers arrived with trays of rich food, there were hired palm trees and an orchestra.

Courtesy of Fall River Historical Society

7 FRENCH STREET.
FALL RIVER,
MASS.

My dear Friend
Where are you, how are you and what are you doing? I dreamed of you the other night but I do not dare to put my dream on paper. Have you been away and has your little niece been to visit you? We have been home all summer & spend much time

been so warm and full of thunder storms. I am quite ready for fall.
~~I should be~~ I am glad to hear from you
Sincerely
L. A. Borden
August twenty second
1897

From Lizzie's letter to a female friend: "I dreamed of you the other night but I do not dare to put my dream on paper."

Courtesy of Fall River Historical Society

7 FRENCH STREET.

Mrs Cummings (Dressmaker)
I received your message last evening and think you are very kind to remember me.
I hope to be in the country some this summer, so think one dress will be all I need; I think an India or China silk as useful as any thin dress, and if you will bring patterns of something with dark ground, something suitable for church wear and for calling. I will go to see you the middle of the week. I suppose you will be home by that time.
I hope this wind will go down before night, that you may have a pleasant and safe passage to New York.
Truly yours
Emma L. Borden
March 23 1894

Emma's letter to dressmaker Mrs. Cummings.

Billy Rose Theater Collection, New York Public Library—Lincoln Center; Astor, Lenox & Tilden Foundations

Nance O'Neil, famous actress of the day, with whom Lizzie had an affair.

Author's collection

The Connor house in Newmarket. Emma made renovations to suit her special needs.

Author's collection

prisoner standing by the stove and she approached her, Miss Emma turned round and said, 'Lizzie, what are you going to do?' The prisoner replied, 'I am going to burn this dress—it is all covered with paint.' "

What point had Moody made? That Lizzie had something to hide. That perhaps what was on the dress was blood, rather than paint—which is why she had to destroy it.

The absence of the murder weapon provided him with a more difficult problem. Holding up the two axes and two hatchets which Officer Mullaly had found in the basement of the Borden house, he admitted that they had been carefully examined and none of their blades "seem to contain the slightest evidence of bloodstain. The appearances which were thought to be blood turned out to be something else."

But one of them *had* to be the murder weapon.

Holding up the hatchet with the broken handle, he began to develop its incriminating possibilities: "It was covered with an adhesion of ashes, not the fine dust which floats about the room where ashes are emptied, but a coarse dust of ashes adhering more or less to all sides of the hatchet."

Moody admitted that the hatchet was rusty—"such rust as might be the result of exposure upon wet grass to the night's dew."*

Obviously Lizzie never had enough time to dispose of a bloody axe, but he was clinging to the prosecution's one slim hope—that this hatchet might be accepted as the fatal weapon. "It will appear that soon after the alarm an officer was attracted by Dr. Bowen doing something at the stove, and he looked in and saw what appeared to be a large roll of burned paper."

But it was not really a roll of burned paper. He insisted it was the charred remains of the hatchet's broken handle.

As he spoke, Moody was holding Lizzie's dress in his hands.

Carelessly he tossed it upon the prosecution table, where it swept over a plain, opened handbag with tissue paper covering its contents.

The tissue fell back, revealing the hideous eyeless plaster casts of Andrew and Abby Borden's skulls.

Lizzie's hands shot up, struggling to cover her eyes with her black fan, as she slid against the police matron beside her and pitched forward.

*Since Professor Wood had stated that the fatal blows had been delivered by a *sharp* weapon, Moody was attempting to shorten the length of time necessary for rust to occur. There was never an opportunity for it to be exposed "to the night's dew."

Reporter Joseph Howard, grabbing for pencil and paper, described Lizzie's face as "blue red with congestive symptoms, an inert, consciousless mass of inanimate flesh."

Moody had stopped speaking.

It was two minutes before Lizzie opened her eyes, and then she closed them again instantly. Feebly she raised her left hand a few inches upward toward her face, then let it fall again listlessly to her lap.

Howard reported: "What must it be to a woman garbed to her very neck in heavy black, her temperature heightened by at least ten percent by the wearing of her hat and gloves? What must she endure as Lizzie Borden, the target for every eye, conscious that her old friends and neighbors regard her only with suspicion? No wonder she fainted. The only wonder is that she recovered."

Moody had gotten to her. Lifting the hatchet he forcefully continued: "Let there be no mistake, Mr. Foreman and gentlemen, about my meaning. The Government does not insist that these homicides were committed by this handleless hatchet. It *may* have been the weapon. It may well have been the weapon."

And then came the dramatic crux of the prosecution's case—Lizzie's own testimony given at the inquest.

"We shall prove that this prisoner made contradictory statements about her whereabouts, and, above all, gave a statement vitally different upon the manner in which she discovered these homicides. . . . then we shall ask you to say, if say you can, whether any reasonable hypothesis except that of the guilt of this prisoner can account for the sad occurrences which happened upon the morning of August 4th."

To those listening, Moody's introduction was impressive. Even reporter Howard had to concede: "Mr. Moody has a good head, clear eye, a firm mouth, a pleasant voice and an engaging manner. But far and better away than that, he has the rare gift of common sense, and without attempts at vocal gymnastics tells a clean-cut, well-matured history of the crime. . . . he has worked upon the case for nearly a year and is satiated with Bordenism and permeated with what seems to him incontrovertible proof of guilt."

The three major elements: the burning of the dress, the hatchet with the broken handle and Lizzie's own distorted version of her whereabouts, provided an outline that Moody promised would be substantially filled in by the revelations to follow. But from the appearance of its first witness, the prosecution suddenly encountered reverses it had never anticipated.

Thomas Kieran, a registered professional engineer, gave an exhaustive account of the measurements he had made.

It seemed that he had measured everything:

The Borden house on Second Street was located 1,300 feet from the Fall River Central Police Station and 900 feet from the Fall River City Hall. He had prepared a detailed map of the neighborhood showing the streets which bordered it, picturing each house that existed. He had fashioned still another plan, drawn to the scale of four feet to one inch, depicting both the ground floor and the upstairs bedrooms of the interior of the house. He had measured closets, doorways, windows . . .

The results of Kieran's research were routinely marked as exhibits and admitted into evidence.

Then Andrew Jennings questioned him: Had he conducted any experiments in connection with the guest bedroom, where Mrs. Borden had been murdered?

Astonishment overtook the courtroom as Kieran admitted he had. Prior to this he had made no mention of any such experiments and the District Attorney had never questioned him about them.

Kieran explained that he had his assistant lie down on the rug in the guest room in the same position in which the police had found Abby Borden's body. The assistant was taller and his feet had extended beyond the bed, while Abby's had not. "Then I went downstairs and came up the stairs in the middle of the stairs, as I would if I had not been trying to see this man."

Knowlton jumped to his feet objecting to the witness giving further testimony. But Jennings insisted that Kieran tell his story. Kieran stated that as he proceeded up the stairs he could not see the stretched-out body of his assistant even though he knew it was there. Only at one spot on the stairway, when his eyes were a little above the level of the floor, did he notice him. And that was only because he knew he was there and deliberately looked for him.

The courtroom went into a frenzy.

Moody had contended in his opening statement that Lizzie climbing the stairs must have seen her stepmother's body.

Chief Justice Mason had to rap his gavel for order.

But Andrew Jennings was not finished with Kieran: "How was it when you stood upon the floor of the hall upstairs in front of the door which we will call Miss Lizzie's room?"

"I couldn't see him," Kieran replied.

"As you stood in the hall did you stand in the hall in front of Miss Lizzie's room and look for him?"

"I did."

"Could you see any portion of his body from that position?"

"No, sir."

The reporters noted the anxious looks on the faces of Prosecutors Knowlton and Moody. Moody had just driven home the point that "Mrs. Borden's body lay within plain view of the hall." Now he was being flatly contradicted by his own expert witness.

The assistant's feet extending beyond the bed should have made him even more visible to someone on the stairs.

Jennings was ruthless: "Could you see his feet from any position on the stairs?"

"I could not."

It was the most damaging beginning possible. The prosecution dismissed Kieran and summoned photographer James A. Walsh to the stand, who identified the photographs he had taken of the bodies.

Their next witness was John Vinnicum Morse.

Short and extremely vital for his sixty-nine years, Morse, who had been the first to be suspected of the murders, recounted his activities leading up to their discovery.

"I was in the yard eating pears only two or three minutes before Mr. Sawyer [the passerby who had been ordered by the panicked Officer Allen to stand guard outside the Borden house—and who had ended up standing there all day], at the door, spoke to me about the occurrences inside. There was no one else in the yard except Sawyer and myself. Inside the house I saw Lizzie. She was sitting in the dining room on the lounge. Mrs. Churchill and Miss Russell were with her, but then they went into the living room where Mr. Borden's body was lying on the sofa. There were two or three police officers in the house and I saw blood spots on the door leading from the sitting room into the dining room and above Mr. Borden's head. I think that Emma washed these off on Sunday."

Governor Robinson cross-examined him about the enormous breakfast served that morning—mutton soup, johnnycakes, bananas, bread—Morse agreed, there had been "plenty of it."

Robinson questioned him about Lizzie's age. Lizzie began to grin as Morse struggled to calculate it. When he finally came out with "thirty-three," she shook her head vigorously. He had added a year.

John Morse was excused, as the prosecution called five successive witnesses who had been with Andrew just prior to his death. The last of them, carpenter Joseph Shirtsleeves, had been working on the new store Jonathan Clegg, the hatter, had rented from Andrew in the Borden Building. Shirtsleeves recalled the incident of the broken lock which Andrew had picked up off the floor:

"He looked at it, put it back on the floor and went upstairs. He came down, picked up the broken lock again and walked out. He was at the store no more than two minutes when he left, headed in the direction of his home. The time was about ten-thirty a.m."

Abraham G. Hart came to the stand. He was treasurer of the Union Savings Bank, which Andrew owned. He testified that Andrew had died without leaving a will. Jennings then stated for the court record that for many years he had been Andrew's attorney (in truth he had been Andrew Borden's attorney for only six years, following a term he served in the Massachusetts senate), and Andrew had never asked him to draw up a will and had never discussed making a will.

Knowlton accepted both statements without comment.*

When Bridget Sullivan entered, Lizzie stiffened. Her former maid

*It would not lessen Lizzie's motive. Despite her vagueness in attempting to disguise it, *she had known about a will.* It was part of her inquest testimony, which Knowlton would soon introduce:

Knowlton: Did you ever know of your father making a will?
Lizzie: I heard somebody say that there was one several years ago. That is all I ever heard.
Knowlton: Who did you hear say so?
Lizzie: Mr. Morse.
Knowlton: What Morse?
Lizzie: Uncle John Morse.
Knowlton: What did he say about it?
Lizzie: Nothing except just that.

It was not a will made "several years ago" that worried Lizzie. It was the one that her father and her uncle, John Vinnicum Morse, had been discussing on the evening before the murders, when she overheard their voices through her upstairs window. The transfer of Andrew's Swansea farm was one of the will's key elements. This was why her father had been so disturbed on that hot day less than a week prior to the murders when the treasurer of the Globe Yarn Mill had asked him about his farm and Andrew replied: "I'm having a lot of trouble at home. I can't talk about Swansea until it's settled."

Andrew had sought help from John Vinnicum Morse. Once before he had asked Morse for advice, before secretly purchasing a house from Abby's sister Mrs. George Whitehead. Andrew had placed the title in Abby's name, an act which had enraged Emma and Lizzie when they later found out about it.

On the day prior to the murders Morse drove his niece, Mrs. Emery, to look over the Swansea farm (according to an interview Morse gave the Providence *Journal*). After that (Morse admitted to the Fall River *Daily Herald*), he and Andrew had "talked about business." John Morse had known about the will; he was Andrew's close confidant concerning financial matters. When Andrew's first wife had died, he had revealed to Morse that he was worth $150,000, invested largely in mill stocks, which were high-paying securities. He also discussed with him his heavy investment in a horsecar line.

Since then, Andrew's wealth had grown to such an extent that his brother-in-law Hiram Harrington was able to state in the Fall River *Globe:* "Money, unquestionably money—he left something over $500,000, and all I say is that, in my opinion, that furnishes the only motive, and a sufficient one, for the double murders."

wore a large black hat and a brown dress with an oval brooch at the throat. The reporters noted that she looked extremely nervous. At the time of the murders she was the only person known to have been in the house, besides Lizzie.

Bridget promised to be the prosecution's key witness.

She began answering Knowlton's questions in a soft, hurried voice. She admitted that she was twenty-six and although she had been called Maggie by Miss Emma and Miss Lizzie, Mr. and Mrs. Borden called her by her proper name. She described her coming from Ireland seven years before and her duties as a housemaid. She then related the events which occurred on the morning of the murders, from her awakening at six-fifteen a.m., "feeling poorly."

She had dressed and gone downstairs, where she helped to prepare the massive breakfast enjoyed by Andrew, Abby and John Morse.

About eight-thirty a.m., unable to stand her feelings of nausea any longer, she had rushed into the yard and vomited and then returned to the house, where Mrs. Borden instructed her to begin washing both the outsides and the insides of the windows.

She had gone into the barn to get the handle for the brush and then began washing the sitting-room windows on the south side of the house. After a while she paused to talk over the fence with Mrs. Kelly's servant girl. She had to make several more trips in and out of the barn to fill her pail with clean water as she washed the parlor and dining-room windows. While washing the outside of those windows, she saw no one in the house.

In her thin Irish brogue she told of Andrew's appearance at the front door, moments before his brutal slaughter.

By now she had worked her way into the house. "I began to wash the windows next to the front door. Then I heard like a person at the door was trying to unlock the door but could not so I went to the front door and unlocked it. The spring lock was locked. I unbolted the door and it was locked with a key—there were three locks. I said 'Oh pshaw,' and Miss Lizzie laughed, upstairs. Her father was out there on the doorstep. She was upstairs."*

*Knowlton: Now I call your attention to the fact that twice yesterday you told me with some explicitness that when your father came in you were just coming downstairs?

Lizzie: No, I did not. I beg your pardon.

Knowlton: That you were on the stairs at the time your father was let in, you said. Do you now say you did not say so?

Lizzie: I said I thought first I was on the stairs. . . . then I remembered I was in the kitchen when he came in.

Why couldn't Andrew unlock the front door?

Because Emma had bolted it from the inside—locking all three locks after she entered (her father's key could unlock only one of the locks) —so that she could proceed upstairs, accompanied by Lizzie, and murder Abby without interruption.

"Had you ever let Mr. Borden in on any other day at the front door?" Knowlton asked.

"No, sir, I don't remember," she replied.

"What?"

"No, sir, I did not."

"After you let Mr. Borden in you say you heard Miss Lizzie laugh?"

"Yes, sir."

According to Bridget, Lizzie came down immediately after her father entered—effectively preventing him from climbing the stairs to find Abby's body. She had to decoy Bridget away, so that Emma could complete her murderous work.

Bridget continued: "Then Lizzie brought in an ironing board from the kitchen, put it on the dining-room table and commenced to iron. She said, 'Maggie, are you going out this afternoon?' I said, 'I don't know—I might and I might not. I don't feel very well.' She says, 'If you go out be sure and lock the door—Mrs. Borden has gone out on a sick call.' "

Lizzie knew what the comment would mean to Bridget: Abby, having left the house, was no longer looking over the maid's shoulder, and even though Bridget had just begun "to wash the dining-room windows," she could quit working—which was exactly what she did when Lizzie followed her from the dining room into the kitchen, tempting her further: "Miss Lizzie came out there and said, 'There is a cheap sale of dress goods at Sargent's this afternoon, at eight cents a yard.' And I said, 'I am going to have one.' Then I went upstairs to my room."

Upstairs in her room Bridget heard nothing . . . then she remembered the City Hall bell ringing eleven . . . then Lizzie shouted up the stairs . . .

"When I got downstairs I saw Miss Lizzie standing with her back to the screen door. I went to go right in the sitting room and she says,

---

Knowlton: First you thought you were in the kitchen, afterwards you remember you were on the stairs?

Lizzie: I said I thought I was on the stairs—then I said I knew I was in the kitchen. I still say that now. I was in the kitchen.

—From Lizzie's inquest testimony,
August 10, 1892

'Oh, Maggie, don't go in. I have got to have a doctor quick. Go over. I have got to have the doctor.' I went over to Dr. Bowen's right away and when I came back I says, 'Miss Lizzie, where was you?' I says, 'Didn't I leave the screen door hooked?' She says, 'I was out in the backyard and heard a groan and came in and the screen door was wide open.' "

Lizzie was planting the possibility that someone could have gotten into the house. At Lizzie's request Bridget ran to get Alice Russell. When she returned she found Lizzie with Mrs. Churchill and Dr. Bowen.

"Dr. Bowen came out from the sitting room and said, 'He is murdered—he is murdered.' And I says, 'Oh Lizzie, if I knew where Mrs. Whitehead was I would go and see if Mrs. Borden was there and tell her that Mr. Borden was very sick.' She says, 'Maggie, I am almost positive I heard her coming in. Won't you go upstairs to see?' "

Lizzie was aware that the frightened Bridget would discover Abby's dismembered body.

But Bridget's cautionary instinct prevailed.

"I said, 'I am not going upstairs alone.' Mrs. Churchill said she would go upstairs with me. As I went upstairs I saw the body under the bed. I ran right into the room and stood at the foot of the bed. The door of the room was open. I did not stop or make any examination. Mrs. Churchill did not go in the room. We came right down."

By the end of Bridget's direct examination, the prosecution had created an even greater enigma for themselves. What new, incriminating evidence had been revealed by her retracing the morning of the murders? Reporter Julian Ralph in the New York *Sun* wrote: "Unless the Government has got more than it has shown, the Borden case will pass into history as one of the most mysterious of the celebrated cases of the century."

But what did the Government have? Endless details separated by great yawning gaps, which they hoped to fill.

Cross-examining Bridget for the defense, Governor Robinson explored the relationships of the Borden household. Moody, in his introduction, had made the strong point that there was such ill-feeling that Lizzie and Emma refused to eat their meals with Mr. and Mrs. Borden.

"Now the daughters, Miss Emma and Miss Lizzie, usually came to the table, did they not, as the father and mother did?" Robinson asked.

"No, sir, they did not."

Robinson abruptly challenged her. "Didn't you testify at the inquest that they seemed to get along congenially?"

"Yes."

This was an apparent contradiction and he jumped on it. Attempting to show that Bridget had been subsequently influenced by the prosecution, he demanded to know where she had been employed since the murders. She admitted that she had been working for Mrs. Hunt, the keeper of the jail.

"And are you still there employed?" he questioned.

"Yes, sir," Bridget replied.

"You came right over from Fall River?"

"Yes, sir."

"And you have been there all the time?"

"Yes, sir."

Bridget then admitted that Marshal Hilliard and State Detective Seaver had gotten her the job.

Nothing Bridget said had hurt Lizzie. Joe Howard commented: "Firstly, she is firmly resolved to say nothing which in her judgment can injure her mistress; second, she has become so permeated with the ideas of the prosecution that she really doesn't know whether she stands on her head or on her heels."

Her interrogation by both the prosecution and the defense had been relentless, leaving her dazed and in tears. The lethal blow had come from Governor Robinson as he brusquely discredited her motives, finally dismissing her from the stand, a pathetic, frightened young woman.

Dr. Seabury Bowen had been a friend of the Borden family for twenty-seven years. He was a tall man, with pointed features and careful, dark eyes. Now on the stand he related that he was their family physician.

At the inquest he had described the dress Lizzie had worn on the morning of the murders as "drab," a morning calico dress, with "not much color to it to attract my attention."

Referring to that prior testimony, Prosecutor Moody now attempted to squeeze a more explicit description out of the evasive doctor: "What do you say as to the color?"

"That is very indefinite there," Bowen answered.

"What do you say as to the 'drab'?"

"I should say the color is very indefinite."

"I did not ask you to criticize your answer, sir."

"I made the best answer at the time that I could."

"Do you desire to say that the dress appeared to you to be a drab dress or not?"

"I merely mean to say that the dress is a common—"

"Answer my question."

"Wait—" Bowen attempted to stop him.

"No, answer my question, and this is the question—Did it appear to you to be a drab-colored dress?"

"It was an ordinary, unattractive, common dress that I did not notice especially."

Judge Mason intervened: "Answer the question if you can—if you cannot, say so."

"I don't think I can answer it better than I did. I don't know."

Moody showed Bowen the blue silk dress. "Is that the dress she had on that morning?"

"I don't know, sir."

"Does it appear to you to be the dress you described at the inquest?"

The defense immediately objected and Moody waived the question, asking it another way.

"Give us your best judgement as to whether this is the dress or not?"

"I have told you once."

"And what is it?"

"That I don't know."

Suddenly Governor Robinson complained that the line of questioning had gone on long enough, but Moody managed to force out the one detail he wanted: "What color do you call this dress, Doctor?" He held up the blue silk.

Robinson objected, but the question was upheld.

Moody repeated: "What color do you call this dress?"

"I should call it dark blue," Bowen replied.

Moody had made his point. The obvious implication was that this was not the dress Lizzie had worn that morning—its vivid "dark blue" could not be described as "drab," having "not much color to it to attract my attention."

Moody then led Bowen to his discovery of Andrew's body.

"I saw the form of Mr. Borden lying on the lounge at the left of the sitting-room door. His face was very badly cut, apparently with a sharp instrument. His face was covered with blood. I felt of his pulse and satisfied myself he was dead. I glanced about the room and saw there was nothing disturbed—neither the furniture nor anything at all. Mr. Borden was lying with his face toward the south, on his right side, and apparently at ease, as if asleep. His face was hardly to be recognized by one who knew him. I asked for a sheet to cover up Mr. Borden. Bridget brought me one. Then Miss Lizzie asked me to telegraph her sister Emma."

While Bowen was at the telegraph office, Abby's body was discovered. Upon his return, he examined it.

"I went downstairs and told the people in the kitchen that Mrs. Borden had been killed by the same instrument, I thought, and that it was fortunate for Lizzie she had been out of the way, or else she would also have been killed."

Bowen's testimony was brief. Melvin Adams, an attorney from Boston whom Jennings had recently called upon to assist Robinson and himself, cross-examined the doctor. Lizzie's immediate desire that the telegram be sent to Emma, prior to the discovery of Abby's body, was significant. It bolstered the defense's contention that Lizzie had no knowledge that Abby had also been murdered.

"You say you received some request from Miss Lizzie to send a telegram?" Adams asked.

"Yes, sir," Bowen replied.

"And you went to the telegraph office?"

"Yes, sir."

"How did you go to the telegraph office?"

"In my carriage."

"You drove quickly?"

"Yes, sir."

"You have a good horse, I suppose, in common with other physicians?"

"Possibly."

"Well, I won't press that. You drove quickly to the telegraph office?"

"Yes, sir."

"And sent this telegram?"

"Yes, sir."

On the afternoon of the murders Bowen had given Lizzie a sedative, Bromo-caffeine. Adams inquired: "Did you have occasion to prescribe for her on account of this mental distress and nervous excitement after that?"

"Yes, sir."

"When was it?"

"Friday."

"Was the prescription or medicine the same as the other?"

"It was different."

"What was it?"

"Sulphate of morphine."

"What is commonly called morphine?"

"Yes, sir."

"In what doses?"

"One-eighth of a grain."

"When?"

"Friday night, at bedtime."

"The next day you changed that?"

"I did not change the medicine but doubled the dose."

"That was on Saturday?"

"On Saturday."

"Did you continue the dose on Sunday?"

"Yes, sir."

"Did you continue it on Monday?"

"Yes, sir."

"And on Tuesday?"

"Yes, sir."

"How long did she continue to have that?"

"She continued to have that all the time she was in the station house."

"After her arrest, was it not?"

"And before," Bowen added.

"In other words she had it all the time up to her arrest, the hearing and while in the station house?"

"Yes, sir."

"Does not morphine given in double doses to allay mental stress and nervous excitement somewhat affect the memory and change and alter the view of things and give people hallucinations?"

"Yes, sir."

By cross-examination the defense had implied a startling point. One week after the murders Lizzie had testified at the inquest hearing. Had she been drugged?

It was Adelaide Churchill's turn.

The Borden's next-door neighbor (according to the New York *World*) "said she was forty-eight years old, though she did not look it. She is a plump, motherly-looking woman, with a bright kindly face."

Joe Howard's description was more colorful: "No May Day queen was ever happier than Sister Churchill on the stand. She smiled perpetually upon the counsel for the prosecution, regarded Lizzie from a lofty point of commiseration, and treated the counsel for the defense with condescension until Governor Robinson charmed her with his graciousness, when she yielded to his blandishment, and gave him smile for smile."

Returning from her shopping at M. T. Hudner's Market on South Main Street shortly after eleven a.m. on August 4th, she had seen Bridget crossing from Dr. Bowen's to the Borden house, walking fast, her face white.

Mrs. Churchill had taken her groceries through her front door into the kitchen and had looked out her kitchen window. Lizzie was inside the screen door at the side of the Borden house opposite.

She called to her.

Lizzie had answered, "Oh, Mrs. Churchill, do come over. Someone has killed Father."

She described how she found Andrew's body in the sitting room and how she later accompanied Bridget to the second-floor guest room, where they discovered Abby.

Prosecutor Moody went right to the dress Lizzie was wearing.

No, it was not the dark blue silk on the prosecutor's table. She was certain of that. It had been a calico, light blue with a dark navy blue diamond printed on it.

But it was during the defense's brief cross-examination that Adelaide Churchill's answers became most significant.

"You had been with Miss Lizzie all the time?" Robinson asked.

"Yes, sir," Mrs. Churchill replied.

"Did you see any blood on her dress?"

"No, sir."

"On a dress as light as that, if there had been any blood you would have seen it, wouldn't you?"

"I don't know. I should think if it was in front I might have seen it."

"You were right over her fanning her?"

"Yes, sir, I stood in front of her."

"You afterwards saw her with Miss Russell and she was lying on the lounge?"

"Yes, sir."

"At that time did you see a particle of blood on her dress?"

"No, sir."

"On her hands?"

"No, sir."

"On her face?"

"No, sir."

"Or any disarrangement of her hair?"

"No, sir."

After Bridget, Mrs. Churchill was the first person on the scene, and her testimony regarding the now-famous light blue calico dress, for the moment, seemed strikingly favorable to Lizzie.

But the prosecution's next witness threatened to blow Lizzie's defense wide open.

Miss Alice Russell was called.

At the sound of that name Lizzie became tense. Her eyes never left Alice's face as the witness took the stand. The reporters noted that from that moment on Lizzie's lips quivered continuously.

They were no longer friends. Alice's testimony in December regarding the burned dress had been the prime cause of Lizzie's Grand Jury indictment.

Tall and angular, lofting her chin upwards above her long, birdlike neck, Alice identified herself as a spinster who had formerly lived next door to the Borden house and now resided in a cottage only a short distance away, next to a bakery shop between Third and Fourth streets. Joe Howard commented: "Precisely why she should throw her eyes at an angle of forty-five degrees toward the northeast corner whenever she answers a question I don't know, but she does."

Alice described the terrors which had gripped Lizzie on the evening before the murders. Alone with her in her cottage, Lizzie had revealed that Andrew and Abby had vomited the night before. She was certain that someone had tampered with the bread. When Alice attempted to allay her fears, she became frightened about the milk. Alice remembered their conversation:

"I think she told me that they were better in the morning and that Mrs. Borden thought they had been poisoned and she went over to Dr. Bowen's—"

"Is there any other thing that she began to talk about?" Moody asked.

"I can't recall anything just now. Of course she talked about something else, because she was there for two hours." Moody prodded her until she recalled Lizzie's statement "I feel afraid sometimes that Father has got an enemy."

"Is there anything else that occurs to you in the conversation?" he asked.

"Oh, she said, 'I am afraid somebody will do something. I don't know but what somebody will do something,' " Alice recalled. On the morning of the murders Alice arrived at the Borden house, finding

Lizzie. "I started to loosen her dress, thinking she was faint, and she said, 'I am not faint.' "

With relish, Moody edged toward his prime target: the dress.

On Sunday morning following the murders the three of them, Emma, Alice and Lizzie, were in the kitchen of the Borden house, having just eaten breakfast. Lizzie had a dress in her hand and Alice recalled Emma asking, "What are you going to do?"

Lizzie replied, "I am going to burn this old thing up—it is covered with paint."

A short time later Alice saw Lizzie standing up toward the cupboard door, either ripping something down or tearing part of the same light blue dress. Alice spoke up: "I wouldn't let anybody see me do that, Lizzie."

"Did she do anything when you said that?" Moody inquired.

"She stepped just one step farther back up towards the cupboard door."

"Do you know Mr. Hanscom?"

"Yes, sir," Alice replied.

"Did you see him at the Borden house on Monday morning, the following day?"

"Yes, sir."

"I do not ask you what he said to you or you to him, but did you have some conversation with him?"

"Yes, sir."

"Did you see anyone after that conversation?"

"I saw Miss Lizzie and Miss Emma."

"What talk passed between you?"

"I said to them—I said, 'I am afraid Lizzie the worst thing you could have done was to burn that dress. I have been asked about your dresses.' "

"What did she reply?"

"She said, 'Oh, what made you let me do it? Why didn't you tell me?' "

Obviously Alice Russell's conversation with O. M. Hanscom had agitated her—she first confessed the dress incident to him, and then, despite the fact that Hanscom advised her to tell no one, she was driven by guilt to reveal it at the Grand Jury hearing four months later. Moody questioned her:

"Will you tell us what kind of a dress—give us a description of the dress that she burned, that you have testified about, on Sunday morning?"

"It was a cheap cotton Bedford cord."

"What was its color?"

"Light-blue ground with a dark figure . . ."

When cross-examined, Alice further remembered that she had seen no blood on the fabric, "not a drop."*

Alice had not gone to the funeral. As the procession passed solemnly up Second Street toward Oak Grove Cemetery she had remained in the Borden house. She revealed that while Emma and Lizzie were at the cemetery the police had ransacked Lizzie's room, ripping apart the drawers in her bureaus, and "what she called her toilet room, pulled the portiere to one side." Then they searched Emma's room, tearing open the cupboard door, which they had difficulty closing again. "I remember one of the officers pressing against a bundle after he shut it, some pillow or blanket, something of that kind, and then Emma's bed was taken to pieces."

Before she was allowed to leave the stand, Moody asked one more time: "What was the material of which the Bedford cord dress was made?"

"All cotton. The dress was all cotton," Alice replied.

"And not silk?"

"No, sir."

Alice Russell's testimony was assayed by the New York *World:* "The one distinctly vulnerable point in Lizzie Borden's movements at the time of the murders and during the few days immediately following them was the burning of the light blue dress with the dark navy diamond figure. It is upon this that the Grand Jury indicted her and it is this which will convict her."

In the days that followed, as the summer heat became more intolerable, the prosecution summoned a stream of people who gave brief, repetitive statements:

*On Saturday night, following the funeral, when Marshal Hilliard and Mayor Coughlin visited her house, Lizzie had questioned Coughlin, "Is there anybody suspected in this house?" Coughlin tried to avoid answering, but Lizzie confronted him. "I want to know the truth." Coughlin admitted, "Well, I regret very much to say, Miss Borden, but you are suspected."

The following morning, in a fit of anxiety, she disposed of the dress.

There seemed to be no reason for Lizzie to burn it. It was one of her best defenses. Every witness who had seen her that morning testified that there was no blood on it. Why did she burn it? Only to incur the probability that her act would incriminate her? Lizzie had not wielded the axe—she had poisoned her parents. This is where her feelings of guilt existed. What if Lizzie's dress had been tested in Boston and its corded cotton fabric had been found to contain traces of arsenic?

John Cunningham, the newsdealer, whose phone call had alerted Marshal Hilliard that possible violence had occurred at 92 Second Street.

George W. Allen, the police officer who bolted in terror from the Borden house back to the Central Police Station after seeing Andrew's body.

Francis X. Wixon, a deputy sheriff of Bristol County, who described Abby's blood as "dark maroon," which "had thickened up" when he saw it.

At the beginning of the fourth day of the trial, Joe Howard described that "Miss Lizzie, escorted by an attentive deputy sheriff, but very pale and nervously anticipating the horrors of the day, took her seat near Governor Robinson where she was pleasantly greeted by her clerical friends from Fall River and her counsel, but not by any one of the wild-eyed, haggard-featured, thick skinned women, who stared at her through their spectacles and opera glasses as though she were a beast on exhibition."

With the testimony of the Deputy City Marshal of Fall River, John Fleet, the prosecution intensified its attack.

Fleet appeared to be everything that Knowlton desired. He had been Deputy City Marshal for five years and was well-thought-of in the community. Moreover, his answers sounded forthright and intelligent as he detailed the investigation the police had conducted.

He had arrived at the Borden house at eleven forty-five a.m. on the morning of the murders. After seeing the bodies, he had questioned Lizzie as to her whereabouts and she told him that when her father had come home she had "advised and assisted him to lay down on the sofa." She had left him to go out into the barn. When she returned half an hour later, she discovered him murdered.

Fleet had asked her if she had any idea who could have killed her father and mother. Lizzie replied, "She is not my mother, sir. She is my stepmother. My mother died when I was a child."

Could Bridget have been the killer? Fleet asked Lizzie.

No—"Maggie" had gone up to her room before her father's lying down on the lounge. When Lizzie returned from the barn, she had called her downstairs.

After his interview with Lizzie, Fleet had gone to the cellar. There, with Officer Mullaly, he had taken down a box from a shelf near an old-fashioned chimney and found the handleless hatchet. He recalled, "The piece of wood that was in the head of the hatchet was broken off close, very close to the hatchet. The hatchet was covered with white ashes—not on one side but on both were ashes on the head of the hatchet. . . . The handle appeared as though it had been newly broken —the break in the wood was new." This was the blade which the prosecution claimed was the murder weapon. The handle was never found and District Attorney Moody in his introductory statement had suggested that Lizzie had burned it in the stove after annihilating her stepmother and father.

It all seemed to make sense. Lizzie had washed the blade clean and covered it with ashes—there were piles of them next to the chimney in the basement, Fleet maintained. The "new break" next to the blade and the absence of the handle made it conclusive.

Governor Robinson rose to begin his cross-examination when the court was adjourned for the day.

Impressed by Fall River's Deputy City Marshal, *The New York Times* commented: "Mr. Fleet's description of the weapon is so minute and his reputation for veracity is so great that belief is general that he found the weapon with which the murder was committed."

But there was something about Fleet's aura of honesty that troubled Robinson. On Friday, June 8th, he went after him with a vengeance.

First of all, Fleet had altered his initial testimony given at the preliminary hearing. He had never mentioned that Lizzie told him she had "assisted and advised" her father to lie down on the sofa, which was the ideal position for him to be slaughtered. Did Fleet mean to say that his memory was sharper now, ten months later, than it had been three weeks after the crime?

Fleet brushed it off as an oversight. He thought he had mentioned it before.

And then he made a startling statement, which sent shivers of anger through his questioner: His men had searched the house—but it had not been a thorough search.

"But you took each dress and looked at it, is that so?" Robinson questioned.

"Yes, sir, I think it is about so," Fleet answered.

"Were you looking to see if you could find any bloody garment?"

"Not very closely—"

Fleet was now creating the impression that the search for the bloodstained dress had been nonchalant, raising the possibility that Lizzie's dress might in fact have been stained with blood and no one noticed.

Robinson felt his patience ebbing. Tersely he took Fleet through the house, room by room—

"Did you see in that room any dresses?"

"I think there was some clothing in one of the rooms," Fleet replied.

"Did you examine it?"

"Just looked at it, that is all."

"Did you take it down to look at it?"

"No, sir."

"You didn't examine that clothing?"

"Not to take them down, but just looked at them."

"Not to take them down? And you three officers were there making a search, weren't you?"

"Yes, sir."

Fleet continued to imply that he had "just looked at" each dress—but Robinson demanded more. He kept at him, relentlessly barraging him with questions, until at last Fleet gave in and conceded that each garment was taken out of closets, drawers, trunks and examined individually for traces of blood.

According to Fleet's testimony to Prosecutor Moody's questions, the blade of the hatchet found in the cellar had been covered with white ashes—yet he described every other object found in the cellar as "dusty."

Fleet's blatant adherence to the prosecution's cause continued to rankle the ex-Governor.

"Had you noticed whether either of the other two hatchets were covered with ashes?" Robinson prodded.

"The smaller one was somewhat dusty."

"Dusty"—an infuriating way of saying that the blade of the so-called murder weapon appeared different—as if someone had purposely covered it with a fine layer of ashes.

Suddenly clutching the handleless hatchet, Robinson roared with anger: "Tell me if you see any ashes on it! Tell me in your judgment as a man, *not a police officer!*"

Knowlton jumped to his feet. "Is that a proper way to address a witness?"

Robinson backed off. "I withdraw it. I don't think it is. We must be very careful of our deportment here."

The next witness called to the stand was former Sergeant Philip Harrington. Since Lizzie's arrest and the publicity his exploits* had

*Two days after the murders, Harrington had revealed in the *Globe* how he had discovered that there were no footprints in the barn loft where Lizzie claimed she had been while her father was being murdered.

received in the Fall River *Globe*, Harrington had been promoted to captain. Wryly, Joe Howard observed: "Nearly everyone who has taken an active part in the endeavor to fasten this awful crime upon Miss Borden, has within the year been promoted until now captains in Fall River must be as thick as flies in a cow pasture."

Harrington swore that he particularly noticed that the shoes on Andrew's feet had been laced. Howard related how, when "confronted with a photograph which showed that they were not laced, but were congress gaiters, the gentleman was not upset. Complacently he remarked that the photograph was wrong."

Captain Harrington stated that he had seen Dr. Bowen throwing scraps of notepaper into the kitchen stove. The word "Emma" was written at the top left-hand corner of one of the pages. He described what he saw inside the stove: "I noticed the firebox. The fire was very near extinguished. On the south end there was a small fire which I judged was a coal fire. The embers were about as large as the palm of my hand. There had been some paper burned in there before, which was rolled up and still held a cylindrical form."*

"Now will you describe that roll of burned paper by measuring it with your hands, please?" Moody asked.

"Well, I should say it was about that long," Harrington indicated with his hands. "Twelve inches, I should say."

"And how large in diameter?"

"Well, not over two inches."

Officer Patrick Doherty was the nineteenth witness for the prosecution, and he briefly described the upstairs guest room: "I saw blood spots on the pillow shams and a bunch of hair on the bed, black hair. It was a piece of hair which had been severed, I think. It was about half as large as my fist. I left it there."

He was followed by Officer Michael Mullaly, who again related the discovery of the handleless hatchet in the cellar. But it was when Robinson was cross-examining him that he came out with the most sensational statement of the day: In the box which held the handleless hatchet, *there had been a broken handle.*

*Eccentric as he may have been, it seems unlikely that Andrew Borden died without some sort of a will. Lizzie's admission that she had heard about one from her uncle, John Morse, had been less than helpful to her—it established a motive. But it was never suggested that what Harrington might have seen was the remains of this missing will, drawn in Andrew's own hand, the provisions of which had been the source of discussion with John Morse on the evening of August 3rd.

The prosecution had been utterly confident that Lizzie had burned the handle in the stove. Now the whole issue had been hurled back into their faces.

Sitting forward in his straightback chair, reporter Joe Howard jotted: "If a small-sized Russell Sage bomb had fallen in the courtroom more astonishment could not have been caused."

Robinson could not contain himself. "What!" he shouted with surprise. Eagerly he showed Mullaly the tiny piece of broken handle which Professor Wood had removed from the hatchet's eye for testing. The words rushed out of him: "That was in the eye, wasn't it?"

"Yes—" Mullaly admitted. "Then there was another piece."

"Another piece of what?"

"Handle."

"Where is it?"

"I don't know."

"Was it a piece of that same handle?"

"It was a piece that corresponded with that."

"The rest of the handle?"

"It was a piece with a fresh break in it."

"The other piece?"

"Yes, sir."

"Well, did you take it out of the box?"

"I did not."

"Did you see it taken out?"

"I did."

"Who took it out?"

"Mr. Fleet took it out."

Mullaly then indicated by his two hands the handle's length and showed by his thumb and forefinger its size. Once again, under oath, he swore he saw Fleet take it out of the box.

Spurred on by the possibility that Fleet's testimony had all been a lie, Robinson pressed the witness: "You were there?"

"I was there."

"Anybody else?"

"Not that I know of."

"Did Mr. Fleet put it back, too?"

"He did."

District Attorney Knowlton was completely caught off-guard. He attempted to backtrack when Robinson demanded the handle. Shaking his head he admitted, "I don't know where it is. This is the first time I ever heard of it."

Hurriedly Robinson recalled Fleet to the stand. Once again he was shown the hatchet blade as both the defense and prosecution laced into him. Robinson began: "Now this is all you found in the box except some old tools, is that right?"

"That is all we found in connection with that hatchet," Fleet replied.

"You did not find the handle—the broken piece—not at all?"

"No, sir."

"You did not see it, did you?"

"No, sir."

"Did Mullaly take it out of the box?"

"Not that I know of."

"It was not there?"

"Not that I know of."

"But you could have seen it if it was there?"

"Yes, sir."

"You have no doubt about that at all?"

"What?"

"That you'd have found the other piece of handle had it been in there?"

"No, sir."

At that point Moody took over: "Did you see anything other than the metallic substance except this piece of wood that was driven into the eye of the hatchet in that box?"

Fleet's reply was less certain: "I don't recollect that I did."

Robinson cut in again: "There was no hatchet handle belonging to that picked up right there?"

"No, sir," Fleet answered.

"Or anywhere around there?"

"No, sir."

"Or any piece of wood besides that that had any fresh break in it?"

"Not that came from the hatchet."

"Or in the box in any way?"

"No, sir, not in the box."

"Or around there?"

"No, sir, not that I'm aware of. I didn't see it."

The prosecution never again brought up the possibility that the handle to the hatchet had been burned in the stove.

The Springfield *Daily Republican* commented: "The handleless hatchet testimony has been emasculated by Officer Mullaly's evidence concerning the finding by Officer Fleet of the handle."

Watching Robinson handle Fleet, Joe Howard went further: "Governor Robinson completely twisted the poor fellow who unfortunately substituted smartness for frankness."

Captain Desmond of the Fall River Police then took the stand and admitted that, contrary to Fleet's description of a less-than-thorough search of the house, nothing had been overlooked. Even the mattresses on all the beds in the house were turned, in the possibility of finding bloodstained items.

The next witness, Detective George Seaver, proved even more damning to Fleet's image. The investigation to locate a bloodstained dress had been extremely exacting. He and Fleet had examined the dresses together: "I removed each dress off the hook and he examined them as well as myself, he [Fleet] more thoroughly than myself, and I took each garment then and hung it back as I found them."*

The point had been driven home. The myth of Inspector Fleet's "veracity," as *The New York Times* had termed it, had been toppled by his own men.

The police offered more, less sensational witnesses:

Officer Charles J. Wilson testified that he had been present when Deputy Marshal Fleet searched Lizzie's room on the day of the murders. Lizzie had been in the room with Dr. Bowen at the time and Bowen had asked if the search was necessary as Lizzie was sick. Fleet insisted that it was.

Lieutenant Francis L. Edson had been part of a further search which had been conducted at the Borden house on Monday, August 8th. He explained that he had accompanied Captain Desmond, Inspector Medley, Officer Quigley, Andrew Jennings and O. M. Hanscom. The search had been a thorough one.

William H. Medley stated that he had found no footprints in the dust of the loft where Lizzie claimed she had been. His reward since Lizzie's arrest had been a promotion from patrolman to inspector.

*In addition, Seaver gave an extremely precise description of over one hundred bloodstains found near Abby's and Andrew's bodies. Andrew's blood had splattered on the frame and glass of the picture hanging over the sofa and all over the wall above his head.

And then came what promised to be the turning point of the trial, the presentation of Lizzie's strange, contradictory testimony. Prosecutor Knowlton was certain it would fix Lizzie as a liar in the minds of all those present. He summoned Miss Annie White.

Governor Robinson immediately objected. Miss White had been the stenographer during the inquest but Robinson charged that her transcript of Lizzie's three-day testimony was inadmissible, for these reasons:

First of all, prior to the inquest the police had kept Lizzie under constant surveillance and she had been informed that she was already a suspect.

Secondly, her request to be represented by counsel had been refused by the district attorney and the judge.

Third, after completing her testimony she was not allowed to leave and was placed under arrest two hours later.

Fourth, a similar warrant had been issued even before the inquest but was not served, and she was not told about the existence of the first warrant.

Fifth, neither the court nor the prosecutor gave her the customary warning that she did not have to testify or that anything she said might be used against her.

From dispatches which poured from the courtroom on the afternoon of June 9th, it was obvious with whom Joe Howard's sentiments lay: "She was helpless. If she had been arrested no person in the State could have forced her to speak unless she was willing. Was it right to take her before a stern magistrate and have answers wrung from her by a trained, professional, astutely vigorous questioner? Was it a fair and equal contest such as chivalry delights in?"

The Court called for a day's recess. They could not decide if the transcript should be admitted.

Finally it was Robinson's hired man, Justice Dewey, who prevailed over the triumvirate of judges. On Monday, June 12th, they presented their controversial decision: ". . . we are of opinion both upon principle and authority that if the accused was at the time of such testimony under arrest, charged with the crime in question, the statements so made are not voluntary and are inadmissible at the trial."

The court then ruled that Lizzie had been under virtual arrest while being questioned.

Her testimony was excluded.

It was a terrible defeat for Knowlton and Moody. If the inquest testimony had been admitted, despite the allegation that Lizzie had been under the influence of morphine, they could have shown that she kept changing her story so radically that she had no alibi at all.

It was with the appearance of Medical Examiner William A. Dolan that the trial entered a new phase. His description of the autopsy was the bloodcurdling first stage of the sensational testimony to follow: "With me at that time was Dr. Francis W. Draper of Boston. Dr. Draper made casts of both skulls . . . we also examined the intestines of both bodies. We measured and closely inspected each of the wounds on each skull. They varied from one half inch to approximately five inches long."

Dolan explained that he personally decapitated both bodies and then he demonstrated how he removed the flesh and eyes and cartilage from the two skulls at the Oak Grove Cemetery.

The autopsy had taken place on the day of the funeral, after the bodies were not permitted to be interred. Neither Emma nor Lizzie had been informed that Abby and Andrew were finally buried in their caskets *without heads.*

Using a plaster cast formed from Andrew's skull, Dolan painstakingly outlined in blue crayon each of the ten blows which had crushed Andrew's face. Dolan felt that the wounds could have been inflicted by a woman of ordinary strength, probably clutching the weapon with both hands. He described the direction in which the blood had spurted from the corpse, the savagery of the wounds and their devastating descent into the brain cavity: "this wound started in what we call the left nasal bone, that is the left nose bone, and extended down through the fleshy part of the side of the nose, over the upper lip and the lower lip and chin, and cut slightly into the bone . . . the next wound came down through the eye and cut the eye completely in half and cut through the cheekbone, severing it, and ended just below the cheekbone . . ."

Suddenly one of the jurors, Louis Hodges, a blacksmith from Taunton, became so overwhelmed by the grisly details that he fainted.

An emergency recess was called to allow the jury to retire before hearing more.

But when they returned, the details became even more gruesome. Dolan, pointing his blue crayon, now outlined the nineteen blows showered upon Abby. "The right side of Mrs. Borden's head was crushed in . . . there was a hole there, one and a half by five and a half inches . . . there was a scalp wound on the left side of the face—a flap wound where the flesh was cut off but not separated from the head . . . on the left side of the middle line of the head there were four wounds—three of them went into the skull—one taking a piece right out of the skull . . ."

It was almost a relief when Edward Wood of Harvard Medical School was called to the stand and questioned about Lizzie's clothing. Dr. Wood had been a professor of chemistry at Harvard for twenty-seven years and had testified in several hundred criminal cases, including a large number of capital cases. Wood had examined all of Lizzie's garments, shoes and stockings and found no blood. However, on the back of a white skirt, which she did not wear on the day of the murders, eight inches above the hem, was found one drop of blood less than the size of a pin's head. Wood concluded, that, "The fact that it was plainer and more extensive on the outside of the skirt, that it was larger in diameter on the outside of the skirt, indicates that it came onto the skirt from the outside and not the inside."*

Wood was then confronted with the crucial point of his testimony: his examination of the hatchet.

He replied: "All the stains on the head of the hatchet were subjected by me to chemical and microscopic tests for blood, and with absolutely negative results."

Specifically, he had removed the broken handle piece from the eye of the handleless hatchet and placed it in iodine of potassium, which removes blood pigment. He allowed it to soak for several days before making his tests. He could not find the slightest trace of blood.

Realizing that the validity of his case depended on the presence of the murder weapon in the house, Prosecutor Knowlton was not about to give up. He asked if blood could have been washed from the hatchet so that it could not be detected.

Wood replied: "It couldn't have been done by a quick washing."

"Why not?" Knowlton asked.

"It would cling in those angles there and couldn't be thoroughly removed. The coagula would cling. It would have to be very thoroughly washed in order to remove it. It could be done by cold water, no question about that. But it couldn't be done by a careless washing."

Knowlton still had some hope, but Melvin Adams, taking over the cross-examination for the defense, sealed the issue. Holding up the handleless hatchet, he asked: "This slot on the inner edge of the head furnishes a good refuge for any blood to gather?"

*Citing this spot of blood as evidence, it would later be claimed that Lizzie was in a menstrual period on or about August 4th. Professor Wood's statement, however, absolutely refutes this claim.

"Yes, sir, on its face," Wood admitted.

"And it would be quite a place to clean, assuming that any blood got on it?"

"It would, and there is white dirt in there, and there is dirt there now."

The presence of white dirt indicated that the handleless hatchet had not been washed. Had there been any blood on the hatchet it would have come in contact with the dirt.

In addition, Wood pointed out that the sides of the weapon after striking twenty-nine lethal blows would have been saturated with blood which would have seeped into the tiny, almost microscopic imperfections in the blade, so that no ordinary scrubbing could have cleansed them.

It was the most illuminating moment of the trial. Once and for all it had been proved that the murder weapon had not been found—that it had disappeared from the house. But if Lizzie never left the house, who removed it?

The evidence seemed clear: There was someone else in the house who performed the murders and took the weapon with them when they left.

Professor Wood's next statement made the fact that the murderer had come and gone even more convincing. When asked if the killer could have avoided being stained by blood, Wood replied: "I don't see how he could avoid being spattered." He pointed out that in Andrew's case the bloodstains would have been from the waist up while the murderer, in the case of Mrs. Borden, would have been spattered "from the lower portions of the body and upward."

Yet each of the witnesses—Bridget, Mrs. Churchill, Dr. Bowen and Alice Russell—had already testified under oath that they had seen no blood on Lizzie's clothing and Dr. Wood had examined and tested all of Lizzie's garments and had found no evidence of blood except a tiny drop on the back of a white skirt which she had not worn on the morning of the killings.

There was one vital point that Knowlton needed to clarify: Had there been any poison in the stomachs of Andrew and Abby?

Professor Wood's response disappointed him. After examining and testing the stomachs of both victims he had reached an unequivocal conclusion: "I found no evidence of poison of any kind."

"Of any kind whatever?" Knowlton asked.

"In either case."*

Obviously Wood realized that he had tested for the wrong poison and had examined the stomachs again following the inquest.

Before Professor Wood stepped down Prosecutor Moody hastened to prepare the jury for what was yet to come.

"What is the nature of prussic acid?" Moody questioned.

"It is a poison acid—gaseous," Wood replied.

"What are its poisonous effects?"

"It is one of the most deadly poisons we know."

"And how instantaneous or otherwise is it?"

"Death is caused anywhere from a few seconds to a couple of minutes."

"What quantity of prussic acid is sufficient to cause the death of a human being?"

"Any solution of prussic acid which contains one grain of acid is a fatal dose."

The parade of medical experts was dizzying. Dr. Frank Draper, Medical Examiner of Boston, was called. He had testified that Abby's killer had chopped into her skull while standing astride her prostrate form as she lay face down on the floor. The one exception he noted was the forehead flap wound: "I think that was given while Mrs. Borden was standing and facing her assailant."

There was an uneasy pause as Prosecutor Moody took a large package, wrapped in brown paper, from the floor and placed it on the prosecution table. The paper rustled as he tore it open. Suddenly he walked toward the witness holding in his hand the actual fleshless, decapitated head of Andrew Borden.

The shock was staggering. Women shrieked, covering their eyes, and members of the jury gasped. Reporters peeked past the starched collars of their colleagues to notice that someone else had fainted.

It was Lizzie.

She was carried from the courtroom as Dr. Draper began inserting the edge of the hatchet into the wounds of the eyeless relic.

It was all over in a few moments.

*Author's note: I discussed the symptoms which Abby and Andrew (as well as Bridget) had experienced prior to the murders—nausea, stomach cramps, vomiting—with Professor Milton Bastos, Head of Toxicology, Medical Examiner's Office for the City of New York. He described these as the usual symptoms of arsenic poison. He explained that Professor Wood's analysis of Andrew's and Abby's stomachs would not have revealed arsenic poisoning, as the Bordens had only experienced a few doses with their food. According to Dr. Bastos, arsenic is the ideal murderer's poison as it can only be detected in the stomach when consumed over a long period of time.

Dr. Draper was followed by Dr. David Cheever, a professor of surgery at Harvard, who took the axe from Dr. Draper. *The New York Times* described what followed: "At Mr. Adams's request the witness gave a representation of the manner in which one of the blows was struck, using Mr. Adams's head for a target. A shudder went over the courtroom as he struck the blow, stopping just short of Mr. Adams's skull."

Cheever believed that the killer must have been stained with blood after committing the murders. He added, "I should think the amount of blood would be a great deal."

The courtroom experienced a respite from the wave of gruesome opinions as Marshal Rufus Hilliard and Mayor John Coughlin took the stand to give brief accounts of their visits to the Borden house. Then Hannah Gifford, a dressmaker, recalled that in March 1892, while speaking with Lizzie, she had referred to Abby as Lizzie's "mother." Lizzie had snapped back at her: "Don't say that to me . . . she is a mean good-for-nothing!"

Mrs. Gifford recalled: "I said, 'Oh, Lizzie, you don't mean that.' And she said, 'Yes, I don't have much to do with her . . . I stay in my room most of the time.' I said, 'You come down to your meals, don't you?' And she said, 'Yes, but we don't eat with them if we can help it.' "

Lizzie's use of the word "we" obviously referred to Emma and herself, but neither the three judges nor the five attorneys present asked for it to be clarified. "Them," of course, included both Andrew and Abby.

There was no reason for Mrs. Gifford to lie about what she had heard —it was apparent from Lizzie's statement that the hostility in the Borden household did not stem from her alone. It involved *we* versus *them.*

Or did it? Lizzie had always loved her father; she had been his confidant. Could the catalyst for her animosity have been Emma?

The prosecution presented the written statement of Miss Anna Borden, Lizzie's cousin and cabin companion during her tour of Europe two years before the murders. According to the statement of Miss Borden, on the trip home Lizzie had remarked that she was not happy to be returning.

After the defense objected, the court ruled: "The character of the testimony, the expressions used, are too ambiguous. If the expressions were distinct of personal ill will to either the father or stepmother, it might not be too remote. We think the evidence should be excluded."

Then came six people who were in the neighborhood on the morning of the murders:

Lucy Collet was at Dr. Chagnon's house, which adjoined the Borden premises on the northeast. Miss Collet sat on the Chagnon veranda all morning and saw nobody cross the yard.

Thomas Bowles was washing a carriage in Mrs. Churchill's yard. No intruders came under his observation.

Patrick McGowan, Joseph Desrosier and John Denny, stonecutters, were at work in John Crowe's stoneyard at the rear of the Bordens'. They saw no stranger escaping by that route.

Aruba P. Kirby, another neighbor with a rear view of the yard, saw nobody.

The press now awaited Mrs. Hannah Reagan.

There was a compelling silence as the matron for female prisoners at the Fall River jail testified that she heard Lizzie accuse Emma of giving her away: "I could not hear what Miss Emma said, only 'I did not, Lizzie. I did not give you away, Lizzie.' Lizzie said. 'You have.' Lizzie spoke in a loud voice."

"What occurred then?" Moody asked.

Mrs. Reagan recalled: "Lizzie laid down on the couch and faced out the window and closed her eyes. Emma got a chair and sat beside sister and stayed until sometime after eleven o'clock in the morning."

The courtroom had become an inferno of rustling crinolines and uncomfortable high-necked gowns. A brief downpour of rain in the afternoon had made the humidity so thick that palm-leaf fans had sprung up everywhere and iced drinks had to be passed out in the adjacent hallways. An unyielding restlessness was created by the steaming atmosphere, and Lizzie seemed more affected than anyone.

Joe Howard noted an oddly informal picture—Lizzie, "flushed and pale by turns, had become so worked up by the testimony of the matron, that she leaned forward upon her tip-tilted chair, running the point of her chin into Counselor Adams's back and leaning somewhat heavily upon Governor Robinson's arm with one elbow, as she feverishly fanned herself with the other hand."

For the first time Andrew Jennings personally conducted the cross-examination. He read the document which he had drawn immediately after the Fall River *Globe* had carried Mrs. Reagan's statement: "This is to certify that my attention has been called to a report said to have been made by me in regard to a quarrel between Lizzie and her sister Emma in which Lizzie said to Emma, 'You have given me away,' and that I expressly and positively deny that I ever heard anything that could be construed as a quarrel between the two sisters."

Jennings then attempted to show that Mrs. Reagan had been willing to sign the document but that her superior, Marshal Hilliard, had stopped her.

Mrs. Reagan denied any knowledge of what he was saying. Suddenly, she caught him by surprise by reminding him of his conversation with Emma that morning in Lizzie's cell: "Have you told her all?" Jennings had asked.

"I said that?"

"Yes, sir, you did. I was standing right beside you."

Jennings's sudden embarrassment went unnoticed; the prosecution had summoned druggist Eli Bence.

Bence had begun his testimony when Robinson leapt up, objecting that the witness's testimony had no bearing on the charge.

The jurors were ordered to withdraw as Moody read Bence's testimony: "This party came in there and inquired if I kept prussic acid. I was standing out there, I walked in ahead. She asked me if we kept prussic acid. I informed her that we did. She asked if she could buy ten cents worth. I informed her that we did not sell prussic acid unless by a physician's prescription. She then said she had bought this several times before. I says, 'Well, my good lady, it is something we don't sell unless by a prescription from the doctor as it is a very dangerous thing to handle.' I understood her to say she wanted it to put on the edge of a sealskin cape."

As Moody finished reading, Knowlton added, "It would be fair to say we have evidence to show some attempt to purchase prussic acid in another place with the same negative results."

Robinson countered: "You propose to bring evidence upon attempts, but no success?"

"Yes, sir," Knowlton replied.

Robinson became adamant that Bence's testimony against Lizzie should not be admitted: "She is charged in this indictment with slaying these two people with a sharp instrument—committing the murder with an axe, for instance—nothing else. Now here is an attempt to charge her with an act causing death by a wholly different means, for which she is not now on trial."

Prosecutor Moody spoke up: "The indictment not only charges that the prisoner killed Mr. and Mrs. Borden but that she did it with a certain intent and premeditation—and the purpose for which the testimony is offered is upon the intent and premeditation—or, in other words, upon the state of mind of the defendant just prior to this homicide."

But Robinson came back at him, and in doing so surprisingly acknowledged that Lizzie, in fact, had attempted to purchase the lethal poison. He insisted that there was nothing in her attempt to buy prussic acid which showed malice to Andrew and Abby. "Where is it? Where is the least tendency? Well, people buy prussic acid to kill animals—it may be the cat. It is not a crime at any rate."

But he was on dangerous ground. Professor Wood, when questioned earlier, had stated that prussic acid was "one of the most deadly poisons we know" and that a solution containing one grain was "a fatal dose."

But Lizzie had said she intended to use it on her sealskin cape, and this became the issue which Judge Dewey cited when once again he proved his invaluable worth to his benefactor, Governor Robinson:

Bence had stated that prussic acid was not used for the purpose of cleaning sealskin capes or capes of any kind. Dewey stated that the prosecution had until the following morning to produce witnesses who would corroborate the druggist's opinion or his entire testimony would be excluded.

That evening, as Knowlton and Moody canvassed New Bedford in a frenzy, searching for people who might testify, Joe Howard's syndicated dispatch became an irritable appeal: "The heat tonight is something frightful and if the Court persists in beginning at nine and sitting until five, a charge of premeditated manslaughter might be suggested against them in case the jurors melt in their seats, the prisoner goes mad, or the correspondents die from exhaustion."

The following morning District Attorney Knowlton presented a pharmacist and a chemist, both of whom insisted that prussic acid had no commercial use, that its lethal fumes ruled it out as an exterminating agent. They were followed by a furrier who stated that prussic acid was never used for cleaning furs and that sealskin was naturally immune to moths.

Governor Robinson tore into the furrier, challenging him to swear that prussic acid would not kill moths in sealskin—*should there ever be* moths in sealskin.

The furrier quietly admitted that prussic acid would kill almost anything.

There were several moments of whispering between the attorneys for the defense and the prosecution, who had all been called to the bench.

Finally the justices reached a decision.

Eli Bence's testimony would be excluded.

During the recess that followed, a Boston attorney, John Cummings, who had arrived to assist the prosecution, found Knowlton and Moody in a private room of the courthouse. He was taken aback to see Knowlton sitting in a chair, pale and depressed, while Moody, young and idealistic, kept stalking up and down. Bristling with impatience Moody shouted that the entire trial was a mockery. He would not go any further. All of their most vital evidence had been rejected. Suddenly he flew into a rage—the judges were thoroughly biased on Lizzie's behalf, but there was one way to get back at them. The prosecution would abandon the case and throw upon the Court the responsibility of freeing her.

Knowlton stopped him, firmly resisting the suggestion.

Meanwhile, upstairs, Joe Howard had not left the press area. He was watching Lizzie when he noticed that "her sister Emma came into the court for the first time during the trial." Howard noted that "their greetings were affectionate and such as might be looked to between sisters conscious that hundreds of critical eyes were upon them."

13

THE DEFENSE

One question which is causing great interest here is whether the defendant will be put on the stand.

—*The New York Times,* June 14, 1893

Knowlton:	Where was your sister Emma that day?
Lizzie:	What day?
Knowlton:	The day your father and Mrs. Borden were killed?
Lizzie:	She had been in Fairhaven.

—From the inquest testimony, August 10, 1892

ANDREW JENNINGS, in his twenty-eight-minute opening speech to the jury, came right to the point: "Fact and fiction have furnished many extraordinary examples of crime that have shocked the feelings and staggered the reason of men, but I think no one of them has ever surpassed in its mystery the case you are now considering."

He was obviously as troubled by the mystery as anyone in the courtroom. He had been Andrew Borden's attorney. He was now defending his former client's accused murderer, who was also the client's daughter. What more disturbing paradox could confront a trial lawyer?

Yet for himself and for all those present, there was one reassuring element which seemed to exonerate Lizzie of the Government's charge: "They have either got to produce the weapon which did the deed . . . or else they have got to account in some reasonable way for its disappearance."

Jennings knew that whatever was left of the prosecution's case hinged on two incriminating factors: Lizzie's hatred for her stepmother and the burning of her blue dress.

Smoothly he dismissed what Knowlton and Moody had already offered: "There are two kinds of evidence—direct evidence and circumstantial evidence. Direct evidence is the testimony of persons who have seen, heard or felt the thing or things about which they are testifying. . . . there is not one particle of direct evidence in this case—from beginning to end—against Lizzie Andrew Borden. There is not a spot of blood—there is not a weapon connected with her—"

As Jennings spoke a correspondent from the New York *Sun* reported: "The prisoner sat with her face buried in her handkerchief. . . . Miss Borden is showing the terrible strain under which she has been brought since the trial began ten days ago."

Vigorously Jennings emphasized: "The Government's claim is that whoever killed Abby Durfee Borden killed Andrew J. Borden—and even if they furnish you with a notion on her part to kill the stepmother they have shown you absolutely none to kill the father."

What he would now do was prove that the prosecution's case against Lizzie was not only entirely circumstantial, but also unfounded. "The proof that the law requires is that Lizzie Andrew Borden did it . . . that there is absolutely no opportunity for anyone else to have done it."

Nowhere in Massachusetts law was there a requirement that proof had to exist that there was "absolutely no opportunity for anyone else" to have committed a crime.

This blatant inaccuracy presaged the odd assortment of witnesses which Jennings had gathered to show that someone else could have been the Borden murderer.

Miss Martha Chagnon, a delicately pretty young lady with a slight French accent, testified that she was the daughter of Dr. Chagnon, who lived on Third Street behind the Borden house. On the night before the murders she had heard a sound, "as though someone were pounding on wood." When District Attorney Knowlton brought out that Miss Chagnon had previously testified that this sound had come from a nearby icehouse, Mrs. Marienne Chagnon, the witness's mother, who had also heard the sound, admitted that, in fact, it was confusing where the sound had actually come from—sometimes dogs in the neighborhood crawled into her wooden trash barrels at night.

Mary A. Durfee had witnessed a man angrily conversing with Andrew Borden in front of his house "sometime before Thanksgiving." She had no idea who the man was or what they were talking about.

On the day before the murders both Charles N. Gifford and Uriah Kirby had seen a man sitting on the steps of a residence on Third Street, a block away from the Borden house. Kirby testified that the man had been sleeping and when he was shaken, his hat fell from his head to the ground.

At nine forty-five a.m. on August 4th, Mrs. Delia S. Manley had noticed a good-looking young man "in a suit of white" on Second Street near the Borden house. Unfortunately she could not identify him.

Sarah B. Hart, Mrs. Manley's sister, testified that she had noticed the very same young man.

More and more the strange tales began to sound as if they were anecdotes from a local newspaper. Spectators in the courtroom had begun to laugh.

Benjamin J. Handy saw a pale, well-dressed young man walking down Second Street on the morning of the murders between ten-twenty and ten-forty a.m. Handy said that the young man's "eyes were on the sidewalk" as he walked and that he "was acting differently from any person I ever saw on the street in my life—he was agitated and seemed weak."

Joseph Lemay required an interpreter, as he spoke only French. On August 16th, ten days after the murders, he had encountered an eccentric-looking person on his farm, four miles from Fall River. The stranger clutched a hatchet in his hand and Lemay understood him to have said, "Poor Mr. Borden." With that the man leaped over a stone wall and ran away.

In the midst of what seemed to be a good time which Jennings had concocted at the expense of the jurors, but which was actually a clever smokescreen of stories to once and for all demolish the prosecution's case, there was one brief statement of significance.

Mark Chase, proprietor of the livery stable on Second Street, remembered the mysterious horse and buggy parked for at least an hour in front of the Borden house on the morning of the murders.

But it was Hiram Lubinsky, an ice-cream vendor, who commanded the court's attention. He said that at eleven a.m. on August 4th, on the way to pick up his daily stock of ice-cream, he had passed the Borden home and saw a woman walking from the barn toward the rear screen door. Unfortunately Lubinsky had arrived at the courthouse without an interpreter and was desperate to find someone who could speak either Russian or Yiddish.

The disjointed statements preceding Lubinsky's had incited within District Attorney Knowlton various degrees of tension, nervousness and fury. With Lubinsky he lost all patience. Pacing up and down he blasted the poor ice-cream vendor with question after question: Why had he been looking into yards? Was that how he found people to buy? Even when he had no ice-cream in his wagon? How did he know the time? Lubinsky held up his hands, pleading, "Please. I don't know what you say. You go too fast."

Jennings's collection of witnesses had been like wasps swarming about the head of the beleaguered prosecutor. Now he would not let up.

Finally Lubinsky left the stand, his testimony in a shambles.

Jennings followed him with two boys, Everett Brown and Thomas Barlow, both very young and obviously either adventurous or excellent storytellers. On the morning of August 4th, they said, they had heard about the murders and tried to get into the Borden house but the guard would not let them in. So they sneaked into the barn and dared one another to climb up into the loft. It was shortly after the murders had been discovered and Barlow, a Fall River youth who worked in the town poolroom stacking up pool balls, related: "Me and Brownie went in the side gate, went to the barn and up to the hayloft. It was cooler in the barn than outside. People were there trying to look in the windows. The police officers put us out of the yard."

Jennings had used the two boys to detract from the evidence given by Officers Medley and Harrington. Allegedly young Barlow and Brown had been in the barn and climbed up into the loft prior to the examination of the dust on the floor which the two policemen stated showed no sign of footprints.

Charles S. Sawyer described himself as "an ornamental painter, a fancy painter." He had been the passerby on the morning of the murders whom Officer Allen, fleeing from the scene, had posted at the side door of the Borden house. Sawyer had ended up there until six that evening. The courtroom rocked with laughter when he admitted that he had been constantly nervous as he stood at the door, apprehensive that the murderer would come up from the cellar and attack him.

Marianna Holmes was Lizzie's friend. She testified as to Lizzie's religious activities, one of which was her role as teacher of a Chinese class in the Sunday school. (One observer, James L. Ford, in an interview with the Providence *Journal,* later theorized that since the deaths were caused by a hatchet—a favorite weapon used in Chinese tong wars—that the murders might have been committed by one of Lizzie's

Oriental pupils—as an act of devotion to his beloved teacher.)

Mrs. Holmes was one of the five witnesses employed by Jennings to undermine Hannah Reagan's account of the argument between Lizzie and Emma. Mrs. Holmes said that she had questioned Mrs. Reagan about the story at the Central Police Station and the matron had told her, "No, Mrs. Holmes, it isn't so."

Thomas F. Hickey, a reporter from the Fall River *Globe,* had asked Mrs. Reagan, the day following the appearance of the story in the newspapers, if there was any truth to it. He claimed Mrs. Reagan had replied, "No, sir, no truth at all."

Finally Marianna's husband, banker Charles J. Holmes, another reporter, John R. Caldwell, and Mrs. Mary Brigham all testified that Mrs. Reagan had admitted to them that her story was a lie.

Yet, a few days before, under oath, Hannah Reagan had stated that she had heard an argument between Lizzie and Emma.

To the eyes of an observer, what had she gained by perjuring herself? Notoriety? A sense of self-importance?

Or had she been telling the truth?

Was Mrs. Reagan threatened with social ostracism in the community if she did not deny what she heard in Lizzie's cell? And then on the witness stand, as in the case of Alice Russell, had she come to the realization that she must lie no longer?*

At seven a.m. on the eleventh day of the trial, long lines of farmers' wagons and buggies surrounded the courthouse in New Bedford. The sky was white, crisscrossed with furrows of unsettled heat, as once again the sweating crowds surging toward the building far exceeded the number of seats inside. Shortly after nine, when the spectators gallery became packed to capacity, several of the expectant faces caught Joe Howard's eye: "I was surprised somewhat to see a large number of young and rather pretty girls, apparently school girls, whose sole interest centered on the artists who drew their pictures and the photographer who took snapshots of their comely countenances and their summer straws."

Yet the vast majority of women present expected the trial's most sensational witness.

There was a long wait after the name was called.

It became absolutely still in the courtroom.

Finally, from a side door near the judges' bench, a small woman

*What Mrs. Reagan thought she overheard will be discussed in a later chapter.

appeared. She was clad completely in black, relieved only by a touch of blue in the plume of her hat. People craning their necks for a full view observed that she wore black gloves and black patent leather boots. It would be the only chance anyone would ever have to study Emma Borden.

Once more she eluded them.

So devoid was she of any outstanding physical characteristics that the reporters watching almost had to create her. They began by trying to capture her eyes.

Julian Ralph of the New York *Sun* noticed that she had "big brown eyes, a high forehead and a strong, coarsely modelled mouth," and that she was "not as tall or as big boned as Lizzie."

The correspondent from the New York *World* found that she possessed "eyes with dark circles" and "a curious, almost weazened little face."

The portrayal given by the man from the New York *Herald* was more incisive. What he saw was a "prim little woman, very frail, with a careworn face and big black eyes that have a scared expression."

Joe Howard had described many of the earlier witnesses with swift jabs of humor. But when it came to Emma, he drew back discreetly: "She is over forty years of age, and looks it—a little, old-fashioned New England maiden, dressed with exceeding neatness in plain black, with the impress of a Borden in every feature."

The New York *World* spotted that "for an instant the sisters' eyes met as they faced each other, but no sign of recognition passed between them."

In his most kindly, gentlemanly manner, Andrew Jennings asked her, "You are the sister of Miss Lizzie Borden?"

"Yes, sir," Emma replied.

"How long have you lived at the home where you were living at the time of the murder, Miss Borden?"

"I think twenty-one years last May."

"Did your sister Lizzie always live there too with you?"

"Yes, sir."

"Yourself, your father, Miss Lizzie and Mrs. Borden?"

"Yes, sir."

"Did your father wear a ring, Miss Emma, upon his finger?"

"Yes, sir."

"Was or was not that the only article of jewelry which he wore?"

"The only article."

"Do you know from whom he received the ring?"

"My sister, Lizzie."

"How long before his death?"

"I should think ten or fifteen years."

"Do you know whether previously to his wearing it she had worn it?"

"Yes, sir."

"Did he constantly wear it after it was given to him?"

"Always."

"Do you know whether or not it was upon his finger at the time he was buried?"

"It was."

Jennings asked about the search which had been conducted following the murders—if Dolan had actually said to her that it had been a thorough search. Knowlton quickly tired to interrupt her but Emma snapped at him: "He told me the search had been as thorough as the search could be made unless the paper was torn from the walls and the carpet taken from the floor!"

Knowlton said no more as Jennings got to the heart of his questioning: the dress.

"Now, then, Miss Emma, I will ask you if you know of a Bedford cord dress which your sister had at that time?"

"I do," Emma answered.

"Won't you describe the dress, tell what kind of a dress it was?"

"It was a blue cotton Bedford cord, very light blue ground with a darker figure about an inch long and I think about three-quarters of an inch wide."

"And do you know when she had that dress made?"

"She had it made the first week in May."

"Who made it?" Jennings asked.

"Mrs. Raymond, the dressmaker."

"Where was it made?"

"At our home."

"What kind of material was it as to cost?"

"Very cheap."

"Do you know, have you any idea what it cost?"

"It was either twelve and a half cents a yard or fifteen cents."

"About how many yards were in it?"

"Not over eight or ten."

"In what way was it trimmed?"

"Trimmed with just a ruffle around the bottom, a narrow ruffle."

"How long were you in making the dress?"

"Not more than two days."

"Did you and Miss Lizzie assist the dressmaker in making the dress?"

"Yes, sir."

"That was your habit, was it?"

"Yes, sir, I always do."

"And where was the dressmaking carried on?"

"In the guestchamber."

Having gotten Emma to describe the dress in detail, Jennings moved on to the incident which caused it to be destroyed: "Do you know whether or not they were painting the house at the time that dress was made?"

"I think they did not begin to paint it until after the dress was done."

"Do you know anything about her getting any paint on it at that time?"

"Yes, she did."

"Where was the paint upon it?"

"I should say along the front and on one side toward the bottom and some on the wrong side of the skirt."

"How soon was that after it was made?"

"Well, I think within two weeks—perhaps less time than that."

"Now where was that dress—if you know—on Saturday—the day of the search?"

"I saw it hanging in the clothes press over the front entry."

"How came you to see it at that time?"

"I went in to hang up the dress that I had been wearing during the day and there was no vacant nail. I searched around to find a nail and I noticed this dress."

As if the dialogue between them had been memorized, each of Jennings's questions was met with a thoroughly descriptive, unhesitatingly apt answer. But when Jennings asked, "Did you say anything to your sister in consequence of your not finding a nail to hang your dress on?" Knowlton objected to the question as being incompetent.

However, Chief Justice Mason wanted to hear her answer.

Emma gave it: "I said, 'You have not destroyed that old dress yet—why don't you?' "

"What was the condition of the dress?" Jennings asked.

"It was very dirty—very much soiled and badly faded."

"Was this material of which this dress was made in a condition to be made over for anything else?"

"It could not possibly be used for anything else."

"Why?"

"Because it was not only soiled, but so badly faded."

"When did you next see that Bedford cord dress?"

"Sunday morning I think—about nine o'clock."

"Now will you tell the Court and the Jury all that you saw or heard that morning in the kitchen?"

"I was washing dishes and I heard my sister's voice and I turned round and saw she was standing at the foot of the stove—between the foot of the stove and the dining-room door. This dress was hanging on her arm and she says, 'I think I shall burn this old dress.' I said, 'Why don't you,' or 'You had better,' or 'I would if I were you,' or something like that, I can't tell the exact words—but it meant—Do it. And I turned back and continued washing the dishes and did not see her burn it and did not pay any more attention to her at that time."

"What was the condition of the kitchen doors and windows at that time?"

"They were all wide open—screens in and blinds open."

"Were the officers all about at the time?"

"They were all about the yard."

"Was Miss Russell there?"

"Yes, sir."

"Was anything said by Miss Russell in the presence of Miss Lizzie in regard to this dress?"

Now, from Emma's lips, came the famous story which had caused Lizzie's indictment:

"Miss Russell came to us in the dining room and said Mr. Hanscom asked her if all the dresses were there that were there the day of the tragedy and she told him 'Yes'—'and of course'—she said 'it is a falsehood.' No—I am ahead of my story. She came and she told Mr. Hanscom a falsehood and I asked her if all the dresses were there that were there the day of the tragedy and she told him 'yes.' There was other conversation—but I don't know what it was—that frightened me so thoroughly I cannot recall it. I know the carriage was waiting for her to go on some errand and when she came back we had some conversation and it was decided to have her go and tell Mr. Hanscom that she had told a falsehood—and to tell him that we told her to do so. She went into the parlor and told him and in a few minutes she returned from the parlor and said she had told him."

Jennings interrupted the winding tale with a quick cue: Miss Russell had said "It was the worst thing that could be done—"

Emma continued: "Oh, yes, sir, she said that Monday morning. When she came into the dining room and said she had told Mr. Hanscom that she had told him a falsehood—we asked what she told it for—and she said, 'The burning of the dress was the worst thing Lizzie could have done'—and my sister said to her 'Why didn't you tell me? Why did you let me do it?' "

"In order that there may be no mistake, Miss Emma, I would like to ask you again—who was it that said she had told a falsehood to Mr. Hanscom?"

"Miss Russell."

"She had told a falsehood?"

"She had told a falsehood."

Emma's direct testimony had been beautifully rehearsed beforehand. During the afternoon recess news spread through New Bedford that she was still on the stand. The streets leading to the courthouse became choked with people fighting to get in.

Within the courtroom not a soul stirred as they awaited Emma's return. Lizzie had received a big box of red and yellow roses from a man named McLean, in Connecticut, whom she had never heard of. When she returned to her seat she carried a single yellow rose wound around her fingers.

Since the trial had begun, although there were many women present—as Joe Howard called them, "women experts who are quite confident that they could prove the guilt of the accused if they had a chance"—none of them would speak to Lizzie. It was as if she were ostracized.

Finally, the Baltimore *Sun* noticed that "Mrs. Fessenden of Boston talked with her during the recess, being the first lady who has spoken to her in the courtroom."

As he began his cross-examination District Attorney Knowlton tried to pin down where Emma was on the day of the murders:

"On the day that this thing happened you were in Fairhaven?"

"Yes, sir," Emma answered.

"How long had you been in Fairhaven?"

"Just two weeks."

"And you were visiting?"

"Mrs. Brownell and her daughter."

"Had you seen Miss Lizzie during the two weeks?"

"Yes, sir."

"When?"

"Well, I can't tell you what day it was. . . . she had been at Fairhaven."

"Was it on her way over to or back from Marion?"

"Oh—I know. She went to New Bedford when I went to Fairhaven. I think it was the Saturday following our going Thursday."

Emma's apparently innocent confusion contradicted Lizzie's inquest testimony that they had parted on the way to Fairhaven.

Knowlton asked her about the interest in the house her father had given to Mrs. Borden's sister Mrs. Whitehead. As Emma related the story, Knowlton attempted to trip her up: "Did that make some trouble in the family?"

"Yes," Emma admitted.

"Did you find fault with it?"

"Yes, sir."

"And did Lizzie find fault with it?"

"Yes, sir."

"And in consequence of your faultfinding did your father also make a purchase for you or give you some money?"

"Not—I don't think because of our faultfinding."

"Did he—after the faultfinding—give you some money?"

"Yes, sir."

"How much?"

"Grandfather's house on Ferry Street."

"And was there some complaint that that was not an equivalent?"

"No, sir. It was more than an equivalent."

"That it wasn't so productive of rent as the other?"

"I don't know what the other house rented for—but I should think that ours rented for more than hers."

"Were the relations between you and Lizzie and your stepmother as cordial after that occurrence of the house that you have spoken of as they were before?"

"Between my sister and Mrs. Borden they were."

"They were entirely the same?"

"I think so."

"Were they so on your part?"

"I think not."

Perhaps Knowlton in his desire to close in on Lizzie simply overlooked what Emma had suddenly revealed. She had dismissed Lizzie's motive—and had given herself one.

Knowlton continued: "And do you say that the relations were entirely cordial between Lizzie and your stepmother after that event?"

"Yes, I do," Emma answered.

"Have you ever said differently?"

"I think not."

"Did your sister change the form of address to her mother at that time?"

"I can't tell you whether it was at that time or not."

"She formerly called her 'Mother'—didn't she?"

"Yes, sir."

"She ceased to call her 'Mother'—didn't she—practically?"

"Yes, sir."

"And wasn't it about at that time that she ceased to call her 'Mother'?"

"I don't remember."

It was the first time that Emma would reply, "I don't remember." From then on, whenever she tired of one of Knowlton's questions—whenever he came too close to getting a definitive answer out of her—she would simply say, "I don't remember."

She would use the expression twelve more times.

"What address did she give her after that time?" Knowlton asked.

" 'Mrs. Borden.' "

"And up to the time she changed she called her 'Mother'?"

"Mostly."

"And don't you recall that was sometime in connection with the transaction in relation to the house?"

"No, sir, I do not know what it was."

Emma's testimony now differed from the answers she gave at the inquest.

"Do you say that you have not said that the relations were not cordial between your sister and your mother?" Knowlton asked.

"I don't remember that I have."

"You testified at the inquest—did you not?"

"I did."

"Were you asked questions in relation to that matter?"

"I don't remember what you asked me."

"Do you remember that I asked you if your relations were cordial between you and your mother?"

"I think you did either then or before the Grand Jury—I don't remember which."

"Do you remember that you said they were not?"

"I don't know whether I did or not."

"Now I want to ask you if you didn't say this—'Were the relations between you and your stepmother cordial?' Answer—'I don't know how to answer that. We always spoke'?"

"That was myself and my stepmother. . . ."

"Do you remember that answer!"

"I do now."

But at the inquest Knowlton had made the point that even though Emma and Abby had spoken, did it mean they were cordial with each other? Emma had replied, "Well, perhaps I should say no then."

Knowlton asked: "Do you remember that—talking about yourself?"

"No, sir—I don't remember it."

But Emma *had* said it.

Taking the inquest transcript in his hand he quoted directly. " 'Were the relations between your sister and your mother what you would call cordial?' Answer—'I think more than they were with me.' Do you remember that answer?"

Suddenly she gave in—"Yes, sir."

For that second he had her. She had attempted to conceal her previous statement.

However, he was not able to dwell on the matter. Emma was not on trial.

Knowlton then recalled a question asked at the inquest to which Emma had answered that the relations between Lizzie and Abby were not cordial.

Emma now attempted to protect Lizzie: "I shall have to recall it—for I think they were."

Knowlton's struggle with Emma to get at Lizzie's motive was fascinating.* Julian Ralph of the New York *Sun* saw Knowlton as a "very large and powerful man with a head as hard as iron set on a neck that is a tower of strength. He is by nature combative. It was worth a great deal to a lover of the sports of the legal arena to see this colossus pitted against the slender sister of the prisoner. He advanced toward her with something like the impetus of a locomotive and he shook her bits of testimony as a bull terrier would shake a rat. She had been smiling and agreeable toward her sister's lawyer, but upon Mr. Knowlton she turned a cold, steely eye, a set mouth and a proudly held head. . . . she never relaxed her cold calm demeanor for an instant."

Knowlton continued quoting the testimony from the inquest: "I will read you this question and answer—'Can you tell me the cause of the lack of cordiality between you and your mother—or was it not any specific thing?' Answer—'Well—we felt that she was not interested in us and at one time Father gave her some property and we felt that we

*Emma's testimony is over twenty pages long; the most significant elements covered here are the cross-examination concerning Lizzie's dress, the relationship with the stepmother, and Emma's stay in Fairhaven, which was never explained.

ought to have some too—and he afterwards gave us some.' Do you remember that?"

"No, sir."

"Is that true?"

"It was true at the time that he gave us the house."

"I will read another question—'That, however, did not heal the breach, whatever breach there was? The giving of the property did not entirely heal the feeling?' Answer—'No, sir.'?"

"It didn't—not with me—but it did with my sister after."

Once again Knowlton had been taken by surprise. The breach between Emma and her father had *not* been healed. Yet with Lizzie it had been. Audaciously Emma had admitted the truth.

During the remainder of Emma's testimony, Knowlton never came close to exposing her. Joe Howard commented: "There was no swaying of her slender form, no drooping of her straight-cut eyes, no quivering of her tight shut mouth."

The district attorney attempted to pin down the truth of Hannah Reagan's story of the argument in the jail—"There was no sitting silent for any length of time that morning?"

"I can't remember. I don't know," Emma admitted.

"She said you remained in your chair—and she on the sofa with her back turned away from you—and you yourself remained an hour and a half. Did that take place?"

"I have no recollection of anything of that kind."

Inadvertently, Knowlton then asked her an extremely revealing series of questions. "Did any of the members of your family have waterproofs?"

"Yes—we all had them," Emma replied.

"What kind were they?"

"Mrs. Borden's was a gossamer—rubber."

"That is—you mean rubber on the outside?"

"Yes, sir."

"Where was that hanging?"

"I think she kept it in the little press at the foot of the front stairs in the front hall."

"Did Miss Lizzie have one too?"

"Yes, sir."

"What kind of one was that?"

"Blue and brown plaid—an American cloth."

"And you had one too?"

"Mine was gossamer. Made of the same material as Abby's—"

"Did you have yours with you in Fairhaven?"*

"I did."

But where was it now? Had it covered her clothing when she committed the murders and then afterward been discarded?

Emma appeared fatigued. She asked for and was given a chair as Knowlton came to the crucial issue of Lizzie's dress.

"Do you recall what the first thing you said was when Miss Lizzie was standing by the stove with the dress?"

"I said, 'You might as well,' or 'Why don't you?'—something like that. I can't tell you the exact words."

"Wasn't the first thing said by anybody, 'Lizzie, what are you doing with that dress?' "

"No, sir—I don't remember it so."

"Do you remember Miss Russell so to testify?"

"I think she did."

"Do you remember whether that was so or not?"

"It doesn't seem so to me—I don't remember it so."

"Why doesn't it seem so to you?"

"Why—because the first I knew about it—my sister spoke to me."

"That is what I thought you would say. You don't recall that the first thing you said to her was—'What are you going to do with that dress, Lizzie?' "

"No, sir. I don't remember saying it."

His next question insinuated that the sisters had planned it all beforehand. "The reason you don't think you said so was because you had previously spoken with your sister Lizzie about destroying the dress?"

Emma flew back at him: "I don't understand your question!"

Robinson intervened: "Is that a question?"

"Yes," Knowlton replied.

Robinson commented, "It doesn't sound like one."

Knowlton calmly rephrased it: "Now isn't that the reason that you say you didn't say that—the argument that you had with her?"

"The reason that I say I didn't say so is because I didn't say so," Emma answered.

"You swear that you didn't say so?"

"I swear that I didn't say it."

*From Knowlton's question it appears that he did not know where Emma's waterproof was, even though a thorough search of the house had been made after she returned from Fairhaven.

Emma had been caught off guard. He now used her own enigmatic "I don't remember" phrase against her. "Did you just tell me that you didn't remember saying it?"

"I did," Emma replied.

"Do you mean to put it any stronger than that?"

"I think I meant it truthfully."

"What has refreshed your recollection since?"

"Nothing. After thinking—I am sure I didn't say it."

Her next critical answers refuted the possibility that Lizzie's dress could have been burned for any reason other than it's having been stained by paint.

"Had she worn it quite a number of mornings?" Knowlton asked.

"When she first had it she did—until it was badly soiled."

"After the paint was on it?"

"She wore it some after the paint was on."

"She got the paint on—if I understand you—immediately after she got it made?"

"I think within a week or two. I don't remember whether the painting was commenced immediately or not."

"But notwithstanding the paint she wore it mornings?"

"She wore it some until the dress got soiled besides that."

"She wasn't interrupted in the wearing of it on account of the paint alone?"

"Well—she was—excepting very early in the mornings."

Perhaps it was the tone of Emma's voice or her unflinching directness but she was extremely believable to at least one observer. Joseph Choate wrote home to his wife: "I suppose that you still read the daily reports of the Lizzie Borden case. Her defense has come out very strong, especially her sister Emma's evidence. . . ."

"Did you see your sister burn the dress?" Knowlton questioned.

"I did not."

"Did you remain in the room?"

"I did."

"Did you see Miss Russell come back again the second time?"

"I don't remember. I think she was wiping the dishes and came back and forth—I didn't pay attention."

"Did you hear Miss Russell say to her—'I wouldn't let anybody see me do that, Lizzie'?"

"I did not."

"Do you mean that you don't remember it or that it was not said?"

"I don't say it was not said—I say that I didn't hear it."

"And did you notice that for any reason your sister Lizzie stepped away after something was said by Miss Russell?"

"I didn't see my sister at all after she left the stove."

Even under Knowlton's cross-examination, Emma's statements had destroyed the impact of Alice Russell's testimony. Lizzie had burned the dress simply because it was soiled and had been stained with paint. What other reason could there possibly have been? There had been no attempt at deception—that was a figment of Alice Russell's frightened imagination.

Before Emma left the witness box Jennings again asked her to substantiate the whereabouts of Lizzie's waterproof. "Do you know where this waterproof of Miss Lizzie's was on the day of the search?"

"Hanging in the clothes press at the top of the stairs," Emma replied.

"Do you know where it is now?"

"It is there now."

"Been there ever since?"

"Every day since."

Jennings never asked about her own gossamer waterproof, which she admitted had been "in Fairhaven."

After Emma left the stand the defense called three witnesses:

Mrs. Mary Raymond, a dressmaker, testified that she made the Bedford cord dress and that she had seen it after it had been stained with paint.

Phoebe Bowen, wife of Dr. Bowen, had been with the prisoner shortly after the discovery of the murders. She related that Lizzie had been pale and faint, but had no blood on her.

Annie White read from her notes of the inquest showing that Bridget had testified that when she had come downstairs in response to Lizzie's cry of finding Andrew murdered, Lizzie was not only more agitated than Bridget had ever seen her but was also in tears.

The testimony was complete. The defense had presented its entire case in a day and a half. It was now left to the tall, erect and strikingly distinguished former Governor of Massachusetts to provide the classic closing argument. He would deliver that final, flowery burst of oratory for which two decades of political speechmaking had prepared him.

"May it please Your Honors, Mr. Foreman and gentlemen: One of the most dastardly and diabolical of crimes that was ever committed in Massachusetts was perpetrated in August, 1892, in the city of Fall River. . . . the terror of those scenes no language can portray. . . . so we are challenged to find somebody that is equal to that enormity—

whose heart is blackened with depravity . . . a maniac or a fiend . . . a lunatic or a devil. . . ."

With a surge of sentiment approaching veneration, Robinson recalled Andrew Borden's love for Lizzie: "Here was a man that wore nothing in the way of ornament, of jewelry but one ring, and that ring was Lizzie's. It had been put on many years ago when Lizzie was a little girl and the old man wore it and it lies buried with him in the cemetery. He liked Lizzie, did he not? He loved her as a child—and the ring that stands as the pledge of plighted faith and love, that typifies and symbolizes the dearest relation that is ever created in life, that ring was the bond of union between the father and the daughter. No man shall be heard to say that she murdered the man that so loved her. . . ."

With scorn he alluded to the Fall River police: "Policemen are human, made out of men and nothing else, and the blue coat and the brass buttons only cover the kind of man that is inside. And you do not get the greatest ability in the world inside a policeman's coat."

And then he ridiculed District Attorney Moody's suggestion that the hatchet handle had been burned: "There was some talk about a roll of burned paper in the stove, where Mr. Philip Harrington, I believe, was the officer. He took off the cover and saw the rolled-up piece of paper, burned. . . . Well, we thought the handle was there. We thought that was the plan, that the Government possessed itself with the idea that that handle was rolled up by the defendant in a piece of paper and put down in there to burn. . . . did you ever see such a funny fire in the world? A hard wood stick inside the newspaper and the hard wood stick would go out beyond recall—and the newspaper that lives forever would stay there! What a theory that is! So we rather think that our handle is still flying in the air, a poor orphan handle without a hatchet, flying around somewhere. For heaven's sake, get the one hundred and twenty-five policemen of Fall River and chase it. . . ."

He recalled the testimonies of Bridget, Alice Russell, Mrs. Churchill, Dr. Bowen . . . before continuing his attack on the credibility of the handleless hatchet.

He identified it as an Underhill hatchet, "one of the kind that you and I remember well when we were young. Why gentlemen, that hatchet has got to be sharp enough to cut the eyeball. . . . it has also got to be sharp enough to cut Mrs. Borden's natural hair off as cleanly as a razor would do it—or a shears. Do you believe it? Cut a mass of hair off like shears? It might tear it, snarl it, break it, but not the other thing."

And then he raised the one issue which everyone had avoided. He suggested that if Lizzie had been tried before the hatchet had been tested by Professor Wood, "she possibly would now have been beyond their recall, although they had actually put her to death wrongfully. . . ."

A second later he once more drove the point home: "You are trying a capital case, a case that involves a human life, a verdict in which against her calls for the imposition of but one penalty, and that is that she shall walk to her death."

It was ominous for the spectre of the death penalty to be raised initially not by the prosecution, but by Lizzie's own attorney.

The ex-Governor finally attempted to coax the jury: "It is not your business to unravel the mystery . . . you are not here to find out the murderer . . . you are simply and solely here to say, is this woman defendant guilty? That is all, and though the real criminal shall never be found, better a million times that than you find a verdict against this woman upon insufficient evidence. . . . In the old days they had sacrifices of lambs and goats, and even human beings were offered in expiation and in sacrifice. But we have got over all that. We do not even burn witches now in Massachusetts."

Beyond rhetoric, Robinson had given the jury a terribly hard choice. Lizzie Borden would have to be either set free—or executed.

Robinson's unsettling challenge to the jury prepared the way for District Attorney Knowlton, in his closing argument, to focus on the horror of the crime. Knowlton's words were not so poetic—yet he was insistent that an act had been committed, so evil that it could not go unpunished.

"What were the feelings that overpowered the community when the news of the tragedy was spread like lightning to the ends of the world? Nay, gentlemen, I need not ask you to imagine it. You were a part of the community."

Knowlton was well aware that he was addressing an all-male jury who had been schooled to look upon women, if not as less than, at least as distinctly unlike, themselves: "They are no better than we. They are no worse than we. If they lack in strength and coarseness and vigor, they make up for it in cunning, in dispatch, in celerity, in ferocity. If their loves are stronger and more enduring than those of men, on the other hand, their hates are more undying, more unyielding, more persistent."

He could still defend the police of Fall River: "Honestly, faithfully, as thoroughly as God had given them ability, they pursued the various avenues by which they thought they might find the criminal. . . . don't you suppose they would be glad today if it could be found that this woman did not do this thing?"

As did Robinson, he reviewed the details of the murders, but when he began describing Abby's relationship to Lizzie he made an unusual comment: "Through all her childhood's sicknesses that woman had cared for her. . . . this girl owed everything to her. Mrs. Borden was the only mother she had ever known. . . . it was a living insult to that woman, a living expression of contempt, and that woman [Lizzie] repeated it day in and day out, saying to her, as Emma has said, you are not interested in us. You have worked round our father and have got a little miserable pittance of fifteen hundred dollars out of him, and you shall be my mother no more. . . ."

"*As Emma has said.*" But Lizzie had not said it. Emma, by her own admission, was the one who had harbored resentment toward Abby Borden.

Once more Knowlton had missed the obvious.

However, when he described Lizzie's presence in the house he drew nearer to the truth than anyone.

"If she was upstairs there was nothing to separate her from the murder but the thinness of that door that you saw. Do you believe for a moment that those blows could have been struck—that woman was struck in a way that did not make her insensible—that she could have been struck without groaning or screaming—that she could have fallen without a jar? Was Lizzie in the passageway when the assassin came in? She alone knows. Was she in her room when that heavy body fell to the floor? She alone knows.

"But we know that when Bridget opened that screen door and went out to wash the windows, that she left in the house this poor woman and the only enemy she had in the world."

Knowlton traced the impossibility of anyone getting into the house without Lizzie's knowledge. It was Lizzie he was after even though there was one point he could not answer: "How could she have avoided the spattering of her dress with blood if she was the author of these crimes? . . . I cannot answer it. You cannot answer it. You are neither murderers nor women. You have neither the craft of the assassin nor the cunning and deftness of the sex. . . . we get down now to the elements of ordinary crime. We get hatred, we get malice, we get falsehood . . . we get absurd and impossible alibis. We get contradictory stories that are not attempted to be verified. We get fraud upon the officers by the substitution of an afternoon silk dress as the one that she was wearing. . . ."

Finally he mentioned the missing attorney general of Massachusetts, Arthur Pillsbury: "He who could have charmed and entertained and inspired you is still detained by sickness and it has fallen to my lot to fill unworthily the place of the chief lawgiver of the commonwealth. . . . I do not put it on so low a ground as to ask you to avenge these horrid deaths . . ."

Yet, with a last cry, he let them know that they must become avengers: "You are merciful men. The wells of mercy, I hope, are not dried up in any of us. But this is not the time nor the place for the exercise of it!"

Neither Andrew Jennings nor Governor Robinson had ever called Lizzie to the stand. There was a loud rustling in the spectator section of the airless courtroom as the chief justice asked her if she had anything that she wished to say to the jury.

Slowly Lizzie rose. She stared at the twelve men sitting motionless before her.

"I am innocent. I leave it to my counsel to speak for me."

14

DEATH SENTENCE

Under cross-examination Miss Borden admitted that there had been ill-feeling between her stepmother and herself. The ill-feeling so far as Lizzie was concerned, however, wore off. So far as she herself was concerned she said that the breach had never been completely healed.

—New York *Herald,* June 17, 1893

Where is the weapon, where's the handle of the hatchet found by Marshal Fleet and since mysteriously disappeared? Any quantity of blood, but not on Lizzie's garments. Considerable ill-feeling toward the stepmother, but in Emma's breast it rested, according to her own testimony. . . .

—Joseph Howard, syndicated throughout the country, June 18, 1893

IT HAD BEEN AN AWESOME RISK. Lizzie had stood trial for two murders that Emma had committed. She had sat listening to testimony about a murder weapon that she had never used, as all the while judges, attorneys and reporters groped for the single fact that would explain it all.

It was ironic that Emma should at last be called upon to furnish the strongest element of Lizzie's defense—admitting that she, alone, possessed the motive.

Her part of the bond was fulfilled.

But it was too late for the mystery to be solved.

If Lizzie was found guilty, her penalty would be the most modern and terrible faced by any woman.

On the morning of August 6, 1890, a convicted axe murderer had been led into the death chamber of Auburn Prison, New York, to test a controversial new invention. The prisoner, who was formally attired in a brown business suit, was introduced by Warden Durston to the newsmen and officials. "Gentlemen, this is William Kemmler."

Kemmler removed his jacket and placed it neatly on another chair in the chamber. His vest and shirt were slit in the back to permit the attachment of an electrode. He was strapped to the chair and the headpiece was lowered with *its* electrode. The signal was given to the nervous executioner. He released one thousand volts through Kemmler's body, and as he did, the chair and the man strapped to it began to rock in grotesque fashion, due to the effect of the current and the fact that the chair had not been bolted to the floor. To the alarmed witnesses it looked as if Kemmler was fighting to get free. Several shouted to the man at the switch to cut off the current, and it was done. As the horrified audience watched, Kemmler's chest heaved and a thick purple foam came from his mouth. At this sign of life the warden, the doctors, the witnesses and the electrocutioner all seemed to go to pieces. There were cries of "Turn it on!" as the man at the switch discharged numerous short bursts of current into the body. When he stopped the doctors listened for a heartbeat. Finding none, they hurried the body off to the autopsy room.

Even though the first experiment had proven unfortunate, an editorial in *The New York Times* predicted that it was a device that would be used in the future: "It would be absurd to talk of abandoning the law and going back to the barbarisms of hanging and it would be puerile to propose to abolish capital punishment because the new mode of electrocution was botched in its first application."

For over a year the State of Massachusetts had been planning to use the electric chair to execute capital criminals. There was no question that within the thoughts of those gazing at Lizzie lurked the highly publicized image of William Kemmler. Speaking to the jurors, Governor Robinson had insisted: "Do I plead for her sister? No. Do I plead for Lizzie Andrew Borden herself? Yes . . . and pleading for her I plead for you and myself that the verdict you shall register in this most important case shall stand sanctioned and commended by the people everywhere in the world, who are listening by the telegraphic wire to know what is the outcome. . . ."

But Robinson could take no chances. He needed one last favor from his trusted appointee, Judge Dewey.

Escaping from the oppressiveness of the courtroom following the closing arguments, Joseph Howard had taken a carriage ride upon the Point along the line of Buzzard's Bay. He later wrote that the area was "swept by breezes from the ocean so strong as to suggest the most vigorous boisterousness of a northeast gale. As we sped along just this side of Fort Taber which, in its dismantled condition, neighbored by a score or more of costly guns and other paraphernalia of war, suggested thoughts of the wastes of the Government, my eye was attracted by a picturesque figure sitting on a rock a little this side of the rolling waters. As I drew near I recognized the classic contour of Judge Dewey's well-known face, and felt a thrill of joy as I saw the refreshment he was getting while the wind toyed playfully with his whitening locks, cooling his fevered brow and toning him up for the herculean labor before him."

What occurred on the following afternoon not only took everyone by surprise but shattered every precedent that had ever been established by judicial law. The climax provided by the white-haired judge was ruthless and sudden.

Abruptly stepping down from the bench, Judge Dewey charged the jurors: "You have listened with attention to the evidence in this case and to the arguments of the defendant's counsel. It now remains for me, acting in behalf of the court, to give you such aid towards a proper performance of your duty. . . ."

With a casual glance at Knowlton, Dewey hammered home the pivotal point: "Now you observe, gentlemen, that the Government submits this case to you upon circumstantial evidence. . . ."

Before the stunned spectators, he began to dismantle the prosecution's case:

The Government had acknowledged that Lizzie's character had been noble and good—that she had actively engaged in religious and charitable work. Did this not raise a reasonable doubt as to her guilt, even in the face of strongly incriminating circumstances?

Mrs. Gifford had recalled Lizzie's hostile remarks about Abby. But wasn't it the habit of young women to use intense expressions that often went far beyond what they really mean?

As to the note received by Mrs. Borden, perhaps it had been used by the real assassin to draw Abby away from the house. But when the murderer came and killed her, didn't it seem obvious that he would have removed that note, which was the only link betraying his identity?

Referring to Lizzie's inconsistent statements as to her whereabouts at the time of the murders, Dewey cautioned that such oral statements were often subject to error.

Never before had a judge been known to give a jury his opinion of a case. Even Joe Howard was taken aback:

> At one forty-five p.m. the mercury having mounted the very tiptop of the thermometer, everybody fagged, worn out, impatient and cross. Judge Dewey standing, the jury, the courtroom perfectly still. . . . Lizzie Borden sat on the edge of her chair, leaning forward and listening with breathless anxiety, you may well believe.
>
> The judge's charge was remarkable. It was a plea for the innocent. Had he been the senior counsel for the defense making the closing plea in behalf of the defendant, he couldn't have more absolutely pointed out the folly of depending upon circumstantial evidence alone. With matchless clearness he set up the case of the prosecution point by point, and in the gentlest and most ingenious manner possible knocked it down.

Dewey even sympathized with Lizzie for not appearing on her own behalf. "Nor is the defendant called upon to offer any explanation of her neglect to testify. If she were required to explain, others might think the explanation insufficient. Then she would lose the protection of the statute. It is a matter which the law submits to her own discretion, and to that alone. The defendant may say: 'I have already told the officers all that I know about this evidence. Whatever is mysterious to others is also a mystery to me. I have no knowledge more than others have. I have never professed to be able to explain how or by whom these homicides were committed.' "

He cautioned the jury that in order to convict her they would have to be certain beyond a reasonable doubt: "If the evidence falls short of providing such conviction in your mind, although it may raise a suspicion of guilt, or even a strong probability of guilt, it would be your plain duty to return a verdict of not guilty."

Joe Howard applauded Dewey's defiance: "Like the saints he continued to the end, throwing bombs of disheartenment into the ranks of the prosecution and causing smiles of joy to play about the lips of Lizzie's friends. And hers too. I doubt if ever there was such a charge before."

Finally, Dewey advised them to disregard all that they might have read in the newspapers, that if they entered on their deliberations "seeking only the truth, you will lift this case above the range of passion and prejudice and excited feeling, into the clear atmosphere of reason and law."

If the jurors were able to do this he assured them, with almost ecclesiastical fervor, "this trial may be adopted into the order of providence, and may express in its results somewhat of that justice with which God governs the world."

It was done.

The witnesses had been questioned and requestioned, Lizzie's skirt, the hatchets and the skulls had been marked and exhibited. There would be no more stirring appeals, it had all been said.

It was Tuesday, June 20, 1893, the thirteenth day of the trial. The jurors were given the case at three twenty-four p.m.

But no one in the courtroom dared move.

One hour and six minutes later, when the foreman rang the bell announcing that a verdict had been reached, the crowd thronging the courthouse went into a frenzy. The thousands milling along the streets poured onto the courthouse lawn. A mass of sweltering bodies flooded the flagstone platform upon which the four massive Doric columns stood. For almost a year they had waited.

Inside the miserably hot courtroom the perspiring spectators could barely stay silent.

The clerk called out, "Lizzie Andrew Borden—stand up!"

Lizzie's face became flushed as she wearily lifted herself up from the hard, straight-backed chair and tottered to her feet. Her lips anxiously tightened as she obeyed the clerk's instruction and stared vacantly into the faces of the twelve men. The wide-brimmed, feathered hat she was wearing, with its great plume jutting upward, gave the impression of a bird poised for flight.

The clerk's voice boomed: "Gentlemen of the jury, have you agreed upon a verdict?"

Foreman Richards responded, "We have."

"What say you, Mr. Fore—"

The Foreman suddenly interrupted.

"Not guilty."

At the sound of the two words Lizzie sank quickly backward into her seat, covering her face with her hands.

A sudden yelling cheer mingling with wild voices swept by surprise trembled through the courtroom. Dozens of spectators leapt from their seats waving their hats and handkerchiefs. The shouting became thunderous. It echoed down the corridors and the stairs, increasing in volume as it reached the throats of the people jamming the streets. Never had New Bedford experienced such a day. The three stately judges gazed straight ahead at the bare walls. Not once during the tremendous excitement, which lasted for several moments, did they make a move to halt the uproar. Sheriff Wright, the husband of Lizzie's matron at the Taunton Jail, whose daughter had played with Lizzie as a child, was also responsible for keeping order but could not do so. He was moved to tears by Lizzie's acquittal.

Lizzie had grasped the rail with her two hands. She was sobbing uncontrollably.

The only person who seemed to have any composure left was Joe Howard. He wrote: "She was no longer friendless. Her sister, her counsels, the women in the courtroom, all the men from everywhere rushed to greet her. Burying her head in her sister's arm she said: " 'Now take me home. . . .' "

Howard quickly stopped writing and glanced up. Lizzie was standing above him. He started to rise when suddenly she grasped his hand. "Thank you," she smiled, her bold blue eyes glistening, ". . . thank you very much."

Surrounded by admirers and friends, Lizzie was taken to the justices' room. Within an hour she and Emma would be leaving in a carriage to catch the train for Fall River.

But already the back of the courthouse, where her carriage was waiting, was mobbed.

Finally she appeared.

Her smiles became brilliant as she saw the multitudes. After she had been helped into her carriage she would not let it drive on until an endless procession of men and women filed past to shake her hand. Small children were lifted up for the privilege, and babies, for her to kiss.

The writer for *Frank Leslie's Weekly* captured the scene with a single phrase: "Public interest increased to an abnormal extent."

The populace would not leave her. They had gathered on the streets and sidewalks to watch her go. As she passed by they began to cheer. The cheers went on and on. Young boys ran ahead of her carriage as from the crowd there arose murmurs of "God bless you . . . God bless you . . . God bless you."

III

TWO SISTERS

AUTHOR'S NOTE

According to popular history, the story ended with Lizzie's acquittal on an exciting, memorable day in 1893. Yet what seemed most fascinating were the dark, sad years afterward.

What finally became of these two women? How were they able to continue living with the guilt of that frightening morning which took place in Andrew Borden's grim, boxlike house, still standing on Second Street in Fall River?

Much of what follows has never been revealed before.

15

MYSTERY

"Yes, it was a glorious surprise . . . and yet how could they do anything else? That charge of Judge Dewey's was so good to us."

—Emma Borden, June 20, 1893

That was the end of one of the greatest of modern criminal trials, and it left the people where they began, asking one another who killed Mr. and Mrs. Borden.

—New York *Sun,* June 21, 1893

EMMA HAD KNOWN THE LAW. It was essential that Abby be done away with before she slaughtered her father. If the path of carnage had been reversed, Abby's sisters, Sarah Whitehead and Priscilla Fish, would have claimed a major share of Andrew Borden's wealth.

Prior to Professor Wood's official determination of who had been the first to die, the probability of such a claim was considered in a brief article which appeared in the Fall River *Daily Herald* on August 6, 1892: "Quite a tidy sum is the issue in the case . . . one-third of an estate, termed the widow's dower. If the wife was killed first this would not be taken into consideration, but if the murderer struck down the old gentleman in the beginning, the one-third share goes to the heirs of Mrs. Borden, even if she was a widow but five seconds. . . ."

By first eliminating Abby, Emma had insured that there would be no widow's dower. Sarah Whitehead and Priscilla Fish were finally awarded only the estate of Abby herself.

It amounted to the paltry sum of $1,626.05 in savings and $90 in cash.

Immediately following the murders, since Andrew had died intestate, Emma, being the elder daughter, applied for her father's fortune. In accordance with the law her application had to be published for three weeks in succession in the Fall River *News.* Twenty-nine days after the butchery of her father and stepmother she gained possession of Andrew Borden's entire estate.* The one-page document granting her this windfall was witnessed not by Andrew Jennings, but by his young assistant, Arthur S. Philipps.

Andrew and Abby Borden were murdered on August 4, 1892.

Lizzie was arrested seven days later, on August 11th.

The preliminary hearing began on August 25th, and lasted until Wednesday, August 31st.

Two days later, on Friday, September 2, 1892, the document giving Emma the entire estate was filed.

It was now a matter of legal record that only one person would profit from the murders.

Emma was in control of half a million dollars.†

Emma's control of the fortune was a new source of fear to Lizzie. Following Lizzie's arrest, the argument which jail matron Hannah Reagan had overheard between Emma and Lizzie concerned the inheritance. Mrs. Reagan thought she heard Lizzie charge: "Emma, you have given me away, haven't you?" But there was nothing about Lizzie that Emma could give away. The crux of Lizzie's anger was that Emma had applied to become sole Administratrix of the estate, with no portion of Andrew's wealth going to Lizzie.

Finally, Lizzie was in such a fury that she could no longer speak to her sister. When Andrew Jennings arrived at the jail he asked Emma, "Have you told her all?"

Emma, according to Mrs. Reagan, replied, "I did."

Lizzie also knew that if she had been convicted, even if she had escaped the death penalty, she might never have seen a penny of Andrew's money. The courts would have sided with the innocent sister

*The results of Professor Wood's examinations of Andrew and Abby to determine the exact times of death would not be publicly announced until the trial. But Emma *knew* who died first.

†Worth twelve million dollars today.

rather than the convicted murderess. Emma could have kept it all.

Emma had a fierce love for her sister—and Lizzie had no one else. And now she was completely dependent on Emma for her new life.

As the two sisters rode triumphantly through New Bedford, while a joyous mob blessed them, Judge Dewey was interviewed by the Boston *Globe*. "I am perfectly satisfied with the verdict," he boasted. "I was satisfied when I made my charge to the jury that the verdict would be not guilty, although we cannot always tell what a jury will do."

In Fall River the news, which flashed over the wires, of Lizzie's acquittal was met with stunned amazement. Immediately a crowd began to gather in front of the Borden house on Second Street awaiting a glimpse of the released prisoner.

By eight-fifteen p.m. Second Street was jammed.

Five blocks away a carriage stopped before the residence of banker Charles J. Holmes, at 67 Pine Street. The first person to step down from the carriage was Charles Holmes, followed by Lizzie and Emma. Lizzie did not wait for Holmes to escort her, but bounded up the steps and disappeared within the house.

At nine p.m. a United Press reporter interviewed her in the Holmeses' front parlor. Lizzie wore a black silk dress and she laughed joyously as she admitted that she was "the happiest woman in the world."

Afterwards there was a party, during which the guests pored over newspapers collected from everywhere in the country, showing full sketches of Lizzie at the trial. Most were terrible likenesses and Lizzie chuckled uncontrollably as she looked at them.

It was a warm, memorable night along the winding streets which led up the hills from the Quequechan River. The summer sky had filled with stars. By ten p.m. the numbers of people who had remained in front of the dark, empty Borden home had swelled to over two thousand. For the people of Fall River it was the finale of months of barbaric sensationalism, of waiting for the grim tragedy to be over. Emotionally, it had taken its toll. The gossip, the stories, the solutions, the theories had been incessant. Their police officials had been vilified, as the gaze of the world was riveted upon their daily lives.

Shortly after ten a band arrived and began playing.

The voices of the crowd joined in, singing "Auld Lang Syne."

During the trial Emma had continued to live in the house on Second Street but Lizzie firmly decided that she could not return to those rooms which had witnessed the bleeding bodies of her father and stepmother. The following day Lizzie and Emma visited their friends the Remingtons in Newport. While there, Lizzie decided that she would not return to Second Street.

For the first ten years of her life she had lived in her grandfather's old house on Ferry Street and for the next twenty-one in a converted two-family dwelling located in the downtown business area so that Andrew could be near the bank and the mill he owned. The thought of living in the more fashionable residential area, known as The Hill, had seemed impossible. But now everything was possible.

Emma fulfilled Lizzie's wishes by immediately purchasing a thirteen-room, gray stone Victorian house at 306 French Street.

They would move in five weeks later.

After returning from Newport, Lizzie went back to Taunton to see Mrs. Wright, whose daughter she had played with when they had all lived down on Ferry Street. Again, tears filled the matron's eyes as Lizzie thanked her for her kindness while she had been imprisoned there.

Within the same week, Knowlton's young prosecutor, William Moody, received an unusual package. It contained press clippings of the trial and pertinent illustrations, including photographs of the bodies. It was accompanied by a polite note from Lizzie. She had sent them "as a memento of an interesting occasion."

It was the most joyous day of Lizzie's life when she and Emma arrived at her fine, rich house. It stood at the top of a quiet hill which looked across the green fields of Somerset toward Providence, Rhode Island. At last the Borden legacy had come full circle. Andrew had recaptured the wealth of his predecessors and now Lizzie could once again take her position beside those scions of other early families the Buffingtons, the Grays, the Chases, the Durfees and the Braytons.

Elegantly situated on extensive, grassy grounds, the east and north sides of the house were flanked by a row of flourishing maple trees.

The front steps led into a long, curving glassed-in porch, which opened into a spacious front entry hall. Connected by cherrywood stairways, three floors of rooms were heated by six coal-burning fireplaces as everywhere the eye rested on Italianate arches, oak mantelpieces, iron gratings and smoothly waxed parquet floors.

For Lizzie, everything about the house was a luxury. Even the laundry room in the basement had exquisite dark wood wainscoting.

There were four bathrooms—four *real* bathrooms—not like the primitive plumbing which had been contrived to accommodate the Borden family in the cellar at 92 Second Street. And each bathroom had a bathtub, on which Lizzie immediately painted delicate floral designs.

And there were windows everywhere, through which light continually radiated, giving the house a refined, almost pastoral feeling.

Lizzie furnished each room, bordering the first-floor windows with heavy rose silk drapes. One either side of the buffet, she installed mother-of-pearl light fixtures. She fashioned a comfortable breakfast room and a well-equipped kitchen; on the glass pane which formed the upper part of the door leading from the kitchen to the backyard a glazier cut a subdued but definite letter "*B.*"

Finally her new home was christened. One word was carved with bold block letters into the top stone riser of the steps facing the street: MAPLECROFT.

But the murders had not been solved.

In its lead editorial on June 21, 1893, the Providence *Journal* fired the opening salvo: "There is no reason now for Miss Borden's silence; let her speak! Let her spare no effort to bring this horrible case to a more satisfactory conclusion than it now has reached, with so much evidence barred out by the Court, and the presumption of innocence so strenuously insisted upon by the Judge in his charge to the jury."

The *Journal* was the most widely read newspaper in Bristol County and its effect on public opinion was chilling.

Two days later it assaulted "Lizzie's other kind of champion, the Reverend W. Walker Jubb, who obviously thinks that the fact of Miss Borden's attendance at his church should immediately hush all inquiry into her connection with the murders."

Even though she did not attend the Reverend Jubb's church, Lizzie and her defenders were emerging as objects of ridicule as other newspapers joined the *Journal*'s attack.

After moving into her new home, Lizzie, for the first time since her acquittal, attended services at the huge, stone Romanesque-styled Congregational Church on Rock Street. She had grown up nearby and it had been the center of her social life. Here she had taught Sunday school before the murders and from its pulpit the Reverend Buck vigorously defended her after she was arrested.

Entering through the side door, she sat in the family pew—pew 21—which had been rented by her father.

Immediately those sitting near her got up and began moving away, leaving her surrounded by empty pews.

Lizzie never went back.

The press was already lampooning her as "the self-made heiress," when the world-famous Northwestern University Law School professor, John H. Wigmore, delivered the shattering blow. In the *American Law Review* he castigated the Court for what had occurred in New Bedford:

> The conduct of the accused after the killing was such that no conceivable hypothesis, except that of guilt, will explain the inconsistencies and improbabilities that were asserted by her. The statements about the barn visit, and about the discovery of her father's death, are frightfully inconsistent; while the story of the note requires for its truth a combination of circumstances almost inconceivable. . . . Why did the accused not take the witness stand to explain these things?

While she was in jail no one had wanted to see Lizzie go to her death in the electric chair, but now that she was free it became glaringly obvious that whoever was responsible for the deaths of Andrew and Abby *had gotten away* with the crime. Either Lizzie or someone vastly clever had fooled the public, the police, the press and the law. Now they were stymied. Lizzie could not be tried again and no new evidence had been discovered to reopen the case. Marshal Hilliard had officially marked his investigation "Closed."

It was not until January 22, 1894, seven months after the acquittal, that Emma gave Lizzie her share of the inheritance. The document, witnessed by Andrew Jennings, was filed in the courthouse at Taunton:

> I Emma L. Borden Administratrix of the goods and estate of Andrew J. Borden on oath depose and say that myself and Lizzie A. Borden are only children and heirs at law of said Andrew J. Borden late of Fall River in said County of Bristol deceased; that by the request of and agreement with said Lizzie I have not filed in said Court any Inventory of said estate on account of my administration; that I have duly paid all debts due from said estate and have divided and distributed the balance of the estate then remaining in my hands equally between myself and said Lizzie A. Borden the only other parties interested therein; and I request that this statement may be accepted and filed in lieu of and as a substitute for an itemized account of such Administratrix.
>
> Emma L. Borden

> I Lizzie A. Borden named in the foregoing statement of Emma L. Borden do hereby certify that the facts stated in the foregoing affidavit are true and I request that said statement be accepted in lieu of and as a substitute

for any further or other account; I also acknowledge the receipt of my full share of the said Estate of Andrew J. Borden and in consideration of the premises hereby release and discharge the said Emma L. Borden as sole Administratrix from any and all liability whatsoever arising from or growing out of the administration of the estate of said Andrew J. Borden.

Lizzie A. Borden

What Emma and Lizzie had begun on a sweltering August morning a year and a half before had finally been settled between them.

In 1894, shortly after the inheritance was divided, reporter Edwin H. Porter of the Fall River *Globe* published his account of the murders and the trial, entitled *The Fall River Tragedy*. It was printed privately by a Fall River press and was the first book on the subject, containing much of the trial testimony. In the preface Porter explained that the book had been written because of "the desire to give the reading public a connected story of the whole case, commencing with the day of the tragedy and ending with the day that Miss Borden was set free. . . . that the grand jury indicted the young lady is no fault of the author, and the story of what brought that indictment about is important—therefore it is given without prejudice."

Porter's evaluation that someone outside of the family could have committed the crime was almost tongue in cheek:

> To those who stopped to contemplate the circumstances surrounding the double murder, it was marvelous to reflect how fortune had favored the assassin. Not once in a million times would fate have paved such a way for him. He had to deal with a family of six persons* in an unpretentious two-and-a-half story house, the rooms of which were all connected and in which it would have been a difficult matter to stifle sound. He must catch Mr. Borden alone and either asleep or off his guard, and kill him with one fell blow. The faintest outcry would have sounded an alarm. He must also encounter Mrs. Borden alone and fell her, a heavy woman, noiselessly. To do this he must either make his way from the sitting room on the ground floor to the spare bedroom above the parlor and avoid five persons in the passage, or he must conceal himself in one of the rooms upstairs and make the descent under the same conditions. . . . He must then conceal the dripping implement of death and depart in broad daylight by a much frequented street. In order to accomplish this he must take a time when Miss Emma L. Borden, the elder daughter of the

*Porter includes Andrew, Abby, Lizzie, Emma, Bridget and John Vinnicum Morse.

> murdered man, was on a visit to relatives out of the city; Miss Lizzie A. Borden, the other daughter, must be in the barn and remain there twenty minutes. A less time than that would not suffice. Bridget Sullivan, the servant, must be in the attic asleep on her own bed. Her presence in the pantry or kitchen or any room on the first or second floors would have frustrated the fiend's designs, unless he also killed her so that she would die without a murmur.

Edwin Porter had examined the house and seen the bodies. He had spoken to Lizzie and Emma. Although his presentation of the evidence made a strong case for Lizzie's guilt, his book ends on a face-saving note: "Thus ended, on the thirteenth day, the famous trial of Lizzie Andrew Borden, and she returned guiltless to her friends and home in Fall River."

Lizzie immediately bought up all the available copies of Porter's book and had them burned.*

At the same time she felt that she was being snubbed by the group of women who had once staunchly defended her—the W.C.T.U., which had rented space in the A. J. Borden Building from her father. According to the Fall River *News,* Lizzie "felt that she should not put up with insults from her tenants, and accordingly the W.C.T.U. has been compelled to seek quarters elsewhere. The affair has caused considerable indignation among the eighty members of the local branch."

But the pressure upon Lizzie was building.

Plymouth, Massachusetts, judge Charles Gideon Davis had just published a series of articles in the Boston *Daily Advertiser* in which he accused Judge Dewey of acting not as an impartial judge but as Lizzie's advocate, "by teaching the jury to distrust every important item of evidence offered by the prosecution in the case." Davis did not accuse Dewey of corrupt motives—and he cautiously overlooked his political connections to ex-Governor Robinson—but he charged that Dewey had been unconsciously overcome by bias and prejudice in Lizzie's favor. Judge Davis's overall view of the case was that "it was not the prisoner but the Commonwealth which did not have a fair trial." He attacked those who had let Lizzie off:

> There is natural and uncontrolled repulsion against the barbarism of coldly putting to death a fellow human being. . . . this repulsion is warping

*As stated previously, only four copies are known to have escaped her. One was originally in the Library of Congress, one is at the Fall River Historical Society, another is at the State House in Boston and a fourth is in the author's possession.

> the law of criminal evidence in capital cases. . . . This feeling exalts a prisoner charged with a crime into a hero, and sends flowers to him. It induces philanthropic women, whose life is spent in going about doing good, to volunteer during a trial their unsworn testimony to the character of the prisoner, even to deposing without cross-examination that women burn their clothes three months old in stoves.

The fickleness of public sentiment had rapidly shifted.

Yet little more than a year before, *The New York Times* had commented on the legal officers who had secured Lizzie's indictment and conducted her trial: "They were guilty of a barbarous wrong to an innocent woman and a gross injury to the community. And we hold it to be a misfortune that their victim has no legal recourse against them and no means of bringing them to account. Her acquittal is only a partial atonement for the wrong that she has suffered."

Andrew Borden's fortune had liberated Lizzie, but it seemed to create no change in Emma's existence. Unlike Lizzie, she acquired no rich furniture, fine carriages, jewels or expensive clothing. She chose to remain in the background, living in her sister's shadow. As she conveyed in a letter to the dressmaker, Mrs. Cummings, even though she would be away for part of the summer her needs would be meager:

> Mrs. Cummings (dressmaker)
>
> I received your message last evening and think you are very kind to remember me.
>
> I hope to be in the country some this Summer, so think one dress will be all I need; I think an India or China silk as useful as any thin dress, and if you will bring patterns of something with dark ground, something suitable for church wear and for calling. I will go to see you the middle of the week. I suppose you will be home by that time.
>
> I hope this wind will go down before night, that you may have a pleasant and safe passage to New York.
>
> Truly yours,
> Emma L. Borden
>
> March 23, 1894

Early one morning Lizzie's carriage and coachman were recognized parked at the curb in front of Fall River's largest dry-goods store, E. S. Brown and Company, at the corner of Main Street and Franklin.

When Lizzie emerged from the store, thirty curiosity-seekers were waiting to catch a glimpse of her. They began passing remarks and pointing at her as she quickly got into her carriage and drove away.

As Joe Howard had once commented: "The great Beecher used to say that a public man couldn't blow his nose on his own doorstep, without its report being echoed through the entire city, and so it has been with Lizzie Borden, whether she washed her face, wiped her eyes, blew her nose, puckered her mouth, or raised her hand, whatever she did, wherever she went, she was an object of curiosity and unmitigated assault by the gossips of the time."

Following her acquittal Lizzie had remarked to a reporter: "A good many persons have talked to me as if they thought I would go and live somewhere else. I don't know what possesses them. I am going home and I am going to stay there. I never thought of doing anything else."

It was a mistake.

Since the incident at the Central Congregational Church she had been shunned by those who had once rallied to her side. Even though her formal trial was over, she was now being tried by the people of the town in which she had lived all her life.

When the industrial boom began in the 1860s the elite of Fall River, who lived on The Hill near Lizzie—on French Street, Grove Street, Pearce, Linden and Prospect—had made their fortunes in the teeming textile mills they built beside the Taunton and Quequechan rivers. Yet the Braytons, the Durfees, the Chases did not—their New England mores *would not let them*—rub shoulders with those who had made their riches possible. Neither religiously nor socially would they mingle with the workers who had immigrated from the seaports of Boston and New York, who had formed the ghettos of wooden frame dwellings scattered throughout the city below—the French, the Polish, the Jewish, the Portuguese. The iron-willed precepts and coolness of manner which Fall River's aristocracy inherited from their Puritanical ancestors remained inbred and inflexible. No stores were open on Sunday, and there were no theaters. Even the food eaten on Sunday had to be cooked on Saturday.

They were bigoted people—and Lizzie Borden was not someone to be proud of knowing. Yet they were relieved when she was acquitted. There would be no more scandal.

But those who had watched her grow into womanhood and then witnessed the sensational upheaval of the past few years, even though they remained tight-lipped, were firmly convinced that she murdered her parents.

The present curator of the Fall River Historical Society, Florence Brigham, whose mother-in-law had been a character witness for Lizzie at the trial, recalled that "after she was acquitted she was ostracized. My mother-in-law, Mary Brigham, who testified that she had always been a good person who worked in the church, had to give up going to see her because her friends were starting to leave her alone."

Shortly after her acquittal, Lizzie, with her curly hair still combed back into auburn waves and dressed expensively in clothes that were the latest fashion, accompanied by the small, thin-faced figure of Emma, was often noticed in the streets of Fall River. Now threatened with mounting recrimination in the press, Lizzie's defense was to withdraw.

But if anything, she became more famous.

At the Fall River Railroad Station, hackers who met the trains from Boston advanced upon passengers yelling: "Come and see the notorious Lizzie Borden home—*where she now lives!*" Carriages of sightseers would pull up in front of Maplecroft as the hacker, taking out his whip and pointing to the house, would deliver a history of Lizzie and the bloody details of the murders. For this, each listener was charged twenty-five cents.

Maplecroft was Lizzie's refuge and her prison, and within it she was determined to become self-sufficient. Unable to shop without being mobbed by staring crowds, she had all her groceries delivered to a designated box at the back of the house.

But the press would not leave her alone.

On December 10, 1896, a brief article which appeared in the Boston *Globe* was picked up by newspapers throughout the country:

IS LIZZIE BORDEN TO MARRY?

Fall River, Mass., Dec. 10—Friends of Lizzie Andrew Borden, who was once accused of the murder of her father and stepmother and whose trial was one of the most famous the country has known, are congratulating her upon the approach of her marriage. The husband-to-be is one Mr. Gardner, a school teacher of the village of Swansea, which lies a few miles across the bay to the west of the city. He has been a friend of Miss Borden since childhood days, which they spent upon adjoining farms. The engagement has been rumored about for weeks, but it lacked confirmation until a few days ago, when it was learned that Miss Borden has given to a well-known dressmaker an order for a trousseau. Mr. Gardner has had erected in South Somerset a fine new house. It is said that the wedding will probably take place about Christmas.

The residents of the farm adjacent to the one which Andrew Borden had owned in Swansea *were* named Gardner. And the eldest son was a school teacher. But the story of Lizzie's romance and impending marriage had been fabricated.

Soon after the article appeared, reporters from out-of-town newspapers flooded Fall River.

Gardner went into hiding and Lizzie withdrew behind the oak doors of Maplecroft, where she was constantly harassed. The incident infuriated and disturbed her. Two days later she wrote to Mrs. Cummings, the dressmaker Emma had written to earlier. The letter's significance was that it revealed the strain Lizzie was under.

It was from Mrs. Cummings, whose shop on Elm Street stood beside Andrew Borden's Union Savings Bank, that Lizzie supposedly had ordered her wedding gown.

My dear Friend

I am more sorry than I can tell you that you have had any trouble over the false and silly story that has been about the last week or so. How or when it started I have not the least idea. But never for a moment did I think you or your girls started it. Of course I am feeling very badly about it but I must just bear as I have in the past. I do hope you will not be annoyed again. Take care of yourself, so you can get well.

Yours sincerely
L. A. Borden

Dec. 12, 1896

But within two months Lizzie was to make the front pages of newspapers again.

A warrant had been issued for her arrest on another charge.

16

THE LIE

THE TILDEN-THURBER COMPANY was a stylish art gallery located on the upper floor of the Westminster Street Building at 60 Westminster Street in Providence, Rhode Island. Since 1790 its collection of silver and art replicas had been considered one of the finest in New England.

On a September day in 1896, Lizzie entered the gallery.

In charge of the salesroom was a Miss Addie B. Smith.

Having been informed who the customer was, Addie Smith paid particular attention to Lizzie as she waited on her. Lizzie asked to see a vase, which Addie had to go to the back of the building to find. When she returned with it, Lizzie declared that it wouldn't do at all and strode hastily away.

Lizzie had been alone on the floor.

Before anyone else entered the gallery Addie Smith noticed that one large and one small porcelain painting were missing from the stand where they had been displayed. Addie also recalled that Lizzie had been wearing a voluminous fur coat.

She immediately reported the matter to her employer, Mr. Henry Tilden.

Tilden told her that there was nothing that could be done.

Five months later, in early February 1897, a lady unknown to Miss Smith entered the art gallery. Walking up to the counter, she undid a package to reveal the larger of the two missing paintings. She explained that she had received the porcelain painting as a Christmas gift from Lizzie Borden. It had been damaged and she wished it repaired.

Addie identified the stolen article immediately by its length of about fourteen inches, its oval shape and gilt frame. She told the woman she would find out how long it would take to repair it, and then excused herself. Hurrying at once to Mr. Tilden, Addie told him what had happened.

"Don't allow the woman to discover that you are suspicious," he warned. "Just take her name and address and tell her to come back in two weeks."

Addie did as she was told. The lady wrote down her name and address and left the gallery.

Immediately Henry Tilden notified the Providence police. Chief Detective Patrick H. Parker was given the particulars and he agreed to leave at once for the Fall River home of Lizzie Borden.

Lizzie was shaken when Parker appeared at her front door. She immediately denied that she had stolen the paintings. They were hers and she had a right to give them to whomever she wished.

The following day when Parker returned to Providence, Henry Tilden swore out a warrant for Lizzie's arrest. Tilden's associate, Morris House, was called in to confer as a member of the firm. He advised that Lizzie should be asked to visit Tilden-Thurber in an attempt to clarify the situation.

The following evening, within the darkened offices of Tilden-Thurber, Lizzie met with Henry Tilden, Morris House and William G. Thurber. Indignantly denying all charges of theft, Lizzie claimed that she had purchased the articles legitimately. She asserted that she was being hounded because of her association with the killings of her stepmother and her father. As the three men were undecided in their minds about what to do next, they asked her to return for another conference.

"Unless the situation is resolved," Tilden told her, "we shall have to publicize the incident."

Henry Tilden had been an avid follower of Lizzie's trial, and he—like many others—was firmly convinced that she had murdered her father and stepmother, and had gotten away with it. A day later he met with Stephen C. Metcalf, an editor on the Providence *Journal.* Tilden confided to Metcalf that he had an opportunity to succeed where everyone else had failed. "Do you realize," Tilden related excitedly, "that with the power I have to send that murderess to jail as a shoplifter, I can make her confess to the murders."

"I don't think she'd confess in a million years—you mean she'd exchange her freedom now for a confession of what she did in 1892?"

Tilden nodded.

Metcalf was dubious.

But Tilden prodded him. "With your ability to publicize the affair, we can make it work. I've got a warrant sworn out for her arrest—with that constant threat hanging over her and the *Journal* backing us, let's scare her into believing that we might put her behind bars."

Metcalf doubted the outcome, but Tilden was persuasive.

Finally Metcalf agreed to go along.

And so it was that five men, Henry Tilden, Morris House, Detective Parker, Stephen C. Metcalf and William G. Thurber, began a battle of wits against Lizzie.

Metcalf ordered a portrait of her drawn by a *Journal* artist. Beside it an article was type-set with a headline reading:

LIZZIE BORDEN AGAIN.

A Warrant for Her Arrest Issued
from a Local Court.

TWO PAINTINGS MISSED FROM
TILDEN-THURBER CO.'S STORE.

Several rollings were made of the combination headlines, picture and story.

When Lizzie returned to the store Henry Tilden showed them to her.

As soon as Lizzie glanced at the proofs she became incensed. "You wouldn't dare publish that," she shrieked, her eyes flashing. "I could sue you for every last cent should that article ever appear!"

Tilden answered, "You could sue us, Miss Borden, but you would never win. We can serve that warrant at any time. We will put this in the paper unless you clarify the situation regarding the Borden murders."

"What have they to do with this?"

"Absolutely nothing. But to avoid jail—we would like you to sign a confession that you committed them."

"You know better than to think I'd agree to such a fantastic plan. I'll never sign anything!"

"Would you rather go to jail? I promise that none of us will ever reveal it if you do sign such a statement."

Lizzie sat still in the chair and simply stared. Finally she stood up. "Never!" she shouted. "I'll never sign anything!"

She rushed out of the room and left the building.

A conference between the five men followed.

"Shall I go ahead?" Metcalf asked.

"Why not?" Tilden replied.

The following morning the story was on the front page of the Providence *Journal.*

The humiliating news was told to Andrew Jennings by a reporter from the Providence *Journal.* Jennings's response appeared in the same edition:

> Andrew J. Jennings of Fall River, who was engaged as counsel by Miss Borden when she was first suspected or murdering her father and mother, and who defended her in the Second District Court at the preliminary hearing of the case, would have nothing to say yesterday when informed that it was reported that a warrant has been issued for her arrest on a complaint charging his former client with shoplifting. That is, Mr. Jennings said nothing to indicate that he had the slightest knowledge of any such offence on Miss Borden's part, and intimated that he did not believe there was any foundation for the story.

As soon as the paper came out, Detective Parker visited Maplecroft. He showed Lizzie the front page. "I am authorized to serve the warrant, but a postponement is possible if you return to Tilden-Thurber's with me now."

"I am suing you for this," declared Lizzie.

"Go ahead and sue, but if you don't leave with me in half an hour, I'll have to serve the warrant."

Blustering and fuming for the next few minutes, Lizzie finally calmed down and left the room. Five minutes later, dressed in her fur coat, she reappeared and went with Parker to his carriage for the drive to Providence.

At six o'clock that night the five men and Lizzie were seated around the conference table.

"Lizzie," began Tilden, "you know that we are not joking. We have taken the first step. We're not trying to make it hard for you. All I am

The Providence Daily Journal.

VOL. LXIX. NO. 40. PROVIDENCE, R. I., TUESDAY, FEBRUARY 16, 1897. TEN PAGES. PRICE TWO CENTS.

LIZZIE BORDEN AGAIN.

A Warrant for Her Arrest Issued from a Local Court.

TWO PAINTINGS MISSED FROM TILDEN-THURBER CO.'S STORE.

Said to have Been Traced to Miss Borden's Home in Fall River.

OFFICIALS LOATH TO FURNISH INFORMATION OF AFFAIR.

The Warrant Was Issued Some Time Ago and Has Not Been Served—It is Understood That Miss Borden Claimed to Have Purchased the Articles and That She Retained Them.

It is but a brief period since notoriety attached itself to Miss Lizzie Borden, daughter of Andrew J. and Abby Borden of Fall River, who were found foully murdered at their home in that city a few years ago. Again is the name of the young woman before the public and this time in a less pleasant character than at the last time, when a story of her alleged engagement was current.

The information published in the Bulletin last evening to the effect that it was alleged that a warrant had been issued against her charging larceny of two paintings from the Tilden-Thurber Company of this city created a sensation. This warrant followed a complaint made against Miss Borden in the proper officials here.

The young woman has been a fre-

... assistance of Fall River officials was also brought into the matter.

Mr. Jennings Hadn't Heard It.

Andrew J. Jennings of Fall River, who was engaged as counsel of Miss Borden when she was first suspected of murdering her father and mother, and who defended her in the Second District Court at the preliminary hearing of the case, would have nothing to say yesterday when informed that it was reported that a warrant has been issued for her arrest on a complaint charging his former client with shoplifting. That is, Mr. Jennings said nothing to indicate that he had the slightest knowledge of any such offence on Miss Borden's part, and intimated that he did not believe there was any foundation for the story.

Fall River authorities, including the Inspectors, who are usually detailed to assist officers from other cities in investigating matters of this kind, also stated that they were ignorant of any accusation of the kind. From other sources, however, it was learned that Detective Parker of Providence arrived in Fall River some little time ago and was heard to inquire of a man with whom he left the train where "she" was living at present.

The news printed in the Bulletin created a profound sensation, as does most news which recalls the remarkable assassination of Mr. and Mrs. Borden, and many tongues discussed the details of the crime once more.

A rumor going the rounds is that Detective Parker was in town last week, inquired for Marshal Hilliard, who did not happen to be in the city, and later called a well-known lawyer out of a place of amusement and disappeared with him.

The Borden Murders Recalled.

Wherever the English language is spoken mention of the name of Lizzie Borden will bring with it remembrance of a crime—a crime still unpunished—one of the most horrid in the history of this country. On the 4th day of August, 1892, in the Borden homestead on Second street, Fall River, the bodies of Andrew J. Borden and his wife Abby were found. They had been murdered, ...

Miss Lizzie Borden.

A warrant for her arrest issued from a local court but has not been served.

[Continued on Page 2.]

GREEK TROOPS LANDED.

Detachments from the Warships at Retimo, Heraklion and Canea.

KING GEORGE NOTIFIED OF THE PROTEST OF THE POWERS.

And That His Torpedo Flotilla Must Retire from Cretan Waters.

ENGLAND SAID TO BE IN ACCORD WITH THE OTHER POWERS.

But Will Take No Isolated Action. Germany Joins the Associated Fleet.—The Greek Navy at Anchor Outside the War Vessels of the Powers.—Turkish Troops Twice Repulsed on Saturday in the Halepa Quarter of Canea and Compelled to Retreat to the Fortress.

Athens, Feb. 15.—Advices received here from the Island of Crete announce that the "corps of occupation," consisting of infantry, artillery and engineers, and numbering 1500 men, which embarked at Piraeus yesterday, have landed at Platanias, 14 kilometres west of Canea. The warships of the Powers, the advices also state, had previously landed strong detachments at Retimo, Heraklion and Canea.

Athens, Feb. 15.—When the announcement was made here that "the corps of occupation" under command of Col. Vassos, Chief Aide de Camp to King George, had landed in Crete, demonstrations of wildest joy were indulged in by the populace.

A dispatch from Canea states that Col. Vassos has issued a proclamation to the Cretans and has demanded that the Turks surrender.

THE POWERS' PROTEST.

Conveyed to Premier Delyannis by the French Minister.

Athens, Feb. 15.—The representatives of the Powers accredited to Greece held two meetings yesterday, their conferences taking place at the French Legation. At the second meeting, which was held in the evening, it was agreed that the Powers, through their Ministers at Athens, should protest against Greek ...

THE GREEK FLOTILLA.

AMERICAN WHEAT.

[Continued on Page 2.]

A NARROW ESCAPE.

Harry McDonald Injured in a Mix-up on the Avenue.

CAPTURED A BURGLAR.

THE STREETS OF NEW YORK.

MR. SIMS RESIGNS.

Severs Connection with Armington & Sims Engine Co.

A "SUIT" CHARGED WITH THEFT.

A SUNKEN WRECK.

New Belgian Minister.

asking is that you admit that the acts of August 4, 1892, were yours, and yours alone. The moment the statement is signed, we will drop everything. We will never serve that warrant, and you can walk out of here a free woman."

"You should know me better than that, Mr. Tilden. I'll never sign anything."

"You will be in serious trouble and in jail if you don't sign it. You have my word and I speak for the others as well. I'll never reveal to a living soul what you write on that piece of paper I have put in the typewriter."

Somewhat startled, Lizzie glanced across at the typing machine. There was a piece of paper awaiting her confession.

The white sheet in the typewriter seemed to unnerve her. But again she became defiant.

The hours went by. Nothing apparently was going to be achieved, and by ten o'clock all were weary. Lizzie seemed more tired than the others. She looked desperate.

At eleven-fifteen William Thurber stood up and motioned to Henry Tilden to follow him out of the room.

"We're getting nowhere," he whispered. "Let me make a final try?"

Tilden nodded.

The two partners re-entered the room.

"Miss Borden," Thurber began, "anything you do in this room tonight will never be revealed in the lifetime of any of us here. All you have to do is to exchange a piece of paper for a jail term of possibly several years. Come, I'll type it out if you wish."

"Never," came the answer. "Never, never, never!"

A hurried consultation was held.

Finally Thurber spoke again. "Miss Borden, it is now eight minutes of twelve. I am authorized to state that if you don't sign within eight minutes Detective Parker will serve you the warrant and you'll go to jail. Eight mintues are left."

Lizzie sat very still, looking across at William Thurber. The hands of the wall clock drew nearer and nearer together as twelve o'clock approached. Finally the hour of midnight was reached.

The five men looked at each other. Their gamble had failed.

William Thurber glanced at Detective Parker and nodded his head. Parker stood up and started across the room for the warrant, which was in the inside pocket of his overcoat.

"Just a minute!" The unexpected words came from Lizzie's lips. Rising slowly from her chair, she walked across to the typewriter.

Every eye watched as she sat down. The silence of the room was broken by the slow clicking of the keys as Lizzie began to type. A minute later she reached across the desk for the pen, dipped it into the black ink and wrote her signature. The scratching of the pen was the only sound to be heard.

Lizzie stood up and strode across the room to her fur coat. Morris House helped her into it. She stood quietly for a moment, apparently uncertain just what she should say. At the door, she paused. Detective Parker was hurriedly putting on his own coat, getting ready to drive her back to Fall River.

A moment later she was gone.

The four men crowded around the typewriter as soon as she had departed to read what she had written and signed.

Unfair means force my signature here admitting the act of August 4, 1892 as mine alone.

Lizbeth A. Borden

Why had Lizzie stolen the paintings? She had become a wealthy woman, worth at least a quarter of a million dollars. She lived in a large, elegant home in the richest section of Fall River. She owned the A. J. Borden Building, the Union Savings Bank and her father's shares in the mills.

The total cost of the porcelain paintings was less than one hundred dollars.

If the doors of Fall River's aristocracy had been shut before, they were now locked and bolted. Because of Henry Tilden's obsession to force her to admit to the murders—even though her confession was a lie—the article which had appeared on the front page of the Providence *Journal* damned her forever. There was no one she could turn to. She no longer went to church. Even the Reverend Jubb had deserted her.

After the incident, there were fewer friends and longer hours of idly sitting in the sun.

Mrs. Edith Coolidge Hart, a long-time resident of Fall River, often saw Lizzie and sympathized with her unhappiness: "Lizzie grew up in a household utterly devoid of affection. Her sister, who was close to her, seemed governed by fear rather than love. Lizzie was only three when her mother died. Her sister, ten years older, was the substitute maternal influence. . . . It is difficult to picture the restraints of an era unless you have lived through it. I never heard the words homosexual or lesbian until after my college days. As you know, we kept our thoughts clothed as we did our bodies. A difficult thing to imagine in this era . . ."

Thirty-five years devoid of physical affection were taking their toll. There was a part of Lizzie that ached to be warmed and cherished. A part so secret—which yearned for someone like herself whom she could embrace and shower with affection.

As the days and nights of loneliness crowded in on her there was someone she desired. According to Mrs. Brigham of the Fall River Historical Society, the following letter was written to a young woman:

> My dear Friend
>
> Where are you how are you and what are you doing? I dreamed of you the other night but I do not dare to put my dreams on paper. Have you been away and has your little niece been to visit you? We have been home all summer. I spend much time on the piazza in my steamer chair reading and building castles in the air. I hope you have been away and are well and strong now. Do you expect to do much this fall and are you going to N.Y.? Every time we pass your corner the pony wants to turn down. The weather has been so warm and full of thunder storms I am quite ready for fall.

In an age which prohibited any expression of one's deepest, most passionate feelings, Lizzie's phrase *I dreamed of you the other night but I do not dare to put my dreams on paper* was revealing. Despite her tendency to lie, she could be explicit about her sexual longings.

Discreetly, Lizzie ended the short letter:

> I should be very glad to hear from you.
>
> Sincerely
> L. A. Borden
>
> August twenty second
> 1897

17

NANCE

> Nance O'Neil is a great actress. A few of them have been seen at the Academy, Mrs. Fiske, Mrs. Leslie Carter and Constance Collier, but none of these possess more native ability than Nance O'Neil. . . . she has been compared to Mary Anderson, but she has a more fervent temperament. She has been compared to Julia Marlowe, but she is radically different. Nance O'Neil is of the order of Duse and Bernhardt, a tragedienne, a great emotional actress.
>
> —Chicago *Journal,* June 18, 1904

ON THE TWELFTH ANNIVERSARY OF THE MURDERS, as it had for each of the prior eleven years, the Fall River *Globe* struck with fury at Lizzie:

August 4, 1904
A DOZEN YEARS
SINCE THE BORDENS WERE BRUTALLY BUTCHERED,
AND YET THE HORRIBLE CRIME IS UNPUNISHED.
PERHAPS MURDERER OR MURDERESS, MAY BE IN THE CITY—
WHO CAN TELL?

The long article which followed stretched down the *Globe*'s front page.

A dozen years!

What a long time it seems, yet how quickly passed in this busy, practical world, where so few people have the time to devote to retrospection or reflection, on all the good, and all the evil that is encompassed in the historic chronicle of such a period of time.

Twelve years ago this morning, when God's radiant sunshine was dispelling its August warmth, and casting its brilliant reflection over all in this peaceful community, the just and the unjust, the rich and the poor, the contented and the envious, the pharisee and publican, there sallied forth from the midsummer peace, on outrage bent, a demon in human form, whose quickly accomplished hellishness, was destined to make Fall River occupy a place in the centre of the stage under the entire country's observation, such as has been the misfortune of few civilized communities to stand in.

The *Globe* recalled every detail of the tragic morning as if exhorting the residents of Fall River never to forget that a disgrace to their lives had occurred which must someday be answered for.

The insinuations in the article left no doubt as to who had caused the murders:

Who that recalls that sultry, sickening gruesome day of an even dozen of years ago, will ever forget the day or the deed? . . . Who knows, even now, that the vile-minded murderer may not be at large in the community walking, stalking, or driving about in carriage or in car, seeking the opportunity to make new criminal history?

Perhaps the good people of Fall River may be daily meeting him—or her—in hall or store, or railroad train, and, oh, what a frightful contemplation there arises, if such be the fact, that it is due to the miscarriage of justice in the grand old State of Massachusetts, the cradle of liberty, of advancement, of just judges and of historic statesmen! And what a saddening and solemn reflection it must be for those who were near and dear to the murdered pair in life, to think that they have never been called upon to pay out that $5000 reward for the detection of the murderer, where they would have been so happy to spend that small portion of his hoarded wealth in hunting down those who robbed them of their father and mother—no, step-mother, please! . . . And how the good and kindly disposed people of the town were shocked to hear the people who know what they were talking about, mention their suspicions as to the identity of the murderer—or murderess! . . . Perhaps before another year rolls around, self-accusing conscience may have taken up the task laid down by the criminal law authorities of the state and the man—or woman—who shocked the people of two continents with one of the most ghastly, cruel, selfish, and brutal of double murders 12 years ago, deliver himself—or herself—into the hands of the avenging law, as an escaped criminal. Who can tell?

The Fall River *Globe* had always been Lizzie's greatest enemy. From the day after the murders, when it published Hiram Harrington's interview which strongly suggested that Lizzie had committed the crimes, the *Globe* had never ceased attempting to convict her in print.

It was 1904, early in the new century. Most of the police officers and officials involved had either died or faded into the past.

But Lizzie's trial had caused the press to focus continually on five men—Andrew Jennings, ex-Governor Robinson, William Knowlton, William Moody and Judge Dewey. During the thirteen days of testimony which led to Lizzie's acquittal, drawings and descriptions of them had appeared in every newspaper in the country:

Although frustrated in his attempts to convict Lizzie, Prosecutor Knowlton realized his ambitions. One year after the trial he replaced Arthur E. Pillsbury as Attorney General of the State of Massachusetts.

Ironically, Andrew Jennings succeeded Knowlton as District Attorney of Bristol County. In exchange for his defense of Lizzie, Jennings was named by Emma and Lizzie to the board of directors of the Globe Yarn Mill, a company Andrew Borden had owned.

Judge Dewey survived the attacks of his colleagues Judge Charles G. Davis and John H. Wigmore, and remained an associate justice until he died in 1900.

Governor Robinson returned to his private law practice in Chicopee, Massachusetts, after collecting his lavish fee of twenty-five thousand dollars.

William Moody, the impassioned young district attorney from Essex County who had assisted Knowlton, gained national prominence. In 1904 President Theodore Roosevelt appointed him Attorney General of the United States. Yet the Fall River *Globe* grimly reminded:

> He—or she—is enjoying at least the waking hours of daily life very much as the neighbors, well fed, well dressed, well waited on, however the still hours of the night may be passed, whether in the solace of refreshing slumber, or in the viewing of phantom pictures of the hideous scenes of twelve years ago this morning. Who can tell?

A savage strain of doggerel from an unknown source was being repeated in singsong by children who played in ghettos beneath The Hill. It was a simple quatrain which left no doubt that Lizzie had murdered her parents. Theodore Roosevelt had remarked that he was immensely amused when he first heard it.

There seemed to be no one who hadn't heard it, just as there was no one who did not accept it as fact:

Lizzie Borden took an axe
And gave her mother forty whacks;
When she saw what she had done
She gave her father forty-one.

Emma continued to wear black. She clothed her small, slim body in long, severe, silk dresses. Much of her time was spent on the second floor of Maplecroft in a white, cell-like room. In one closet she kept her few personal belongings, which included a fur coat for the winter. She rarely traveled and took no part in social activities.

Edith Coolidge Hart recalled Emma as being "colorless" with "no ambition, no particular interests." Prior to the murders she had seldom gone to services, but now she steadfastly attended the Central Congregational Church. It was seven blocks from French Street and each Sunday morning she walked there. Sitting alone in the Borden family pew, Emma prayed and sang hymns with the other members of the congregation. It was if she had blotted out all involvement with her terrible crimes. Religion had become her life.

She turned to the Reverend Jubb for spiritual guidance.

She and Alice Russell had parted, so she became increasingly friendly with the Reverend Jubb's sister.

Emma had never been a problem to the community. Even though she had defended Lizzie at the trial, her own innocence was never questioned. Those who knew her could only empathize with the terrible strain under which she had been placed as a result of her notorious sister.

The staff at Maplecroft was Lizzie's. There was a housekeeper, a cook, a second maid and a coachman. Besieged by reporters eager to concoct a story that they could explode into some bizarre revelation about her life, Lizzie ordered the glazed windows of the cellar barred so that no intruder could gain entrance.

Her neighbors were dismayed. Residents on The Hill did not put up bars over the windows of their houses.

In that basement, cut off from the world, surrounded by various small rooms for storage, she installed a billiards room with felt cue holders lining the walls.

On the second floor, the ceilings of all the rooms were covered in white linen, except for one: the front sunroom leading from Lizzie's bedchamber. It was done in gold leaf. The walls beneath it shimmered in chocolate brown wallpaper embossed with radiant pink flowers. In this room, which looked out over French Street, Lizzie kept the large library of leather-bound volumes which she had amassed over the years.

In the adjacent room, near her bed, was a brick fireplace. Into its cherry mahogany mantelpiece she had carved a phrase from a little-known Scottish poem: "In-my-ain-at-hame countrie." The verse of the poem went:

> The green leaf of loyalty's beginning to fall.
> The bonnie White Rose it is withering an' all.
> But I'll water it with the blood of usurping tyranny.
> And green it will grow in my ain countrie.

In 1901, Lizzie had thousands of pounds of stone carted to build a fireplace onto the back of the house. It became part of a private bedroom with a separate staircase she constructed to move her farther away from Emma's room and give her the seclusion to look out over the multitude of feeders below, where early morning visitations of cardinals, downy woodpeckers, catbirds, orioles and black-capped chickadees gathered.

But none of it fulfilled her. The restlessness which had grown over the years since her trial caused her to disappear from Fall River for days at a time. Alone, she slipped away to Washington, New York, and finally to Boston.

She made an attempt to depict herself more elegantly. Ridding herself forever of the raffish-sounding "Lizzie," she changed her name to Lizbeth A. Borden.

In Boston, a hack driver met her at the Back Bay Station and drove her to the Bellevue Hotel, near the State House. It was always the same driver, paid handsomely to remain at her disposal.

The staff at the Bellevue discreetly pretended not to know who she was.

Lizzie would leave in the morning to go out shopping. In the afternoon she would visit the art museums. Finally, by evening, she was ready for the theater.

The theater had always been her greatest love, ever since her trip to Europe, when she had seen Sarah Bernhardt and Lillie Langtry perform.

In February 1904 she attended a performance of *Macbeth* at Boston's Colonial Theatre. In the part of Lady Macbeth was an actress Lizzie had never seen before. She was cool and beautiful, a tall, light-haired young woman with haunting blue eyes. Onstage, as the young actress awakened to the demons she had unleashed by encouraging her husband to murder the king, she suddenly became fiery and incredibly emotional. The Boston *Daily Transcript* had remarked about the actress's ability to effect "a portrayal of supreme power, a rage bordering on madness."

Lizzie went back to see *Macbeth* again and again. As her fascination with the young actress grew she recklessly began to slide open the door that would place her pact with Emma in everlasting jeopardy.

Coincidentally, it was on a summer day in 1893, about the time of Lizzie's acquittal, that a nineteen-year-old stagestruck Oakland, California, teenager had arrived at the Alcazar Theater in San Francisco. The young lady's name was Gertrude Lamson. There was a new drama about to go into production and the young lady had brought with her a letter to the director, McKee Rankin, from a family acquaintance who was a newspaper critic. It read: "Here is a young friend of mine who wants to go on the stage. Kindly discourage her."

Rankin attempted to discourage her, but young Gertrude was insistent. Finally he allowed her to audition.

Within moments, she had the part.

Rankin had adapted a version of *Trilby* from the du Maurier novel.

Miss Lamson was signed to portray the heroine.

Shortly before the play's opening Gertrude decided to change her name, combining the names of two famous actresses, the eighteenth-century British actress Nance Oldfield, and the Irish Eliza O'Neill. When *Trilby* premiered in San Francisco on October 16, 1893, the billboard announced the debut of a new actress: Nance O'Neil.

The opening-night audience went into an uproar. The young woman had chosen to play one of the scenes, which took place in an artist's studio, with bare feet. McKee Rankin was promptly haled into court, where he finally agreed to drop the play from his repertoire.

But Nance O'Neil was undaunted. In 1896 she arrived in New York City in the smash hit play *True to Life.* The critic for the New York *Sun* raved: "Where has she gained her stage experience? New York has never heard of Nance O'Neil before, but surely the art of giving such a finely graduated performance does not come by instinct alone. But wherever she hails from, and whoever she may be, Miss O'Neil is an actress with a future."

The *New York Times* critic added: "I didn't expect such a wonderfully clever girl as Miss O'Neil proved herself to be. How anyone can call her crude passes any comprehension, unless crude means being perfectly natural, for that she certainly is, and may she remain so. Naturalness is one of the greatest charms of an actress, and one of the most rare as well."

At the age of twenty-two Nance began a tour of the country in the arduous role of Hedda Gabler. The critic for the St. Louis *Post Dispatch* was enthralled. He found her to be "a real woman. Her hair is tawny, her thick, well-refined eye-brows are brown, and there is a golden glint in her eyes—eyes that have not decided whether to be grey, green, blue or brown, but are soft, clear and expressive. Her mouth is small and exquisitely formed. She is probably five feet five inches tall, slender and graceful in figure. Her hands are small and soft, and crumple like rose leaves in her grasp."

In 1899, she left the United States and traveled to Australia, where she was immediately acclaimed as one of the great actresses in the world, to New Zealand, South Africa and Egypt, where she appeared by royal command before the khedive in Cairo.

Her next challenge was London. On September 1, 1902, she opened at the Adelphi Theatre in the title role of Sudermann's *Magda.* The critic for the London *Sphere* remarked: "Miss Nance O'Neil made a daring attempt at the Adelphi Theatre on Monday by challenging comparison with Eleanora Duse, Sarah Bernhardt and Mrs. Patrick Campbell in the role of Magda. But her boldness won, and the audience, inclined to be critical at the outset, was fairly conquered."

One week later, when she starred in Giacometti's tragedy *Elizabeth, Queen of England,* the London *Morning Post* added to the accolades: "Miss O'Neil showed that she had fully grasped the character of the great Queen. She played with a passion and often with a subtlety that completely captured her audience."

When Nance traveled to Boston in October 1903, a reporter from the Boston *Herald* asked to visit her in her hotel suite. He found her sitting in the middle of the floor having a romp with her pets, a Boston terrier and an Angora cat. She invited the reporter to join in the revel. He later commented: "In her sun-flooded apartments her masses of glorious golden hair were caught loosely on the top of her shapely head, and held in place by a huge Spanish comb. Nance O'Neil is not always tragic, nor even serious-minded. She impresses one from the start as a girl, a very, very young girl. She is as unaffected by her great success as a child. It may be truthfully said that she is even more interesting personally than she is as an actress—and that is saying a very great deal."

The *Herald* reporter asked her why she never smiled onstage.

She replied, "I can't very well tell why. I have a sense of humor, though people may not believe it, and I love fun, though I may not appear to. But in most of my plays I have no occasion to smile. I am usually in tears."

The reporter concluded: "She is subject to melancholy. She is decidedly moody in temperament. There is a constant intermingling of sunshine and shadow in her nature. And it is this that makes her so entirely fascinating."

She told the reporter that Lady Macbeth was to be her greatest challenge. She would be opening at the Colonial Theatre in Boston on February 23, 1904.

This is the performance that Lizzie attended—and fell in love with her.

It was not until six months later, at a large summer hotel in Tyngsboro, Massachusetts, that Lizzie finally met her idolized Nance. The young actress, about to star in a new play, *Judith,* at Boston's Tremont Theatre, had purchased a beautiful summer home nearby, known as the Brindley Farm.

She barely could afford the down payment.

Despite her successes, she was in desperate need of money.

Her finances, managed by her mentor, McKee Rankin, were in chaos. Most of the expenses of the acting company in which she toured had been deducted from her share of the profits. In December 1903, all of her properties and costumes had been attached by a theatrical manager in Chicago, William Cleveland, who charged that she and Rankin had defrauded him of several hundred dollars.

She had been forced to borrow money to open in Boston. Heavily in debt, she was now being sued by E. J. Ratcliff, a Boston manager, for commissions he claimed she owed him when he attempted to raise money for her company.

Nance and Lizzie hit it off immediately. Lizzie was so taken with her that she began to shower her with gifts. Finally she not only paid Nance's legal expenses in the suit instituted by Ratcliff but followed her into the courtroom throughout the proceedings.

The two women became inseparable.

Nance could be as unpredictable and rebellious as Lizzie, yet there was a difference. She was from the West and possessed neither the Puritanical moralism nor the tense prudishness of a New Englander. She was endowed with many of the traits of those performers and writers who had grown up in San Francisco in the turbulent years following the Gold Rush—such wildly eccentric, colorful figures as Isadora Duncan, Ambrose Bierce, Jack London and David Belasco. Like them, Nance was fiery and uncontrollably passionate. She plunged forward into her art with such blinding emotionalism that she abandoned much of what was considered to be a normal style of living for a young woman in the early 1900s. She admitted to a reporter: "I have ground my very soul to get as far as I have on the stage. A home life? —that is ever a tender spot with me. It is one of the vain regrets of my life. I have schooled myself to say to all who talk to me about a home life, that I have no thoughts about home life."

Emma despised Nance. As the intimacy between Lizzie and Nance grew, Emma became more resentful. There was ample priggishness in her nature to cause her to look down on Lizzie's new-found friend. Even though a woman working in the theater might be admired while on the stage, in New England there existed a caste system which prohibited her from ever being socially acceptable. Indigenous to the Puritan-Quaker ethic was an attitude which still regarded an actress as a loose woman.

But perhaps, what most disturbed Emma was that Lizzie, in a trusting moment, might reveal what had actually occurred on that morning of August 4th, 1892.

Emma was haunted by the constant publicity which Lizzie had attracted in the decade following the murders.

The world would not forget.

In Emma's eyes, her pact with Lizzie had withstood the trial, the condemnations, the waves of newspaper articles and even Lizzie's own thoughtless behavior, which led to the Tilden-Thurber incident. But the liaison with Nance was a different matter. It was more than an act of betrayal. It was an agonizing threat.

Finally, after several months, Lizzie's invitation to Nance to stay with her in Fall River was more than Emma could bear. Emma had attempted to isolate herself in her cell-like, colorless void on the second floor of Maplecroft when Lizzie delivered the final blow.

One night Lizzie threw a tremendous party for Nance and her whole company. Caterers arrived with trays of rich food, there were hired palm trees and an orchestra. Gaslight chandeliers fashioned of brass and crystal and flowery gilt lamps blazed through white scalloped shades illuminating the inner walls, the intricate-patterned doorknobs and ornate tin ceilings. Maplecroft blared with music. It was the fulfillment of Lizzie's dreams: the lavish home that as a child she never had, filled with interesting, exotic, talented people.

Emma was in a fury. That night she left.

For a while she stayed with the Reverend Jubb's sister, and then with friends in Fairhaven. Finally she moved to the Minden House, a residential hotel in Providence.

Meanwhile Lizzie was thoroughly entranced by the aura of the woman she adored. She followed Nance to Tyngsboro, where the merriment continued. Subsequent reports of raucous behavior and alcoholic improprieties reached the establishment of Fall River and were discussed by members of the W.C.T.U., of which Lizzie had once been a member.

There were people in Fall River who had become suspicious of Lizzie. The rumor quickly spread that her relationship with Nance was a blatant homosexual affair.

Lizzie made no attempt to conceal her feelings for the desirable young actress. In June 1905, one year after their meeting, a provocative article appeared in newspapers across the country:

LIZZIE BORDEN TO BE A PLAYWRIGHT

Woman Once Tried for Murder Makes Friends With Nance O'Neil—Sister Leaves Home.

ECHO OF FALL RIVER TRAGEDY

(Special Dispatch to The Morning Telegraph.)

FALL RIVER, Mass., June 4.

Emma and Lizzie Borden have parted company.

After being tried for murder together, and clinging to each other for many years, although of widely different tastes and wholly antagonistic temperaments, they have agreed to disagree, and Emma has removed her belongings from the French street house.

The stage is held responsible—

Lizzie is said to be a warm friend of Nance O'Neil, for whom she is writing a play. Once Lizzie entertained Miss O'Neil's whole company at midnight, to which Emma, who is puritanic and austere, objected vigorously.

A few days later the differences culminated in the separation, which is believed to be permanent.

The entertainment given to Miss O'Neil's company is said to have been of the quietest character. Lizzie Borden is a woman of rare accomplishments, and her wealth and isolation from the society in which she moved before her father's death, have enabled her to read much and travel extensively. She is an inveterate playgoer. No hint is given of the character of the play she is to write.

It was never revealed what Lizzie's play was about, but it would have been a sensation if it had been autobiographical.

Just as Lizzie identified with Nance, as both an actress and a wondrously free-spirited woman, Nance must have recognized in Lizzie elements of the tragic women she had portrayed.

In a magazine article which she wrote sometime later, Nance's analysis of such women could easily have described Lizzie: "Someone has pointed out to me recently that I have nearly always interpreted the unloved woman in the theatre, the woman crucified by the unseen, the conventional traditions. . . . Often in women who live out their destinies in the small places into which they have been driven, there is a storm that broods but never bursts."

With a sudden outpouring of anger, Nance included herself as one of these women: "With the blind intuition that children sometimes have, I wrote in my first diary this defiant rule of life: *'Better an outlaw than not free.'* We are rebels because those who govern us often, blindly, no doubt, betray us. The unloved woman is usually just such, the victim of some man too stupid to know the difference between heaven and earth."

Two months after the article mentioning Lizzie's friendship with Nance and the play she was writing, the Fall River *Globe* went after Lizzie again.

It was the thirteenth anniversary of the Borden murders, and for the first time the antagonistic *Globe* revealed a sardonic sense of humor:

August 4, 1905
GREAT WRONG
IS RIGHTED AFTER 13 YEARS OF MISREPRESENTATION.
NO MURDERS WERE COMMITTED ON AUGUST 4, 1892,
DESPITE THE BELIEF THAT ANDREW AND ABBY
BORDEN DIED IN THAT MANNER.

As usual, the long article that followed stretched the length of the *Globe*'s front page—but this time it was laced with gallows wit:

THIRTEEN YEARS!
THIRTEEN YEARS AGO TODAY!!

How time does fly and how well that fact is comprehended when intelligent men and women, if blessed with memory, recall that on the fourth day of August, 1892—thirteen years ago today—when the midsummer sun was scorching and shrivelling up everything from dandelion boutonnieres to straw hats and peek-a-boo waists, the town was terribly shocked and startled by the false but frightful alarm of murder, which went forth at midday from the Second Street home of the late Andrew J. and Abby Drew Borden!

How the intense excitement grew and the wonder, too, that on that peaceful August morning, there should have been human beings existing in this orderly community so lost to the manifold considerations of truth and honor, as to have given credence to the foul and baseless rumors of inhuman slaughter, that flashed through the city like wildfire wherein it was alleged that a man—or a woman—had raised the blood-stained hand of brutal violence and cut off the mortal career of two unoffending and reputable members of society.

Perhaps the city and its reputation have never suffered more vindictive, unwarranted and libellous assaults upon their stainless honor, than by the unbridled tongues of such people, as at that time gave circulation to the vile calumny that an axe had been swung by the strong and vengeful arm of some demoniac man—or woman—bent on murder and with mercenary motive.

And why, it will be asked, were such calumnies circulated, and such monstrous stories told when there was neither shadow nor substance on which to base them?"

After summoning up the familiar litany of details surrounding the deaths and poking fun at Bridget ("who had taken an overdose of morphine pills and could see and hear nothing"), the enormous breakfast of mutton and pears ("Why couldn't the provider of the household loosen up to the extent of a porterhouse steak, French fried potatoes and mushrooms as a wholesome, refreshing and welcome change?") and the witnesses ("Has Lubinsky ever come forward to confess? No he's never been heard of this side of Poland from that day to this"), the *Globe* zeroed in on Lizzie:

There was no cause for murder. There was nobody who could profit by any such crime. No man—or woman—has ever secured possession of a single cent as the result of the deaths. Not one. No man—or woman—has entered into the realms of swell society, or is likely to as a result of the passing from earth's troubles of the old fashioned home loving and plain mannered Bordens. Not one?

The article ended with a final admonition:

The Globe suggests that its readers forget the past with its cruel errors of judgment, and its suspicions of pure and lofty souls and remember just this one thing for all time:

THERE WERE NO BORDEN MURDERS!
BOTH THE VICTIMS OF 13 YEARS AGO
DIED AS THE RESULT OF EXCESSIVE HEAT!

18

THE LITTLE MOTHER

Is this sort of thing to last forever? Is murder really the safest of all crimes? Is society powerless to help itself? Is the law necessarily a terror to evil-doers only when their evil doings are completely trivial?

—Boston *Daily Advertiser*,
June 15, 1893

"Several years ago I played all of one season at three of the principal Boston theatres, the Tremont, Colonial and Hollis Street."

—Nance O'Neil

AFTER YEARS OF TOURING the country on her own, Nance was suddenly "discovered" by David Belasco. The famed director had lost his major leading lady, Mrs. Leslie Carter, and immediately needed a star to replace her.

Belasco offered Nance a part in his new play, *The Lily,* with the stipulation that he sign her to an exclusive contract so that he could manage her career.

In order to join with Belasco, in December 1909, Nance parted from McKee Rankin, the director who had first hired her, years before at the Alcazar Theater in San Francisco. Rankin immediately sued in the Superior Court in New York City.

The New York Times reported: "Counsel for Miss O'Neil contended that Mr. Rankin had no claim on her exclusive management. Mr. Rankin, counsel said, had borrowed money on her jewels, and the last thing he did was to require seventy-five dollars a week from her."

Finally Belasco settled with Rankin for Nance's contract.

Nance had dropped Lizzie from her life as well.

There is no evidence as to what occurred between the two women, except that Nance's financial condition had continued to worsen. When in February 1906 the mortgage for Brindley Farm in Tyngsboro was due, Lizzie did not assist her. Nance lost the farm because she could not come up with the $7,500 necessary to avoid foreclosure.

Possibly her association with someone as notorious as Lizzie had finally troubled her to the point that she saw it as being detrimental to her career. Or perhaps she eventually felt so stifled that she had to free herself from any trace of that New England temperament which looked upon both actresses and unconvicted murderesses as social pariahs. In an interview Nance admitted that originally she had gone to New England because, being from the West, the people fascinated her—their speech patterns and pronouncements—she had wanted "to study them. . . . I've got to lay bare one of the real secrets of my life—Every evening when the train came bringing me home from Boston, the one long street I had to walk to reach home was lined with the 'blue-nosed' inhabitants. Hundreds and hundreds of them were lined up inside gates to 'see that actress woman pass.' And some of their audible comments did not endear any of them to me. So one day I gathered my pets and belongings and moved back to the hotel in Boston. I had not studied them, while they had torn me to shreds."

The two sisters had not spoken to each other since the night Lizzie had given the festive party for Nance, and Emma had departed from Maplecroft in a rage.

Emma gave some explanation as to what had happened to Edwin J. Maguire, a reporter for the Boston *Sunday Post.*

It was 1913, the twentieth anniversary of Lizzie's world-famous murder trial.

At first Maguire attempted to see Lizzie. As he approached Maplecroft he noticed that the shades were drawn on all the windows. Repeatedly he rang the front and rear doorbells, but there was no response.

Leaving the house, he found a telephone. When he called, the maid summoned Lizzie to the phone.

Maguire asked if he could come and see her, but Lizzie curtly let him know that she had nothing to say. When he further urged her, she slammed down the phone.

Fortunately Maguire was persistent. He learned that Emma was staying in Fall River at the home of Reverend Buck. Obviously Maguire was aware of what he was on to when he called at the house on Rock Street adjacent to the Central Congregational Church.

What follows is an incredible interview. As the reporter commented, Emma's statement "is the first declaration to the outside world that either sister has made regarding that most notable murder mystery—a butchery on which the faintest light is yet to be shed."

In Emma, he saw "a gentle-mannered woman, who unhesitatingly led the way from the front portal of the Buck residence to the quaint parlor at the left. She was courtesy and gentility personified. Her tranquil face, sweet of expression and enhanced by a pink and white complexion that a debutante might envy, was crowned with heavy, snow white hair, parted in the center and rippling to the side of the head in curly billows. There was a look of sadness, even of resignation in Miss Borden's large brown eyes. They seemed to reflect the sorrow and grief that were part of the heritage she received through the untimely death of her father. A gray dress, rich in material, but unostentatious in style, bespoke the quiet, retiring character of the woman. . . . The parlor in which the *Post* representative interviewed Miss Borden seemed consecrated to the memory of the Rev. Mr. Buck, who was one of the most beloved clergymen in Fall River. . . . On the walls of the room, which during Rev. Mr. Buck's lifetime had served as his study, hung framed scriptural texts and religious paintings. One of the latter was 'The Last Supper.' Another art work dealt with angels and cherubs. On tables and shelves were religious volumes and pamphlets."

Within this demure sanctuary Emma admitted to Maguire that the Reverend Buck was "my best friend in the world." It was he "who advised me when matters reached such a pass that I could not stay longer in the same house with Lizzie."

Why had she parted from her sister?

Emma refused to divulge the details. However, she commented, "I did not go until conditions became absolutely unbearable. . . . I consulted Reverend Buck . . . after listening to my story he said it was imperative that I should make my home elsewhere. . . . Under the agreement we entered into, Lizzie is to occupy the house as long as she lives, and is to pay me rent for the use of my half." She added:

"I do not expect ever to set foot on the place while she lives."

When Maguire asked her about the stories involving Lizzie with Nance O'Neil, Emma had a ready answer: "Nance O'Neil has for years been a close friend of Lizzie, and she holds that relation to this very day."*

With that, Emma decided to set the record straight regarding the inheritance: "Someone, who knows more about the Borden estate than I and my sister do, has declared that our combined wealth would go over the million mark. Now here is the truth in respect to that. If all the property that we owned jointly should, through our lawyers, be turned into cash, the total amount of our worldly possessions would not go beyond one-quarter of a million dollars.† That is a large amount of money, but is certainly less than a million."

At this point it would seem incongruous that Emma, after twenty-one years, could be so open in her remarks to a member of the press: "The day the crime took place I was at Fairhaven on a visit to friends, I hurried home in response to a telegram, and one of the first persons I met was Lizzie. She was very much affected. Later, when veiled accusations began to be made, she came to me and said, 'Emma, it is awful for them to say that I killed poor father and our stepmother. You know that I would not dream of such an awful thing, Emma.' Later, after her arrest and during her trial, Lizzie many times reiterated her protest of innocence to me. And after her acquittal she declared her guiltlessness during conversations that we had at the French Street mansion. Here is the strongest thing that has convinced me of Lizzie's innocence. The authorities never found the axe or whatever implement it was that figured in the killing. Lizzie, if she had done that deed, could never have hidden the instrument of death so that the police could not find it. Why, there was no hiding palce in the old house that would serve for effectual concealment. Neither did she have the time."

Thus far, the purpose of Emma's words seemed to be that she intended to defend Lizzie. But gradually it became apparent that Emma was attempting to unburden her own feelings: "Perhaps people wondered why I stood so staunchly by Lizzie during the trial. I'll tell them why. Aside from my feeling as a sister, it was because I constantly had in mind our dear mother. She died when Lizzie was only three years of age, while I had reached twelve years. When my darling

*It is questionable how Emma could know this. She had not spoken to Lizzie in nine years and most probably she had no occasion to communicate with Nance.

†In actuality, Emma's personal fortune alone had grown to almost twice that amount.

mother was on her deathbed she summoned me, and exacted a promise that I would always watch over 'baby Lizzie.' From childhood to womanhood and up to the time the murder occurred, I tried to safeguard Lizzie. . . ."

Again, she mentioned the promise she had made to her mother, *that she would care for Lizzie as if she were her own child:* "I did my duty at the time of the trial and I am still going to do it in defending my sister even though circumstances have separated us. The vision of my dear mother always is bright in my mind. I want to feel that when Mother and I meet in the hereafter, she will tell me that I was faithful to her trust and that I looked after 'baby Lizzie' to the best of my ability."

Unexpectedly the impact of her own words seemed to drastically affect her. As Edwin Maguire watched, Emma's voice became a low moan. And then a howl. Convulsively she began to sob. Clutching the arm of the low rocking chair she abruptly stood up. She began pacing to and fro, attempting to control herself by pressing a black-bordered handkerchief against her lips.

Maguire noted that, "For several minutes the paroxysm of grief continued. Then the little figure straightened slowly to dignified posture, the remaining traces of tears were removed by soft dabs of the handkerchief, and Miss Borden became quite herself once more."

Quietly, she went on. "I intend to defend Lizzie against the harsh public so that Mother will say I have been Faithful to my trust. . . . Every Memorial Day I carry flowers to Father's grave. And Lizzie does not forget him. But she generally sends her tribute by a florist."

Suddenly Emma asked that he leave. The interview was over.

As she led him to the door, Maguire commented that Emma "murmured, as if to herself: 'Though we must live as strangers . . . I am still the little mother. . . .' "

19

NEWMARKET

> The preposterous trial that followed the slaughter in the Borden house focused and held the eyes of this country as no other trial ever did before or since. . . . there were those who felt it was not humanly possible for this young woman, with all the bad will in the world, to have accomplished the murder and effaced every evidence of her guilt in the few fleeting moments when no eye was on her. There were as many others who found it even harder to imagine how some motiveless stranger could have entered, struck, and gone his way without Lizzie seeing or hearing him. . . . this cleavage of opinion has persisted to this day and it is that which has kept the Borden case alive long after those who attended the trial had themselves followed old man Borden to the churchyard.
>
> —Alexander Woollcott, *Vanity Fair*, 1927

IT WAS THE MIDDLE OF THE JAZZ AGE, 1925.

Cecil B. De Mille had completed his spectacular *The Ten Commandments* and Rudolph Valentino, after a two-year absence, returned to the screen in *Monsieur Beaucaire.* On June 12th, Mussolini declared Facism to be a religion, a denial of which was, in his words, "a sin against the light."

England's Chancellor of the Exchequer, Winston Churchill, announced to the British Parliament a return to the gold standard, which immediately enhanced Britain's credit and prestige, causing the sterling bill to again replace the dollar bill as the international medium of commercial payment.

Following a special investigation, the Department of Research and Education of the Federal Council of Churches of Christ in America declared that as a result of national Prohibition, juvenile drinking had increased and respect for law decreased. But that the conditions and the morale of workers were vastly improved. . . . Women wore shorter skirts, knee-length evening gowns, straight, long-waisted dresses and shingled hair. . . . George Gershwin was completing his "Concerto in F" to be performed in December in New York City. . . . F. Scott Fitzgerald's novel *The Great Gatsby* had just been published. . . . London's theatergoers were attending Noël Coward's new play *The Vortex*. . . . Radio had become the craze, and Americans were going to the movies at an average of once a week. . . .

Although defended by famed criminal attorney Clarence Darrow, on July 21st, John T. Scopes, a biology teacher, was found guilty of teaching evolution in a high school in Dayton, Tennessee. Darrow's opponent, William Jennings Bryan, declared that the "evolutionists" and their religious co-workers, the "modernists," were leading the modern world "to perdition."

Nance O'Neil's opening in New York in Louis Bromfield's new play *The House of Women* caused *The New York Times* drama critic Brooks Atkinson to observe: "That cliché of the reviewing trade, a 'triumph,' inevitably turns up in any complete description of Miss O'Neil's acting." Percy Hammond of the New York *Herald Tribune* concurred: "Nance O'Neil gives a performance that is deeply moving. . . . her present part is one of the best this fine actress has had in years."

Jack Dempsey was preparing for his fight with Gene Tunney. . . . On September 20th, Bill Tilden won the National Singles Tennis Championship. . . .

In October, newspapers noted that a legal battle had erupted in Taunton, Massachusetts, between attorneys for Emma and Lizzie Borden.

Emma was attempting to sell her share in the A. J. Borden Building, once owned by her father, located in the center of Fall River's business district at South Main and Anawan streets. Andrew Borden had built the building two years before his murder in 1892. Emma had petitioned the Probate Court at Taunton to sell the property and make an equal distribution between herself and Lizzie.

The significant fact was that the world had not forgotten Lizzie Borden. The news articles that were immediately published revived the story of her trial as if it had just occurred, despite the fact that the participants—Andrew Jennings, Hosea Knowlton, Governor Robinson, William Moody, Alice Russell, Adelaide Churchill, Dr. Bowen, the detectives, the police patrolmen, the medical examiners—all were deceased.

Lizzie personally appeared in the Taunton courtroom.

She was sixty-six years old, corpulent, white-haired and elderly, wearing tiny wire-rimmed glasses.

She was furious at Emma for attempting to have the building sold. Like her father, she felt that the roots of the Borden name should be held intact. That was the reason she had stayed in Fall River all these years, despite the reproach of her neighbors. Above all, she considered herself a Borden. Her family had founded the town.

As reporters descended upon Taunton, Lizzie quietly bought Emma out.

Even though Fall River's condemnatory view of Lizzie had not wavered in three decades, one young neighbor, Russell Lake, liked her: "She made a big hit with me by being my best customer when I had a lemonade stand. Later on, when I left for boarding school, she gave me my first fifty cents. I was one of the privileged children who could run through her yard and climb over the stone wall to get away from the neighborhood bully. . . . Most other children reflected their parents' views and treated Miss Borden and her house like she was a witch or some person to fear."

Lizzie chose her visitors carefully.

She had surrounded Maplecroft and its lawned yard by a wrought-iron fence with a locked gate. Her driveway led back to a sleek, windowed coach house, wood paneled inside, where she kept her black Packard limousine. Closeted in one corner was a gas pump, the only private one in town. Edith Coolidge Hart recalled, "Many times I saw her in her automobile, driving around Fall River. Her face was always set in a glum, unhappy pattern." Librarian Helen Leighton had become one of her few friends. To her Lizzie spoke longingly of how lovely it had been to take trips to Boston, to New York, to Washington, to be in places where nobody recognized her.

Animals became Lizzie's passion, especially the helpless, the orphaned, the abused. There were always several cats and litters of kittens around Maplecroft. She purchased peanuts regularly and put them on the lawn for the squirrels. She took in stray dogs and when they died had them buried in Pine Ridge Cemetery of the Animal Rescue League, near a marker she erected which read SLEEPING AWHILE.

Occasionally, she would allow a number of children to wander through her backyard reciting the poetry of Tennyson and Longfellow. Lizzie would listen from an enclosed porch. If it was a cold day, she would invite them in. Some would be too afraid, but to the few who were brave she would offer cups of hot chocolate.

Russell Lake recalled that as he grew older—". . . I still continued to go across the street to visit with Miss Borden whenever I came home from boarding school. . . . she was very generous and kind to anyone who worked for her or was associated with her. A Mrs. McFarland was Miss Borden's dressmaker, as well as my mother's. I know that Miss Borden helped her out financially. Miss Borden also helped her coachman buy a house. Mother told me she also helped his children through college. . . . as kind and good a woman as Miss Borden could never have committed such a gruesome murder. . . . It would have to be done by someone with a great hatred and absolutely furious at their victims. . . . Miss Borden was never that kind of person."

By railroad, the tiny town of Newmarket, New Hampshire, was one hundred and twenty-nine miles from Fall River. Although reachable by departing from Boston's North Station on the Boston and Maine Railroad Line which steamed upward through Haverhill, Newton and Kensington, Newmarket was not a place that one would normally visit.

The population was little more than a thousand and it was far enough removed from the seaside resort of Hampton Beach or the main thoroughfares to Boston and Portsmouth to preclude travelers from passing through. It was quietly withdrawn, hidden away amid green rolling farms that had been cultivated by English settlers in the 1600s.

On Main Street, near the railroad tracks leading through the center of town, stood a large, white, two-story house, situated on three-fourths of an acre of land. On November 9, 1915, according to the official records kept in the county courthouse in nearby Rockingham, this wooden frame Victorian home was purchased from its owner, George K. Leavitt, by a Miss Mary Connor for $2,500.

But there were certain puzzling elements surrounding the purchase. Mary Connor and her sister, Annie Connor, were middle-aged spinsters who had lived all their lives on a sixty-five-acre farm in Wadleigh Falls, New Hampshire, approximately two miles down the road from Newmarket. Neither of the Connor sisters was employed and between them they possessed only a small inheritance left by their father, Patrick J. Connor, amounting to a few hundred dollars. Consequently, there seemed to be no practical reason why the eldest sister, Mary, should suddenly purchase a second residence for her sister and herself—a much larger house in town—while continuing to own and pay taxes on their farm and residence in Wadleigh Falls.

Immediately after the Connor sisters moved into their new house, in 1916, a third woman, whom no one in the town had ever seen before, quietly joined them, taking over the second-floor front bedroom facing the street. Her identity was unknown, or, as one long-time resident, Sylvia Fitts Getchell, expressed it, "No one made it their business to know who she was."

The mysterious woman never appeared in public, although she immediately had installed a modern bathroom leading from her second floor bedroom, and steam heating throughout the house. The Connor sisters drove the parcel wagon to Newmarket and did all the shopping while the identity of the woman living with them remained a secret.

And then postman Robert Bennett began receiving letters addressed to her.

It took some time, however, before the residents of Newmarket began to realize that the stranger sharing the house with Mary and Annie Connor was Emma Borden, sister of the notorious Lizzie Borden of Fall River, Massachusetts.

Thirteen-year-old Royce Carpenter, who lived down the road from the house, did chores for Mary and Annie Connor. At the back of the house was a barn where the Connors kept their two Jersey cows, which Royce milked in the afternoon when he came home from school. Cluthing two metal pails, Royce would carry the warm milk from the barn into the kitchen. There his job was to churn the milk to get the butterfat out.

He remembered Emma sitting in the rocking chair, her dark eyes watching him as he entered the house.

Royce never saw her wear black. He recalled that she dressed in the pale-colored shifts which were fashionable at the time. Her hair was mostly white, done up on top of her head. As he came through the door she would nod—he always had the feeling that she was studying him closely.

They never met, they never had a conversation, yet he remembered, "Somehow she knew my name—she always called me Royce."

George Bennett, brother of the postman, Robert, often visited the Connor sisters, as he had been their neighbor in Wadleigh Falls. He recalled that Mary and Annie were maiden ladies and that Annie dressed well and was very friendly. Mary was pale and on in years, while Annie had a rosy Irish face.

If he should drop in unexpectedly, he remembered, "that lady living with them would instantly slip away and disappear up the stairs."

Afterward, George Bennett would sit chatting with the two sisters in their kitchen, aware that the mysterious woman was on the floor above.

He recalled that "she never came down, though, or made an appearance."

But it was through the eyes of a young girl who lived across the street from the Connor house that Emma made the most haunting impression. Eva Edgeley was seventeen. There was a screened-in porch on the side of the house where Emma sat day after day, watching the street.

Finally, Eva would notice Emma slip out through the screen door and stand for several moments in front of the house. But she never came out in the daytime.

Dressed in black, she would appear only at dusk.

"She was alone, always alone," Eva remembered.

When one chooses anonymity, what are the reasons?

Are they to avoid the glare of public curiosity, or do they sometimes go deeper?

Could they be to hide from the repercussions of an act which must one day be found out?

Why did Emma choose to hide herself?

Could she have suspected that the unsolved murders of her father and stepmother might prompt someone, someday, to persistently pursue the long-overdue, but obvious question: Who else had a motive beside Lizzie?

In 1921, Mary Connor died. At the time of probate, when it was revealed that Mary's entire financial worth was $365 in savings, her younger sister, Annie, made an astonishing statement.

She maintained that Mary had only put up $500 for the purchase of the house in Newmarket.

It was to Emma's advantage to conceal the details of her arrangement with the Connor sisters. Newmarket, an obscure little town where no one knew her, was where she had chosen to hide from the world. As Annie's constant guest, Emma's shadowy presence occupied the house, while she maintained her official address at the Minden House in Providence.

Two mornings a year, once in the spring and once in the fall, a sedan picked her up and took her to the Jordan Marsh department store in Boston.

The car returned with her late the same evening.

Jordan Marsh was where Emma kept her fur coat in storage.

Ione Kent lived nearby and was well acquainted with Annie Connor. At different times she had asked Annie about the woman living with her, and finally Annie confirmed the fact that it was Lizzie Borden's sister. Annie disclosed two peculiarities about Emma, which Ione never forgot.

The first was that Emma was addicted to cubes of sugar, which she sucked on continually.

The second facet of information was more disturbing. When Emma moved into the house, besides installing an upstairs bathroom and steam heating, she paid for the construction of a second stairway down the back of the house to the kitchen.

The stairway was hidden by a closet door, beside which was a narrow auxiliary pantry where a large axe was kept for chopping wood.

On the wall next to the pantry was an extremely unusual lighting panel, which could instantly illuminate the entire downstairs.*

It was a protective measure.

"*One night they will come for me,*" Emma told Annie in terror.

Startled by the revelation, Ione pressed Annie as to who *they* were.

Annie admitted that she did not know.

*Author's note: Through the courtesy of the present owner of the house I saw both the hidden stairway and the light panel which Emma installed. With a single movement, the panel lights the foyer, parlor, living room, hallways, kitchen, dining room, porch and front of the house.

20

DEATH

IN 1926, LIZZIE ENTERED TRUESDALE HOSPITAL in Fall River for a gallbladder operation.

The astonishing fact was that she had herself admitted under the pseudonym Emma Borden of the Hotel Biltmore, Providence.

Her attempt at disguising who she was proved ineffective. Finally, the south corridor of one floor had to be cleared for her privacy.

The nurses found her an uncooperative patient. They had difficulty keeping Lizzie, her bed or her room in proper hospital order. She would not eat the food. Perhaps she experienced the same abhorrence for institutional food that she had felt years before while imprisoned in the Taunton Jail. Her chauffeur brought her daily rations from Laura Carr's, a well-known caterer in Providence, fourteen miles away.

Lizzie's favorite delicacy was orange sherbet.

A Fall River lady who was in the hospital at the same time had just given birth to her second daughter.

Lizzie asked to see the infant.

As Lizzie caressed her, she remarked to the nurses present that it was the first baby she had ever held.

After several months, Lizzie returned to Maplecroft, but she never recovered from the operation.

She suffered drastic complications on the night of June 1, 1927.

. . .

Emma had no idea that Lizzie was dying. . . .

The sea breeze from Hampton Beach was cut off by the tall pine trees which circled the tiny town of Newmarket, with its farms, its one church, its railroad station. The summer night was warm and still.

During the early morning hours of June 2nd, the moon and stars had faded into the thick, New Hampshire sky.

The night before, her sleep had been interrupted by delusions and wild, frightening dreams.

Dr. Towle had given her a sedative.

Now, once again, Emma awoke as she heard a noise on the first floor.

She was certain that someone was breaking into the house.

Overcome by dread, the seventy-six-year-old woman wrenched herself up out of her bed, got to her feet and crept silently through Annie Connor's back bedroom. Annie appeared to be asleep as Emma started down the dark stairway leading to the kitchen. She knew that she had to reach the bottom of the stairs and the central panel of switches, which would flood the first floor with light.

Next to the panel of switches was the auxiliary pantry with the axe.

She descended the steps one by one. There was no banister and the stairway curved and narrowed. Halfway down she lost her footing and plunged the rest of the way.

She hit the bottom and shattered her hip.

The night was pitch-black.

There was no sound except Emma's helpless whining, which Annie heard, and went to assist her.

Lizzie died on the morning of June 2nd.

The Fall River *Globe* published her obituary and for the first time wrote about her with no hint of condemnation or malice:

June 2, 1927

LIZBETH BORDEN

DIES AFTER SHORT ILLNESS, AGE 68

Miss Lizbeth A. Borden died this morning at 306 French Street, where she had made her home for about 30 years. She had been ill with pneumonia for about a week, although for some time she had been in failing health.

A member of one of the old Fall River families, having been the daughter of Andrew J. and Sarah (Anthony) Borden, she had lived here all of her life. With her two maids she lived a quiet, retired life, paying occasional visits to out-of-town friends and receiving a few callers, whose staunch friendship she valued highly.

Taking an intense pride in the surroundings in which she lived, she did much to improve the locality, purchasing adjoining property that the same refined atmosphere might be maintained. Greatly interested in nature, she was daily seen providing for the hundreds of birds that frequented the trees in her yard, taking care that the shallow box where they gathered was filled with crumbs, seeds and other foods that they favored. She had miniature houses erected in her trees, and in these, frivolous squirrels made their homes. Her figure as she visited with her wild callers, many of whom became so friendly that they never seemed to mind her approach, was a familiar one in that section.

Another pastime in which she greatly delighted was riding through the country roads and lanes. She made frequent trips about the town in her motor car but was never so pleased as when winding through the shady country by-ways.

Surviving Miss Borden is a sister, Miss Emma Borden of New Hampshire, formerly of Providence.

The obituary in *The New York Times* was longer and more pointed, going into great detail about the murders and Lizzie's trial. Toward the end of the obituary, Lizzie was misquoted: "Miss Borden testified that she was not in the house at the time of the murders. She said that Mr. and Mrs. Borden were alive when she went out to the barn to look for some fishing tackle, and when she returned, she found them dead. Her sister, it was established, was away on an errand."

At no time had Lizzie stated that both her father and stepmother were alive when she went out to the barn and dead when she returned.

And it was never "established"—only accepted—that her sister was away. In thirty-five years the facts had faded out of focus.

Mrs. Vida Pearson Turner sang in the choir at the Congregational Church on Rock Street. On the night before Lizzie Borden's funeral she received a call from the undertaker asking her to come to Lizzie's home on French Street the following morning to sing "In My Ain Countrie."

When Vida Turner arrived at Maplecroft the undertaker unlocked the door, let her in and locked the door immediately.

Mrs. Turner was startled. The house was empty except for the two of them.

She was led into the parlor—where the undertaker left her.

All alone, Mrs. Turner was surrounded by Lizzie's crystal, scalloped sconces, exotic flowered walls and white linen ceilings. In her rich contralto voice, she began to sing. It was Lizzie's favorite hymn, the title of which had been carved into the fireplace mantel of her bedroom following her acquittal in 1893. The words, taken from the verse of an obscure Scottish poet, Allan Cunningham, epitomized Lizzie's feelings of being betrayed—and the awful violence which followed:

The green leaf of loyalty's beginning to fall.
The bonnie White Rose it is withering an' all.
But I'll water it with the blood of usurping tyranny.
And green it will grow in my ain countrie.

When she finished singing, Mrs. Turner was paid and ushered out.

She had no idea that Lizzie had already been buried during the night.

The undertaker told her, "Go straight home and don't tell anyone where you have been."

EPILOGUE

The final ironic episode in the bizarre case occurred two years after her death. The new owners of the house on Second Street decided to demolish a backyard barn which Lizzie had visited on the morning of the murders. When it was pulled down, a cooper's hammer, described as an 'ax' by reporters hopefully covering the demolition, was found under the barn floor. In actuality, the hammer, because of its short blunt edge, could not have been the weapon involved in the Borden deaths, but it cost Bristol County $200 for the services of an analytical chemist to quiet the agitated Fall River newspapers. Even Lizzie, who had little enough to laugh about in her lonely and bitter life, might have smiled at that.

—Attorney William M. Kunstler,
The New York Times, May 13, 1979

EMMA DIED ON JUNE 10TH, 1927, eight days after Lizzie. Dr. George Towle, her physician, when completing her death certificate, capsulized her wild dreams and delusions under the heading "contributory cause of death—senility. Duration—unknown."

Brown and Prottier, an undertaking firm in Newmarket, shipped her body by train to be buried. They listed the cost of services in their ledger:

Embalming	$25.00
Transportation to Warren, R.I. 110 miles	110.00
Use of basket and obtaining permit	5.00
	$140.00

The bill was paid on December 1, 1927, by B. M. C. Durfee Trust Co., Fall River, which handled Emma's estate.

The undertaker's ledger stated that Emma was interred June 13, 1927, at Oak Grove Cemetery in Fall River. It described Emma as white, single, female, age 76 years, 2 months and 10 days. Under the heading which noted the occupation of Emma's father was written: "Retired undertaker."

The story was finished, except for the money. It was money which had bound the two sisters in their desperate cause. Money had driven their father to become a cold, tight-fisted victim of Emma's rage. Money had imposed upon Lizzie thirty-five years of solitude and social recrimination. And finally, money was what remained. . . .

Lizzie's will handsomely provided for animals, rather than people.

To the Animal Rescue League of Fall River she bequeathed thirty thousand dollars and all of her stock in the Stevens Manufacturing Company left to her by her father. An additional two thousand dollars was left to the Animal Rescue League of Washington, D.C. She commented in her will: "I have been fond of animals and their need is great and there are so few who care for them."

She left other gifts: a parcel of real estate adjacent to Maplecroft and two thousand dollars to her chauffeur, Ernest Terry, two thousand dollars to his wife, Ellen, and two thousand dollars to his daughter, Grace. To Charles Cook, to whom she entrusted her business affairs, she left ten thousand dollars and some land directly across the street from where she lived. There were bequests of five thousand dollars each to two friends she had made outside of Fall River, Margaret Streeter and Minnie Lacombe of Washington, D.C.

To her most faithful friend, librarian Helen Leighton, and her favorite cousin, Grace Howe, Lizzie left the A. J. Borden Building, in addition to all of her jewelry and furnishings.

Finally, five hundred dollars was given to the City of Fall River, the income derived therefrom to be used for the perpetual care of her father's grave in Oak Grove Cemetery.

The bequests totaled $280,000.

Toward Emma she made no gesture: "I have not given my sister, Emma L. Borden, anything as she had her share of her father's estate and is supposed to have enough to make her comfortable."

Emma, on the other hand, emerged as one of Fall River's most benevolent humanitarians. Her estate, which almost doubled Lizzie's, bestowed large bequests to children's homes, homes for the aged, the Girl Scouts, the Boys Club, the Y.M.C.A. and the Society for the Prevention of Cruelty to Children. There were scholarships to the Durfee High School and gifts to hospitals.

One thousand dollars was left to Lizzie.

One thousand dollars was allotted for the perpetual care of "the family burial plot."

One thousand dollars was left to Andrew Jennings "as a remembrance . . . in appreciation of all that he has done for me."

Immediately following Emma's death, Annie Connor sold the house in Newmarket, New Hampshire, and moved back to her farm two miles down the road in Wadleigh Falls. According to her neighbor, Renata Dodge, within a short time Annie lost her sanity. She would wander, no longer knowing where she was.

The one remaining character was Bridget Sullivan.

Bridget had disappeared after the trial.

According to Florence Brigham, whose mother-in-law had been a character witness for Lizzie, "I think Bridget was given money to go back to Ireland. She may have known more than she told. Maids in those days liked to gossip, and Lizzie wouldn't have wanted her around."

But what could Bridget have known?

In his letter to Attorney General Pillsbury, Prosecutor Knowlton had expressed his certainty that Bridget had known more than she admitted. She had lived with and waited upon the Bordens for two years prior to the murders. She was aware of the tension which existed in the household and must have overheard conversations between the two sisters and their father and stepmother. Even though she never voiced her feelings during the inquest or the trial, it seems probable that she suspected Emma. On the evening of the murders, Bridget fled from the Borden house, never to return, not because she was afraid of Lizzie but because she was terrified that she might be the killer's next victim. Perhaps she felt that she had observed too much. She remained silent because that was her only protection.

In the early 1900s Bridget reappeared in Anaconda, Montana. There she married a man with the same last name, a smelter named Sullivan. Nearby lived her girlhood friend Minnie Green.

During the forty years which followed, Bridget made no mention of the Borden murders, but in 1943 she was stricken with pneumonia and urgently summoned her friend Minnie to her bedside. She had a secret to confide before she passed away.

By the time Minnie Green arrived, Bridget had recovered.

She revealed nothing.

Bridget died in Butte, Montana, on March 26, 1948, at the age of eighty-two. She was buried in Mt. Olivet Cemetery in Anaconda. Before her death she told Minnie Green about Lizzie—that she had always liked her. According to Bridget, during the trial every word she had spoken was true. Lizzie had been appreciative, giving her the money to visit her parents in Ireland. Lizzie's attorney had made Bridget promise that she would never return.

Obviously Bridget had tried her best to keep her promise. When she returned to the United States she journeyed as far as she could from Fall River, to the town of Anaconda, Montana, population 2,140, near her girlhood friend Minnie Green.

Yet one wonders if Lizzie was the one who paid her way back to Ireland after the trial in 1893, when the sole executrix of Andrew Borden's estate was Emma.

Lizzie was born on Thursday, July 19th, 1860, in her grandfather's cottage at 12 Ferry Street. At the time of her birth, a procession of steamboats docked nearby, loading vast shipments of textile goods to be carried to the markets of New York and Boston.

Twelve Ferry Street is now a refuse-filled vacant lot in the middle of the Portuguese section of Fall River.

In the 1920s, when the cotton mills which stood on the edge of the Taunton River failed, the mass exodus of workers left the huge red brick buildings deserted and useless.

The business life of the world's leading textile manufacturing center had come to a standstill.

An era of wealth ended.

In the fifty years which followed, the aging mills with their cold, towering smokestacks continued to decay. And the town did not revive.

Today, Fall River is no longer a bustling mercantile community. Its most modern structure is the superhighway which cuts through its heart like an ugly, elevated scar.

Second Street does not resemble the elm-lined carriage way which it was in the 1890s. The gracious, wooden frame houses have vanished. The block which Andrew Borden climbed on his way home that sweltering August 4th morning in 1892 has been replaced by a sprawling underground mall populated by teeming little shops vending hit records, discount drugs, cut-rate clothing and pizza by the slice.

The narrow house where the murders occurred still stands, yet the yard, the barn, the surrounding picket fence and gate are gone. The house has been renovated, turned into a commercial printing business by its present owner, John McGinn.

Two blocks away is a recently opened singles bar named *Lizzie's*.

On the once-fashionable Hill, housed in a Victorian mansion, is the Fall River Historical Society, which displays Andrew Borden's skull, a wooden stool from Lizzie's cell in the Taunton Jail, a bedspread splattered with Abby Borden's blood, and a severed lock of Abby's brown hair. Five blocks away is Lizzie's home, with a single word still chiseled in its top step: MAPLECROFT.

The streets are quiet which lead through the nearby gates of Oak Grove Cemetery. The founders of Fall River are all buried there. Sixteen-foot marble columns stand as reminders: Brayton, Durfee, Buffington, Chase. . . .

A little way down the path is a small, grassy knoll, perpetually cared for. Sheltered beneath the branches of four large oak trees is a row of slim granite stones, which stand above the graves of Abby Durfee Borden, Sarah Morse Borden and Sarah's second child, Alice, who died in infancy.

Between Sarah and Abby is Andrew's plot, containing his headless corpse.

At Andrew's feet, bordered by pink verbena, are two small plaques imbedded in the earth, side by side. They mark the graves of Andrew's two adult daughters, Emma and her sister, Lizbeth.

NOTES

NONE OF THE CHARACTERS in this book seemed as elusive as Emma Borden. There existed several photographs of Lizzie, Andrew and Abby, and even a sketch of John Vinnicum Morse. There are photographs of every major witness who appeared at the trial, of the judges and the jury. But Emma apparently never stepped within range of a camera. Few people recalled what she looked like and even Andrew Jennings's grandson, Jack Waring, could tell me only that she was "shy and retiring" (the phrase which everyone seemed to use to describe Emma), and that his grandfather refused to talk about either her or her sister.

Roy Kent, the undertaker of Newmarket, New Hampshire, was certain that Emma had not died there; however, he agreed to make a thorough search of his company's funeral records. He was amazed to discover, since he had searched before without finding it, the list of burial costs and the handwritten facts surrounding Emma's death. His company had indeed embalmed her body and shipped it by train to Warren, Rhode Island, on June 12, 1927.

Since the interview she had given the *Sunday Post* on April 13, 1913, Emma's life had been a mystery. It was through the assistance of Newmarket's hospitable, friendly residents, who had never been interviewed before about Emma, that I learned the details of her final years.

Robert Bennett remembered Emma, as did the Kents, Eva Edgeley (Mrs. Don Melville) and Royce Carpenter. The present owner of the house in which Emma lived allowed me to inspect the rear stairway, down which Emma plunged, fracturing her hip, on the night of Lizzie's death. I walked through Emma's bedroom, adjacent to her modern bathroom. I tested the unusual lighting panel Emma installed, which illuminates the entire downstairs of the house and is located near the narrow pantry where she kept the axe.

Renata Dodge supplied information about the Connor sisters, especially Annie. There was some vagueness as to who had owned the house Emma lived in, which I clarified by studying the deeds in the Rockingham County Courthouse in nearby Exeter, New Hampshire.

In 1921, when Mary Connor died, Annie claimed that Mary had put up only $500 and that she had provided the necessary balance of $2,000 to purchase the house in Newmarket—*although her name had never been entered on the deed.*

The subtleties of why Annie would have provided four-fifths of the money to buy a house and then had her name left off the deed were not challenged by the Register of Probate. In addition, he apparently did not suspect that someone else who desired to keep his—or her—identity a secret might have put up the money to purchase it, using Mary's name.

What seemed equally mysterious was that according to the inquest and trial testimony, on the morning of the murders Emma was visiting Jennie Brownell in Fairhaven, yet no one substantiated Emma's presence there. Even though Emma was never a suspect, it would appear to have been routine procedure for a police officer or a newspaper reporter to have interviewed Jennie Brownell.

With the help of Mary Cabral from the New Bedford Free Public Library, I attempted to find some trace of Jennie Brownell. Although she was not listed in the 1892 Fairhaven Directory, a brief notice in the Fairhaven *Standard Times,* June 22, 1948, stated that "Mrs. Jennie P. Brownell, widow of Thomas Brownell, died Sunday in a Brockton rest home." Following the funeral she was buried in the Riverside Cemetery in Fairhaven.

According to the records of the county clerk which I checked in Brockton, Jennie had no surviving relatives. Sensing that she must hold a key to the story, I learned that she was born in Fairhaven in 1868, which meant that in 1892, she was twenty-four. Emma at that time was forty, which casts some doubt as to the similarity of their interests and the closeness of their relationship. And yet, according to both Emma and Lizzie, Emma had traveled to Fairhaven specifically to visit her friend Jennie Brownell.

It seemed that Emma's real purpose in going to Fairhaven was not to spend time with a young woman with whom she might have little in common, but to be away from the house in Fall River. Subsequently, her visit with Jennie Brownell provided her with an alibi that no one questioned.

One coincidence as never brought up at the trial: Emma had explained that she was close enough to dressmaker Mrs. Hannah H. Gifford to assist in making clothing for Lizzie. Mrs. Gifford had been Lizzie's dressmaker for a period of eight years prior to the murders.

What was never disclosed, which I found in the Fairhaven Star Index kept in the archives of the Millicent Library in Fairhaven, was that twenty-four-year-old Jennie Brownell's maiden name was Gifford.

In the Taunton County Courthouse, the wills of Lizzie and Emma are filed and are a constant source of inquiry to those interested in Lizzie and the unsolved murders. There are no wills for Andrew and Abby, yet a lady working there, Louise Beauvais, located an index number, 8691, in the county record book dated 1892. Under the index number she found in the Bristol County archives the document which Emma filed on September 2, 1892, naming her sole Administratrix of Andrew Borden's estate.

The one person who knows more about Lizzie than anyone I interviewed is Florence Brigham. Mrs. Brigham is the Curator of the Fall River Historical Society. Her mother-in-law, Mary E. Brigham, had been a character witness at Lizzie's trial. Mrs. Brigham graciously turned over to me every detail of information that she had on Lizzie, including her entire collection of photographs and letters.

Through the courtesy of Mary Silvia, who owned Maplecroft, I became the first writer allowed to see the inside of the home where Lizzie lived after her acquittal until her death. It was virtually unchanged, with the same white linen ceilings (except for the one in the second-floor summer room that was tin covered with goldleaf), chocolate wallpaper, stained-glass window and Lizzie's bedroom mantelpiece inscribed with the words "In-my-ain at-hame countrie."

There were other people who helped and encouraged me: Bernie Sullivan of the Providence *Journal,* Edwina Bennett, Bonnie Mendes of the Fall River Public Library; Sylvia Fitts Getchell, Robert H. Maucione and Ruth Gamson of the Fall River *Herald News.*

Sources and documentation supporting certain portions of *Lizzie* are given below.

PART I: 92 SECOND STREET

All dialogue is taken from the testimony of witnesses contained in the 1,930-page transcript of Lizzie's trial.

Descriptions of physical settings were drawn from the author's visits to the settings and his research into changes which have occurred since the events described. References to weather and climatic conditions have been verified by the daily records of the National Weather Service.

Newspaper accounts and the accounts of witnesses form the basis of the narrative. A most helpful source was the rare volume written by Fall River *Globe* reporter Edwin H. Porter, *The Fall River Tragedy* (Fall River: George R. H. Buffington, 1893).

In addition, there were those who obtained valuable interviews from others about what occurred.

Edmund Pearson, author of *The Trial of Lizzie Borden* (New York: Doubleday, Doran & Company, 1937), visited Fall River in 1923 and interviewed a man who had worked with druggist Eli Bence. Bence had sworn that Lizzie attempted to purchase prussic acid the day prior to the murders. Bence's co-worker assured Pearson that Bence knew Lizzie by sight, as her house was a short distance away and she often passed the drugstore. He further stated that Bence was a careful man, not inclined to making rash statements.

Descriptions of Fall River, its growth and industrial history, were based upon the writings of Reverend Orin Fowler, *History of Fall River* (Fall River: Almy & Milne Press, 1862), as well as information supplied by the Fall River Public Library and the Fall River Chamber of Commerce.

PART II: THE TRIAL

Accounts of the events in the courtroom were taken from the New York *Herald*, the Baltimore *Sun*, the New York *World*, the New York *American*, the Boston *Globe*, the New York *Sun*, the Springfield *Daily Republican* and the Providence *Journal*.

The trial, which appeared daily on the front pages of every major American newspaper, was one of the most publicized murder cases in American history.

Initially, the murders had been covered internationally by Reuters, but by the time of the trial correspondents from several European dailies had arrived in New Bedford.

Excerpts from the articles of America's first syndicated columnist, Joe Howard, were taken from the Boston *Globe* and the New York *Recorder*. Howard's newspaper background is discussed in some detail in *Abraham Lincoln, A History*, by John G. Nicolay and John Hay (New York: The Century Company, 1890).

The excerpt from the letter of Joseph Choate to his wife (June 16, 1893) is from the *Life of Joseph Hodges Choate* by E. S. Martin (New York: Scribner's Publishing Company, 1920).

The description of the execution of William Kemmler in the electric chair is taken from accounts in *The New York Times* and the New York

World, in addition to Elinor Horwitz's well-researched book, *Capital Punishment U.S.A.* (Philadelphia: J. B. Lippincott & Company, 1973).

Accounts of Lizzie's departure from the courthouse in New Bedford were given in the Baltimore *Sun* and the New York *American.*

PART III: TWO SISTERS

The description of the interior of Maplecroft is based on the author's personal observation as well as information provided by the owner of the house, Mary Silvia. Despite its large size, it is a very livable residence, which Lizzie obviously made as comfortable as possible—indicated by the private apartment with its huge stone fireplace which she added to the rear of the second floor, and her splendid coach house, where she kept her limousine and her own gas pump.

Professor Wigmore's comments are taken from "The Borden Case," by John H. Wigmore (27 *American Law Review,* 1893).

The details of the shoplifting incident at Tilden-Thurber in Providence are taken from the private notes, written in the 1930s, of William G. Thurber. They were discovered by his son William H. Thurber, in August 1983, and given to the author.

Edward D. Radin, in his book *Lizzie Borden, The Untold Story* (New York: Simon and Schuster, 1961), discusses a copy of Lizzie's confession that came from a photographer's assistant, who claimed that he had secretly kept it for a period of fifty-five years and then sold it to newspaper columnist Edward Rowe Snow in 1952 for fifty dollars. With the assistance of handwriting analyst Ordway Hilton, Radin proved the copy of the confession to be a forgery. The appearance of the forged copy did, however, indicate that one of the five men who had vowed to Lizzie never to divulge that she had signed the confession had broken his promise. It was obviously too good a story—and one could imagine Henry Tilden boasting afterward of his accomplishment in getting Lizzie to confess to the murders.

Nance O'Neil's lesbian relationship with Lizzie is briefly mentioned in *A Private Disgrace* by Victoria Lincoln (New York: G. P. Putnam's Sons, 1967). I learned that Nance lived at the Shoreham Hotel on West Fifty-sixth Street in Manhattan until 1947, when she moved to the Actor's Home in Englewood, New Jersey. She died in 1948.

I gained access to all of Nance's scrapbooks and writings as I felt it was essential to present as exactly as possible the woman Lizzie idolized.

Nance emerged as a passionate, extremely individualistic artist who, it would seem from the letters she kept, was adored by a great many women in addition to Lizzie.

Joyce G. Williams, J. Eric Smithburn and M. Jeanne Peterson edited an excellent study, *Lizzie Borden: A Case Book of Family and Crime in the 1890's,* published by the University of Indiana, T.I.S. Publication Division, Bloomington, Indiana. My appreciation to them for the remembrances by Lizzie's neighbors Edith Coolidge and Russell B. Lake.

Lizzie's final years were recounted in part by Florence Brigham, who told me the fascinating story of funeral soloist Vida Turner.

INDEX

ABOUT THE AUTHOR

Frank Spiering is the author of the controversial book *Prince Jack,* which named a member of the British royal family as Jack the Ripper. He has also written for the theater and films. Mr. Spiering is a graduate of the University of California, Berkeley, and currently lives in New York City. His fascination with the story of Lizzie Borden involved him in over a decade of research, which led him ultimately to solve one of the most elusive of all mysteries.